Understanding Healthcare Economics

Managing Your Career in an Evolving Healthcare System, Second Edition

Understanding Healthcare Economics

Managing Your Career in an Evolving Healthcare System, Second Edition

By
Jeanne Wendel, PhD, Teresa Serratt, PhD, RN, and
William O'Donohue, PhD

CRC Press
Taylor & Francis Group
Boca Raton London New York

CRC Press is an imprint of the
Taylor & Francis Group, an **informa** business

A PRODUCTIVITY PRESS BOOK

CRC Press
Taylor & Francis Group
6000 Broken Sound Parkway NW, Suite 300
Boca Raton, FL 33487-2742

© 2018 by Taylor & Francis Group, LLC

CRC Press is an imprint of Taylor & Francis Group, an Informa business

No claim to original U.S. Government works

Printed on acid-free paper

International Standard Book Number-13: 978-1-138-72301-6 (Hardback)
International Standard Book Number-13: 978-1-315-19328-1 (eBook)

Library of Congress Cataloging-in-Publication Data

Names: Wendel, Jeanne, author. | Serratt, Teresa D., author. | O'Donohue, William T., author.
Title: Understanding healthcare economics : managing your career in an evolving healthcare system / Jeanne Wendel, Teresa Serratt, William O'Donohue.
Description: Second edition. | Boca Raton : Taylor & Francis, 2018. | "A CRC title, part of the Taylor & Francis imprint, a member of the Taylor & Francis Group, the academic division of T&F Informa plc." | Includes bibliographical references and index.
Identifiers: LCCN 2017030798| ISBN 9781138723016 (hardback : alk. paper) | ISBN 9781315193281 (ebook)
Subjects: LCSH: Medical economics--United States.
Classification: LCC RA410.5 .W46 2018 | DDC 338.4/73621--dc23
LC record available at https://lccn.loc.gov/2017030798

Visit the Taylor & Francis Web site at
http://www.taylorandfrancis.com

and the CRC Press Web site at
http://www.crcpress.com

We dedicate this book to our families: Tom, Nathan, Jane, Katie, Anna, Jim, and Madi, for their support and encouragement.

Contents

Foreword xv

Preface xxi

Acknowledgments xxix

Authors xxxi

Introduction xxxiii

SECTION I   PRESSURES FOR CHANGE

1   Access 5

Introduction 5

Sources of Insurance and Characteristics of People Who Are Uninsured 6

    Insurance Sources and Trends 6

Who Is Uninsured and Why? 8

    Who Is Uninsured? 8

    Why Are Some People Uninsured? 12

Private Insurance Markets 12

    Insurance Principles: Insurance Is a Mechanism for Managing Risk 13

        How Will the Insurance Company Compute the Premium for a
Specific Type of Insurance? 13

        When Will an Individual Decide to Purchase Insurance? 14

    Application of Insurance Principles in Markets for Health Insurance 16

        Health Insurance for Preexisting Conditions: Risk versus Subsidy 17

        Insuring Risk versus Subsidizing an Expenditure 17

    Summary of Explanation of Insurance Premiums and When to
Buy Insurance 19

Why Do Some Employers Offer Health Insurance While Others Do
Not? 22

    Employers Don't Actually Pay for Employer-Sponsored Healthcare ... 23

What Forces Shift the Cost of Employer-Sponsored Health
Insurance onto Workers? 24
  Basic Economic Tools: Supply and Demand................................24
  Basic Economic Tools: At the Equilibrium Wage, Quantity
  Supplied Is Equal to Quantity Demanded 25
  What Happens When the Actual Wage Is above (or below) the
  Equilibrium Wage?..26
  Why Is the Equilibrium Concept Useful? 27
  How Does Employer-Sponsored Health Insurance Affect the
  Equilibrium Wage?..29
  Scenario 1 31
  Scenario 2 34
  Implications of Scenarios 1 and 2 36
  An Inefficient Healthcare System Means Lower Wages for Workers....36
  Healthcare Coverage Mandates Lead to Higher Costs for Health
  Insurance and Lower Wages for Workers......................................37
Why Do Some Individuals Remain Uninsured, Even Though They
Are Eligible for Public Insurance or ESI? 39
Why Do Insurance Companies Utilize Restrictive Practices That
Make It Impossible for Some Individuals to Purchase Insurance..........42
  Industry Reasons for Using Restrictive Practices............................43
  The "Lemons Problem" 43
    Lemons Problem in Health Insurance Markets 44
    Employer-Sponsored Health Insurance Mitigates the Lemons
    Problem..45
Solution Strategies 47
  Pre-PPACA Legislation to Restrict the Use of Preexisting
  Condition Exclusions..47
    Title I of HIPAA: Prohibit Restrictive Practices in the Markets
    for Small Group and Large Group Health Insurance....................47
    State Reforms That Preceded PPACA Reforms 49
  Pre-PPACA Estimates of the Impacts of Alternate Strategies for
  Increasing Access 50
    Employer Mandate with or without Individual Mandate................50
    Expand Public Programs, Chiefly Medicaid 51
    Tax Credit 51
ACA Solution Strategy for Increasing the Proportion of Individuals
Covered by Health Insurance..51
  ACA Strategy for Increasing Health Insurance Coverage 52

Mandates That Employers Must Offer Group Insurance,
Mandates That Individuals Must Obtain Insurance Coverage,
and Ban on Provisions in Health Insurance Policies That
Exclude Preexisting Conditions from Coverage 52
Creation of State-Level Health Insurance Exchanges.....................52
Expansion of Medicaid Eligibility for Adults with Incomes up
to 100% of the FPL 54
Impacts 55
Conclusion..56

2 Cost...59
Introduction...59
Background Information..61
Definitions: Cost, Price, and Expenditures....................................61
Healthcare Expenditures by Type 62
Sources of Funding for Healthcare Expenditures.................................63
Sustainability of the Public Expenditures 65
Diagnosing the Problem: What Is Fueling the Cost Increases? 69
Technology Is a Key Driver of Healthcare Expenditure Increases 70
Value Produced by the New Technologies Compared with the
Costs of the Treatments 72
Do the New Treatments Improve Health?......................................72
Are the New Treatments a Good Investment as Measured by
Cost per Life Saved (or Cost per Life-Year Saved)? 74
Solution Options 77
Option 1: Continue to Spend More on Healthcare Every Year,
and Accommodate This by Spending Less on Other Goods..............77
Option 2: Restrain the Quantities of Healthcare Services That Are
Utilized Annually in the United States 78
Ration by Price 78
Ration by Wait Time 79
Ration by Setting Priorities..79
Option 3: Reduce the Rate of Technological Innovation by
Reducing the Incentive for Firms to Invest in R&D............................80
Option 4: Reduce the Cost of Delivering Care by Regulating
Prices and/or Profits of Healthcare Providers and Pharmaceutical
Companies..80
Regulate Prices and/or Profits of Healthcare Providers and
Pharmaceutical Companies 80

Option 5: Implement Strategies to Make Our Healthcare System More Efficient 82
Conclusion..83

3 Quality 85
Introduction..85
Background Information: Three Types of Evidence Indicate That Quality Is Not Consistently High..87
International Comparisons Indicate That Other Countries Are Doing More With Less 87
What Can We Conclude about This Evidence? 90
Diagnosing the Root Cause of the Quality Problem 91
Evidence Documents the Occurrence of Preventable Medical Errors.... 91
Evidence Documents Variations in Regional Treatment Patterns........94
What Is Influencing Physician Decisions? 94
Does Higher Healthcare Spending Produce Better Outcomes?.......95
Are the Regional Differences Large Enough to Be Important? 95
Solution Options: How Can We Make Our Healthcare System More Systematic?..96
Applying Total Quality Management Principals to Healthcare 96
Brief History 97
Implement Systematic Protocols: Clinical Pathways and Guidelines ...100
Clinical Pathways..100
Clinical Guidelines 101
Conclusion: Some Strategies for Strengthening Quality Are Clear, but the Concept of Healthcare Quality Is Complex and Multidimensional..109

Conclusion to Section I 113

SECTION II STRATEGIES TO INCREASE EFFICIENCY
Introduction..115
Do Healthcare Markets Operate Efficiently?.........................116
Two Key "Market Failures" in Healthcare........................117
How Should Government Address These Market Failures?..........118

4 Align Incentives via Payment System Design 121
Introduction..121
Background: Alternate Hospital Payment Designs 121
Strategies to Control Cost: Rate Design Replaced Certificate of Need Programs 123

FFS Payments for Hospital Services and Certificate of Need Programs.... 123
Rate Redesign 124
DRG Payment for Hospital Services 125
Capitated Payment for Physicians; Accountable Care Organizations
for Wider Sets of Providers 128
Bundled Payment: Eliminate Silos 128
Selective Contracting 129
Pay for Performance and Consumer Information to Incentivize
Increased Quality 130
Current Efforts: Value-Based Purchasing for Hospitals 132
Physician Payment Systems: RBRVS and MACRA 132
Implications of Public and Private Payment Systems for Hospitals 134
Conclusions 138

5 **Managed Care Organizations, Accountable Care
Organizations, and Patient-Centered Medical Homes.............. 139**
Introduction 139
Background: Managed Care Organizations 140
Managed Care: Historical Trends 141
Managed Care: The Backlash 142
Current Issues: Lessons Learned 144
Defining Consumer Protection Is Complex 144
Shifting to Managed Care and/or ACOs Focuses on a Definition
of Quality that is New for Many Patients 148
Growth of Managed Care Organizations Raised Two Types of
Market Power Issues 149
Reducing Healthcare Cost by Reducing Provider
Reimbursement Sounds Good, if You Are a Consumer, but
Providers See a Different Side of the Issue 150
Providers Responded in Two Ways 151
Managed Care Organizations Also Raised Questions about
Physician Risk Taking and Solvency Regulation 152
Mental Health Parity Mandate May Constitute a Special Case 154
Physician Rating Systems Raise Concerns 157
Do ACOs and PCMHs Deliver on Improving Quality and
Coordination of Care at a Reduced Cost? 159
Conclusion: Experiences with Managed Care Organizations Provide
Significant Lessons Learned, as Providers Begin Forming ACOs and
PCMHs 160

6 Wellness, Prevention, and Disease Management 163
Introduction 163
  Background: PPACA Focuses Increased Attention on Prevention
  and Wellness 164
    Current Issues 165
  After We Identify Individuals Who Are Most Likely to Benefit
  from Prevention Programs, Can We Design Programs to
  Successfully Induce Them to Participate? 167
  Effectiveness of Prevention and Wellness Programs 172
Conclusions 174

**7 Regulatory Challenges Posed by New Types of Competition
  in Healthcare 177**
Introduction 177
Background 178
Current Issues 179
  New Types of Providers: Retail Clinics, SSHs, Telemedicine, and
  Integrated Care Providers 180
    Retail Clinics 180
    Single-Specialty Hospitals 185
    Telemedicine 189
    Integrated Care Providers 191
Conclusion 194

8 HIT = EMR + HIE 197
Introduction 197
Background 199
If HIT Can Generate Net Benefits, Why Are Federal Subsidies
Needed to Boost Adoption? 200
  Expected Benefits versus Costs 200
  Potential Market Failures 200
Rationale for Investing Taxpayer Dollars in HITECH Subsidies 202
HIT Adoption Rates Prior to the HITECH Act 204
Challenges 204
Impact of the HITECH Act 205
Impact on HIT Adoption 205
Impact on Outcomes 206
Statewide versus Private-Sector HIE 207
Conclusions 208

Conclusion to Section II 211

Conclusion 213

References 219

Index 239

Foreword

It is a privilege to introduce this important book to healthcare professionals. All of us in the provider community have been confounded by the complex problems we face in our healthcare system. Many of these problems arrive in our offices as we watch our patients present their insurance cards. As providers, we are the end of a long line of policy makers, payers, healthcare administrators, corporations, and interest groups. At the end of this line we stand along with our patients, the last stop on the journey through the health insurance, healthcare regulatory, and healthcare delivery maze. Despite whatever policies we confront, such as necessary preauthorization, required second opinions, preferred provider lists, and authorized lengths of stay, we are ethically and morally responsible to use our knowledge and skill to help and heal. It is the rare provider, facing a patient in need, who has not at times been so frustrated by the system that he or she wanted to do something to change it, or just do something else. The question is, what should be done? How can we be effective agents for change? What change should we be looking for? Although this book does not pretend to provide the final answers for any of these questions, it gives the committed reader much deeper insights into the economics of the system and the factors that need to be understood before the system can be improved.

The first section of the book presents economic evidence to support a more nuanced understanding of the three components of the system: access, cost, and quality. Aaron Carroll (2012) referred to these three components as the iron triangle. According to Carroll, the trade-offs among the three components of the iron triangle are an inescapable fact of health system change. For example, you can increase access to services for some or all of the population, but when you do this, you will almost always increase cost. This is particularly true if you also define a minimum level of quality for the newly accessible services. If you want to control cost, you will likely constrain either access or quality. Most architects of health system change suggest that you can improve two, but not all three of these components with any given policy. This book provides a basic introduction to all three components and some insights into the nature of the trade-offs between them. It also provides excellent insights into why trade-offs are an essential part of any discussion about the healthcare system. This is critical knowledge for providers seeking to influence health system change.

"Wait a minute," I hear some of you saying. "Who said I wanted to try to influence health system change? As a provider, let me tend to the job at hand—giving the best care possible to my patients. Let someone else worry about changing the system." Before you get too comfortable with that thought, perhaps we should consider how that has worked out for us so far, since the evidence suggests that we haven't been involved. The research on public involvement in healthcare policy is limited, but a recent study (Conklin et al., 2010) reviews the available literature on this topic and concludes that not only is evidence scarce, but that the range and scope of involvement with policy are not well understood, measured, or defined. In fact, according to the study conclusions, there is a considerable lack of clarity about who the public is and what involvement of the public is intended to achieve. This lack of evidence suggests that healthcare providers, like other members of the public, have not assumed a commanding role in shaping health policy and have not been at all clear about what, if anything, we would like to happen. There is no doubt that providers and the organizations that represent them, such as the American Medical Association, the American Nurses Association, and the American Public Health Association, all engage in lobbying efforts and try to get a place at the table when major health policies are discussed, yet the individual professional is frequently silent on these important issues, preferring to let someone else do it. For example, one of the most fundamental indicators of involvement in policy is certainly voting participation. According to the joint voter turnout study by the Bipartisan Policy Center and the Center for the Study of the American Electorate (2012), participation in the 2012 election was 57.5% of all eligible voters. This is a rate lower than the past two presidential elections. Since many commentators say the 2012 election was largely a referendum focused on the Patient Care Affordability Act, is it safe to assume that healthcare providers, along with many other members of the American electorate, just didn't show up at the polls? Thomas Jefferson once suggested that in a democracy you get the government you deserve. Perhaps we as healthcare providers have got the health system we deserve. In order to change this state of affairs, we need to decide to use the knowledge provided in this book and get involved.

So what should we do? Important options for changing the system are presented in Part II of this book, as the authors review some major solution sets including adjusting incentives, managing care, promoting health, and using information more efficiently and effectively. The evidence for implementing these strategic solutions, as well as some of the concerns inherent in implementing them, is thoughtfully presented to us. Familiarity with these discussions provides not only an insight into the strategy under discussion, but also insight into the questions that need to be asked about any proposed solution. Since there are no magic bullets out there, the conclusions presented at the end of the section are worth much discussion and study. The authors suggest, for example, that if the drive for increased consumer choice and participation in the system has its intended result, we need to worry about what will become of those who lack fundamental skills in health literacy. Further questions occur to me. Will this deepen the already developing social divide between those who have and those who have not in U.S. society? How are providers going to cope with the increasing policy mandate to engage with the community and its health needs if the community lacks sufficient skill to define its needs? What if the needs it defines are unlikely to yield optimal or even beneficial results? How are we going to remedy deficiencies in basic health literacy or education? The basic economic models and analytic approaches provided in this text help frame these questions most clearly so that evidence can be considered and some answers can be found. At the end of the day, it is up to us to understand the information this book presents and use it wisely.

If I haven't convinced you that the content of this book is as important to you as the latest clinical information, let me introduce you to yet another compelling concept, that of healthcare as social justice. The Nobel laureate Amartya Sen was asked to deliver the keynote address to the third conference of the International Health Economics Association in 2001. What he said to the economists present at that meeting is in itself a good policy guide for healthcare providers:

> Any conception of social justice that accepts the need for a fair distribution as well as efficient formation of human capabilities cannot ignore the role of health in human life and the opportunities that persons, respectively, have to achieve good health—free from escapable illness, avoidable afflictions and premature mortality*

---

* Sen, A. (2002). Why health equity? *Health Economics*, 11: 659–666.

In his address, Sen makes the important point that a just society must be one that does not tolerate profound healthcare inequities. What about our society—what do we tolerate? The Commonwealth Fund (2012) provides important evidence to us concerning this issue in its 2012 report Rising to the Challenge, Results from a Scorecard on Local Health System Performance. This report examines access to care, quality of care, and health outcomes in 306 local healthcare areas known as hospital regions. The authors of the report found wide variations in all three indicators, often a two to three-fold variation between leading and lagging health systems on these key indicators. There is a familiar saying in real estate: "Location, location, location." Apparently, where you live is not only important for your real estate values, but also for your life. How long we live, how well we live, and how successful we are going to be in life is significantly determined by where we locate ourselves geographically. I suggest you read this report before you dismiss the idea that health disparities are somebody else's problem in someone else's location. Unfortunately the report suggests that we have met the enemy—and it is us. Our cities and towns often present far less than optimal performance on access, quality, and outcomes. Even the best performing systems do not perform consistently well across all three indicators. Regardless of where you live and where you practice, there is significant room for improvement. Even the best of us can sometimes be the worst of us, and we need knowledge and skills beyond clinical competencies to fix the problem.

As this book suggests, the situation we find ourselves in has been evolving over time into a complex tangle of interrelated components. We might fix one and make another worse. For example, as we improve the electronic medical records systems in our hospitals, we find that the infrastructure for data exchange between hospital and ambulatory care providers is in need of improvement, and that patient privacy concerns require costly system safeguards that may impede data exchange and increase overall costs. Sorting out these relationships and understanding these trade-offs require the skills you will learn as you explore the economic frameworks presented to you, then taking the new knowledge forward into your professional life. Yogi Berra observed that "The future ain't what it used to be." Moreover, the future seems to become the present so much faster these days. Most healthcare providers want a future that gives them the opportunity to deliver care to people who need it without the nagging fear that many are completely excluded (and some are lost) before any results can be achieved. If we are to realize that future, we need more knowledge than we have now. I recommend this book as a way to begin.

Mary A. Paterson, PhD, MSN
Ordinary Professor and Director, Assessment and Evaluation
School of Nursing
The Catholic University of America

Preface

The U.S. healthcare system faces important problems—so much so that many describe the situation as a crisis. As advances in medical science create ever-more powerful tools for giving patients more years in their lives and more life in their years, the implications of rising costs and unequal access to health insurance and healthcare become more troublesome. The increasing availability of electronic healthcare data on patterns of care highlights many quality deficiencies in growing detail—so much so that an influential report has called the gap between the healthcare that we have and high-quality healthcare a "chasm." Continued growth in per capita healthcare expenditures generates fiscal pressures for government budgets and financial strains for patients and private-sector payers that many regard as "unsustainable." As these trends continue, the task of finding solutions becomes more vexing.

Controversies concerning healthcare are often in the headlines. Politicians propose certain laws while others, who hold different worldviews, argue that these laws will create more problems than they solve. At a minimum, new laws create fresh debates. The 2010 Patient Protection and Affordable Care Act (PPACA) generated debates, legal challenges, and proposals—from both conservatives and liberals—for significant changes. This act created two new mechanisms for addressing the problem of access inequality, along with numerous provisions to address cost and quality issues.

While the debates continue, much new has occurred since 2010, including

- Implementation of the provisions of the 2009 Health Information Technology for Economic and Clinical Health Act (which are essential for supporting the quality improvement strategies embedded in the PPACA).

- The Obama administration announced several enforcement and implementation decisions that modified the implications of the language of the PPACA.
- The Supreme Court made a significant change in a 2012 decision, giving states the option to decide whether to expand the income threshold for Medicaid eligibility.
- The 2015 Medicare Access and CHIP Reauthorization Act reshaped the structure of quality-based incentive payments for clinicians.

Also, we are in a better position to assess the actual versus the promised effects of the PPACA, which include

- The number of uninsured Americans dropped dramatically—although about 30 million Americans remain uninsured.
- Health insurance premiums increased for many Americans, due to continued increases in the cost of healthcare.
- The system was not transformed into a "healthcare system," from what was viewed as an outmoded "sickness care system."
- Newly insured individuals face deductibles and copayments when they utilize the healthcare system.
- Some insurers dropped out of exchanges, leaving some Americans with limited options to buy insurance under the act.

The PPACA was not developed in a vacuum. In fact, the PPACA is one—in a sequence—of "major" healthcare or health insurance reforms that laid important foundations for the PPACA:

- The 1996 Health Insurance Portability and Accountability Act restricted the use of preexisting conditions exclusions in the group insurance markets that provide coverage for 90% of individuals with private-sector coverage.
- Private-sector managed care companies pioneered care management strategies in the 1990s (and states passed hundreds of laws to restrict the use of some of these strategies in the "managed care backlash").
- The 2003 Medicare Modernization Act provided federal funding for prescription drug insurance, and it also included provisions to structure the favorable tax status for health savings accounts.
- Several states implemented "health reform" policies prior to 2010, with varying degrees of success.

■ Coding systems were developed and widely adopted to support electronic characterization of reasons for hospital admissions (Diagnostic
Related Group codes) and patient diagnoses (International Classification
of Diseases codes and clinical procedural terminology [CPT] codes).
Large healthcare providers began utilizing electronic medical records
systems, and the Centers for Medicare and Medicaid Services initiated
pay-for-performance payment to incentivize hospitals to strengthen
quality of care.

Pre-PPACA experience with these initiatives provided a base of information that was used to estimate likely impacts of the law, and to assess likely
side effects. Available evidence was summarized, prior to the congressional
debate, in a Congressional Budget Office report.

Health policy debates are frequently described in political terms:
Democrats traditionally advocate some solution strategies, while Republicans
advocate other strategies. (See Table 0.1 for a sample of debate issues
described through a political lens.) Unfortunately, this approach has limited usefulness because two elements are missing. First, proponents of each
potential solution strategy focus on its advantages, while opponents focus
on its disadvantages. Thoughtful comparisons of relative costs and benefits
of alternative strategies for accomplishing important goals are not widely
reported in the media. Second, the political ads and media sound bites
tend to ignore the important distinction between *goals* and potential *solution strategies*. "Single payer" is a tool that could potentially accomplish a
goal, but it is not a goal in itself. Patient advocates who care about universal
access to healthcare services could consider accomplishing this goal via a
single-payer system, or subsidies for insurance purchased through the insurance exchanges. In fact, the distinction between the two solution options has
become blurry in recent years. The Obama administration approved waiver
applications from two states, to implement Medicaid expansion by using
Medicaid funds to provide vouchers that allow the newly eligible individuals
to purchase insurance through the exchanges. Similarly, 97% of Americans
over age 65 are covered by Medicare; hence, Medicare is a government-run
single-payer system for individuals in this age group. Individuals covered by
Medicare choose whether to enroll in the traditional Medicare system (which
utilizes fee-for-service payment to reimburse providers for services) or to
enroll in a privately administered managed care plan (known as the Medicare
Advantage component of Medicare). Under the second option, federal funds

Table 0.1 Advantages and Disadvantages of Potential Solution Strategies, as Viewed through a Political Lens

Potential Solution Strategies	Conservatives	Liberals	Issues That Are Not Typically Addressed
Single-payer system with a single risk pool	*Disadvantage*: A single-payer system would dampen private-sector competition and innovation.	*Advantage*: A single-payer system would reduce costs associated with provider billing systems, by reducing billing complexity.	What group will be included? U.S. citizens? Noncitizens who are legal residents of the United States? Noncitizens who are undocumented? Single-payer healthcare at Medicaid rates will lead to long wait times for care; single-payer healthcare at Medicare rates will require substantial tax increases.
Waiting periods for coverage of preexisting conditions or penalties for gaps in health insurance coverage	*Advantage*: Prevents individuals from "gaming the system," by waiting to pay for health insurance until they need healthcare.	*Disadvantage*: Unfairly penalizes individuals with low-income and/or high-cost health conditions.	
High-risk pools (HRPs) that provide coverage for individuals with high-cost conditions (1% of individuals incur 23% of annual healthcare expenditures)	*Advantage*: Stabilize the broader insurance market.	*Disadvantage*: Difficult to maintain the political support needed to maintain appropriate funding for HRPs.	

(Continued)

Table 0.1 (Continued)   Advantages and Disadvantages of Potential Solution Strategies, as Viewed through a Political Lens

Potential Solution Strategies	*Conservatives*	*Liberals*	*Issues That Are Not Typically Addressed*
Risk adjustment strategies to stabilize insurance markets	*Disadvantage*: Insurance companies will seek (and find) ways to game these systems.	*Advantage*: Strategy has been used in Medicaid managed care markets with reasonable success.	
Individual responsibility for lifestyle strategies to build health, for compliance with medical advice, and for cost-effective utilization of the healthcare system	*Advantage*: Individual efforts to obtain cost-effective care create incentives for provider organizations to develop efficient strategies for delivering care.	*Disadvantage*: Overemphasis on individual responsibility may hinder provider efforts to coordinate care, reduce willingness to obtain preventive care, and penalize individuals with low cognitive ability.	

(Continued)

Table 0.1 (Continued) Advantages and Disadvantages of Potential Solution Strategies, as Viewed through a Political Lens

Potential Solution Strategies	Conservatives	Liberals	Issues That Are Not Typically Addressed
State-level decisions, rather than federal-level decisions	*Advantage:* Economic conditions, urban versus rural issues, and the availability of providers vary across states.	*Disadvantage:* National-level competition among insurers and healthcare provider organizations could generate efficiencies and reduce prices. Supports expanded use of telemedicine.	
Publicly run programs (e.g., Medicare) rather than privately run programs	*Disadvantage:* "Disruptive" innovation (needed to substantially reduce the cost of delivering healthcare) is more likely to start in the private sector.	*Advantage:* Centers for Medicare and Medicaid Services payment design innovations incentivize providers to increase healthcare coordination and quality. These efforts can generate a large impact on care patterns due to Medicare's large market share.	The distinction between publicly run and privately run programs is blurred by the fact that some publicly run programs subcontract to private-sector managed care companies.

are used to pay the monthly premium to enroll the individual in the private-sector managed care plan.

Instead of back-and-forth debates that do not resolve issues or generate consensus, important problems (such as healthcare access, cost, and quality) deserve serious solutions. Good problem-solving methods include clear specification of the problem, in-depth analysis of the root causes of the problem, formulation of alternate solution strategies, and evidence-based estimation of the costs and benefits of these strategies. Importantly, good problem-solving methods require completion of these steps *before* process participants form opinions about recommended solutions. Experience applying these methods in quality improvement initiatives in healthcare organization suggests that

- Many individuals embark on the problem-solving process with preconceived opinions about the root causes of the problem, and the preferred solution strategy.
- As the problem-solving group collects and analyzes data on the root causes of the problem, members of the group build a shared understanding of basic facts.
- By the time the group members complete the steps of identifying potential solution strategies, they may identify new options that were not included among the initial preconceived ideas. By the time the group members complete estimation of the costs and benefits of the proposed strategies, members of the problem-solving group may have new opinions that are quite different from their initial views.

Dr. Edward Bono (1985) argues that good problem-solving methods focus on helping individuals postpone formulation of opinions, until *after* facts have been gathered, options have been explored, and diverse views have been shared.

This book provides information to help you form this type of evidence-based assessment of current strategic options. Basic information about root causes of the access, cost, and quality issues is discussed in Section I. The chapters in Section II discuss five components of strategic options for increasing healthcare system efficiency and performance. We present evidence to help you assess advantages and disadvantages of current—and future—policy options. We leave the task of weighing the relative importance of the advantages and disadvantages of each option to you.

Acknowledgments

We thank Kimberly Brown and the Jody DeMeyer Endowment at Boise State University School of Nursing for providing support and assistance in for updating the content of this book.

Authors

Jeanne Wendel, Ph.D., is an economics professor in the College of Business at the University of Nevada, Reno. She teaches classes on health economics, the economics of government regulation, and microeconomics. Her research focuses on health policy issues, including evaluating the impacts of prenatal care and employer wellness programs, hospital decisions to provide uncompensated care, the conceptual framework for analyzing bundled payments, and the federal strategy for encouraging development of statewide Health Information Exchange. Her current research focuses on the impacts of state decisions regarding Medicaid expansion and operation of state high-risk pools. Dr. Wendel also has experience working supporting a hospital quality improvement program.

Teresa Serratt, RN, Ph.D., is an associate professor in the School of Nursing at Boise State University and an adjunct associate professor in the Department of Social and Behavioral Sciences at the University of California, San Francisco. She earned her doctorate in nursing from the University of California, San Francisco, with a specialty in health policy. She currently teaches courses in healthcare project management, leadership, economics, and evidence-based practice. As a health services researcher, her primary research focus is health policy, healthcare workforce, and organizational analysis of economic and quality issues in acute care facilities. As a registered nurse for over 25 years, she has spent the majority of her career at the bedside providing care to critically ill adult patients. She has also held hospital education and administrative positions. In these various roles, she has experienced firsthand some of the failures of our healthcare system and feels it is imperative that healthcare professionals understand the reform issues and join the debate.

William O'Donohue is a professor of psychology at the University of Nevada, Reno and a licensed clinical psychologist. He has published over 80 books and 200 journal articles and book chapters. He has also directed, for over 20 years, a clinic that provides free psychotherapy to children who have been sexually or physically abused and adults who have been sexually assaulted. This clinic is supported by a Victims of Crime Act from the National Institute of Justice and the Nevada Attorney General. His work focuses on sexual abuse, evidence-based treatment, and philosophical issues in psychology.

Introduction

> It is not the strongest of the species that survive, nor the most intelligent, but the one most responsive to change.
>
> **Charles Darwin**

Health economics will be an increasingly important topic for healthcare professionals in the coming years because many substantial changes—despite the passage of the Patient Protection and Affordable Care Act (PPACA)—are clearly in the offing that will continue to radically alter the ways Americans obtain and finance healthcare. Systems for obtaining healthcare and paying the providers are continuously evolving. Consider the advent of Medicaid and Medicare in 1965, the rise of managed care in the 1980s, the incentives for increased reliance on electronic health records (embedded in the 2009 American Reinvestment and Recovery Act), and the sweeping changes brought about by the passage of the PPACA of 2010. However, the pace and magnitude of change will probably increase in the coming decades. Our population is aging and older people often require more healthcare, technological advances offer better diagnostic and treatment options, and the population continues to grow so there will be increasing numbers of people seeking services, and there will be new types of services to deliver. In addition, we have seen in 2017 that shifts in the balance of power between the two major political parties can significantly impact the way Americans receive and pay for their healthcare.

Healthcare delivery necessarily requires scarce resources: in the words of economist Thomas Sowell (1993, p. 83), "There is never enough of anything to satisfy all those who want it." Because healthcare is scarce, it comes at a cost—thus, the key economic questions become

- What actually is healthcare? Erectile dysfunction medication? Seat belt use programming?

- How much healthcare should be covered under publicly funded versus privately funded health insurance policies?
  - How much will it cost in total? What sources of funds will be used to cover publicly funded expenditures?
  - Who should receive healthcare services—and which services should they receive?
  - How will the services be delivered?
  - How will we provide and fund safety net services?

State and federal healthcare laws, regulations, and payment systems play an important role in shaping the U.S. healthcare and health insurance systems. Key federal policies include the 2010 PPACA (widely known by the shorter acronym ACA), the 1996 Health Insurance Portability and Accountability Act, the 2015 federal legislation that established the new Medicare Access and CHIP Reauthorization Act (MACRA) quality-based payment incentives, and the evolving structure of the payment system administered by the Centers for Medicare and Medicaid Services. State-level policies are also evolving. Key state regulatory policies include state regulations that define licensure requirements and the scope of practice for medical professionals, and state-level insurance regulations. Other state issues focus on operation of state-run high-risk pools and Medicaid system design. While continual changes in our healthcare and health insurance systems pose complex issues for state policy makers and regulators, the ACA receives particular scrutiny due to the broad reach of this federal legislation.

Three Important Issues Addressed by the ACA

During the congressional debate over the ACA, legislators and analysts focused on three important issues:

1. The proportion of U.S. citizens and noncitizen residents who were uninsured was increasing prior to passage of the PPACA in 2010. While the issues faced by individuals with preexisting conditions were widely reported, a larger number of individuals faced economic barriers to purchasing insurance. As per capita healthcare expenditures increased, it became increasingly difficult (or impossible) for low-income individuals to purchase health insurance. The ACA created two mechanisms to address these issues. First, the ACA provided federal funding for states

that increased the income threshold for Medicaid eligibility, for adults who were not covered under specific programs. Second, the ACA provided federal funding to subsidize insurance premiums for low- and middle-income individuals who purchased insurance through newly created state health insurance exchanges. Following implementation of these policies, the proportion of individuals who are uninsured has decreased.

2. Projected cost increases are "unaffordable" in the sense that our society will not have sufficient resources to pay for healthcare (as it is currently delivered), as technology continues to advance. The PPACA included provision to address this issue by increasing efficiency in the care delivery system. These efforts include restructuring the Medicare payment system, incentivizing providers to organize new systems for care delivery, and developing new workforce policies.

At the same time, private-sector innovators are working to develop and implement new strategies for more efficient delivery of healthcare services. Some of these innovations are blocked by current state licensure and scope of practice regulations, and this intersection of private-sector innovation with state regulation is generating pressure for states to revisit these regulatory provisions. These innovations will also generate pressure for state and federal regulators to address new types of consumer protection issues.

In addition, the Health Information Technology and Economic and Clinical Health Act provided funding to support a long-term cost control effort based on electronic health or electronic medical records (EMRs) and health information exchange (HIE). This act was included in the 2009 American Recovery and Reinvestment Act, widely known as the "stimulus bill." Compared with paper charts, electronic health records can potentially

- Support more efficient retention and retrieval of health information
- Provide new types of decision support tools, such as improved access to evidence-based guidelines
- Provide efficient communication among providers, to avoid redundancies (such as duplicate tests), improve continuity of care, and improve the efficiency of care

However, these systems pose trade-offs. The cost to purchase, implement, and maintain EMR and HIE systems is high, and the systems vary in their user-friendliness, reliability, and ability to support healthcare providers' workflows.

3. Clear gaps have been identified in the quality of healthcare delivered in the United States.
   - Geographic variations in care delivery patterns suggest that it would be useful to identify—and utilize—"best practices," such as evidence-based care.
   - There is room for improvement in care coordination when several providers jointly care for an individual patient.
   - Increased utilization of preventive care, wellness, and disease management services could potentially strengthen patient health while reducing total expenditures.

Increased utilization of EMR and HIE systems could support efforts to address each of these healthcare quality issues.

Short-Term Assessment of the ACA

The ambitious goal of addressing all three of these issues has been dubbed the "Triple Aim." Blumenthal (2016) assessed the early impact (first 5 years) of the ACA in each of the three areas. He concludes that the ACA has reduced the proportion of individuals who are uninsured. We should note, however, that issues remain:

- Some individuals—about 33 million, in fact (about 1 in 10 Americans)—are still uninsured.
- Several states have applied for "waivers" to modify traditional Medicaid policies, and the Centers for Medicare and Medicaid Services has approved some these applications—to permit work requirements and/or small monthly premiums or small copayment requirements for enrollees.
- Analysts express concerns about health insurance exchange market stability in some areas.

Blumenthal (2016) also cited improvements in healthcare quality in specific areas: for example, the number of hospital readmissions has decreased. However, he concluded that it is too early to assess whether the strategies specified in the ACA will successfully reduce per capita healthcare expenditures while increasing overall healthcare quality. Achieving those objectives will require significant changes in the organization and management of healthcare delivery systems and in patient healthcare utilization patterns.

Ongoing Debates about the ACA Strategy

Ongoing debates about the ACA strategy address significant, substantive and complex issues.

- Will healthcare providers respond to the new MACRA quality incentives (for Medicare providers) by developing efficient systems for enhancing healthcare quality? Under the new MACRA system, the overall level of physician reimbursement is not scheduled to increase over time. In 2020, physicians who are not participating in risk-based payment models will be eligible to earn bonuses up to 27%, or they may incur penalties of 9%, of payments earned by treating Medicare patients. This system encompasses new measures of quality improvement activities, along with measures that were previously included in the Physician Quality Reporting System and the Value-Based Payment Modifier and Meaningful Use systems. This effort to use clinician incentive payments and penalties to trigger a substantial increase in healthcare quality raises questions. Do the measures built into the new payment system pinpoint key quality issues? If providers increase performance on these measures, will these changes generate meaningful improvement in population health? (We will address payment design issues in Chapter 4.)
- Will the accountable care organizations and patient-centered medical homes defined in the ACA develop successful care integration and population health management strategies? This strategy seeks to build on—and improve—the model demonstrated by managed care organizations. (We will address issues regarding managed care organizations, accountable care organizations, and patient-centered medical homes in Chapter 5.)
- If patients had more financial "skin in the game," would they utilize the healthcare system in more effective ways (e.g., primary care visits instead of emergency department visits), invest more effort in wellness and disease prevention behaviors, and increase compliance with medical advice? If so, what is the most effective strategy for incentivizing healthy patient behaviors—insurance copayments, employer wellness incentives, or other strategies? (We will discuss strategies designed to strengthen prevention and wellness in Chapter 6.)
- Will innovations such as retail clinics (perhaps located in places like Walmart) successfully reduce the cost of delivering care without impairing healthcare quality? Will increased use of integrated care models

successfully strengthen healthcare quality without increasing cost? (We will discuss new types of providers in Chapter 7.)

■ The ACA strategies for increasing healthcare quality and reducing cost rely on increased adoption and use of information technology by healthcare provider organizations. This raises the following question: What factors explain the relatively slow penetration of information technology in the healthcare industry? Were healthcare providers less likely to embrace information technology than organizations in other industries because the healthcare software systems are not sufficiently useful, or was the dispersion of these systems hindered by market failures? If the answer to this question lies primarily in the utility of the software systems, the federal effort to speed the dispersion process is unlikely to produce beneficial results. However, if the answer lies in market failures, the federal effort could potentially be valuable. Given the ambitious nature of the Health Information Technology and Economic and Clinical Health initiative, it is too early to assess the long-term outcome of this effort. (We will discuss health information technology in Chapter 8.)

Goal of This Book

The information provided in this book does not provide definitive answers to these questions, and it does not provide definitive analyses of any specific current controversy. Instead, it better equips healthcare professions to assess the ongoing stream of policy issues that are likely to arise in coming years through the lens of economics. This book will help healthcare providers understand evidence-based economic analysis of our healthcare crisis, healthcare reform strategies, the forces that are shaping our nation's healthcare system, and the efforts to achieve the Triple Aim as defined by the Institute for Healthcare Improvement (2017):

■ Improving the patient experience of care—including quality and satisfaction
■ Improving population health
■ Reducing the per capita cost of healthcare

We provide empirical evidence, explain the economic concepts that illuminate the implications of this evidence, and summarize the results of empirical studies regarding (1) our healthcare system's access, cost, and quality problems, and (2) five types of changes that are reforming our system.

We understand that healthcare change poses significant challenges: the issues are complex, and developing effective strategies for responding to industry and policy changes is not an easy task. Practitioners, consumers, and even policy makers can feel that a tsunami of change is about to engulf them. This book will help you understand the terminology and facts, and help you acquire a working knowledge of types of changes that are underway.

While we acknowledge the political nature of healthcare reform debate, we have endeavored to present the economic concepts, analyses, and summaries in a politically neutral manner. Additionally, it is important to note that there are many lenses by which to analyze health policy (e.g., social justice, legal, and ethical). We have intentionally maintained a singular focus on the economics lens. Understanding the economics concepts and evidence provides a strong starting point for assessing the costs and benefits of alternate policy options for addressing social justice, and ethical concerns.

Whether you applaud or decry specific policies, knowledge of the underlying issues will help you navigate the changing landscape in ways that best serve you and your patients. Assessing these issues will help you assess practice opportunities (and threats), and identify viable strategies for adapting to the changes that optimize your practice and the care you provide. In addition, understanding economic principles, and the empirical evidence provided by health economists, will help you assess policy controversies and identify sound policy options.

In every crisis, there is an opportunity, and the ongoing changes in healthcare payment and delivery systems will generate interesting opportunities for the astute, proactive healthcare professional. In fact, policy makers are depending on the cooperation (and sometimes the abdication) of healthcare professions: careful thinking is needed to assess realistic options, the welfare of patients, and the financial viability of possible reforms.

This book is divided into two main sections. Section I identifies the pressures for change in our healthcare system. It focuses on issues related to access to care, cost of care, and quality of care. We examine hypotheses that underlie our current reform efforts and related political debates, and the empirical evidence that validates or negates these hypotheses—to develop an evidence-based foundation for assessing issues and options. Section II examines five ongoing strategies for increasing the efficiency of our healthcare—as dramatic improvements in efficiency and productivity are the keys to resolving the problem. For now, we can think of efficiency as maximizing the healthcare services delivered with a given set of resources, or minimizing the cost to deliver a given set of services. Efficiency will be examined as it relates to past, present, and proposed innovations. We will look at the federal government's strategies, market-based innovations that are impacting our healthcare industry, and the interaction between government policy innovations and private-sector innovations.

We start Section I by identifying the pressures for change generated by the ongoing failures of the current U.S. healthcare system, and then we delve into the specifics over the next three chapters. Although the material is presented in three distinct categories (access, cost, and quality), these pressures for change are inextricably intertwined. In fact, the web of issues that link the access, cost, and quality problems is a major reason that the healthcare crisis has been so intractable for so long. As we examine these issues throughout this book, it will become apparent that simplistic solutions will not resolve the problems. So let's begin!

PRESSURES FOR CHANGE

Introduction

There are no solutions … there are only tradeoffs.

Thomas Sowell (1995, p. 142)

What Is Causing All These Pressures to Reform the Healthcare System?

We frequently hear that "the healthcare system is broken." What exactly does this mean? Why is the debate about healthcare reform so complex, lengthy, and vehement? What changes were triggered by the Patient Protection and Affordable Care Act (PPACA)? What problems still remain?

To understand the system-wide changes that are underway, we begin by examining detailed evidence about the problems that triggered the enactment of the PPACA and the ongoing issues that remain to be solved. The specific problems are relatively well known:

- Employers, who pay healthcare premiums for many Americans, complain about the escalating cost of premiums. With mandated benefits and other requirements, employers have little room to maneuver; hence, they pass on cost increases to their employees.
- Despite the increase in healthcare coverage brought about by the PPACA, 28.5 million individuals in the United States did not have health insurance at the end of 2015 (Kaiser Family Foundation, 2016). Yet

they need healthcare: they either access healthcare inefficiently (by, e.g., using emergency rooms), declare bankruptcy because they can't pay their bills, or postpone—or forego—care. The uninsured individuals face unnecessary health issues due to the fact that they obtain less healthcare than insured people, while society must address the issue of paying for the "uncompensated" care that uninsured individuals do utilize. PPACA's health insurance mandate and Medicaid expansion reduced the magnitude of this problem, but they did not eliminate it.

◼ High costs of health insurance are causing employers to shift those costs to the employees through higher premiums, deductibles, and copays—raising access and cost issues even for those with insurance (Kaiser Family Foundation, 2017).

◼ Low-income individuals still struggle to afford insurance premiums, copayments, and deductibles.

◼ The proportions of individuals who are uninsured dropped in states that expanded Medicaid eligibility. In states that did not expand Medicaid, individuals can be caught between the low-income ceiling for Medicaid eligibility and the higher threshold for eligibility for subsidies offered through the health insurance exchanges (HIXs).

◼ Additionally, undocumented immigrants are not eligible for the subsidies offered through the HIXs and are not eligible for Medicaid coverage.

Despite the inclusion of two insurance reforms that enjoyed broad support (coverage expansion of adult children up to age 26 and the prohibiting of insurance coverage denials due to preexisting conditions), no one seems satisfied with the changes created by the passage of the PPACA; policy makers, employers, consumers (and remember, we all are consumers sooner or later), and providers express dissatisfaction. *Fundamentally, it means there are still problems with access, cost, and quality* (issues often targeted by the Triple Aim*).

We explore these three issues in the coming chapters, from both a pre- and a post-PPACA perspective. Chapter 1 examines access issues, with a particular focus on health insurance. We look at the characteristics of people who are not insured, and we explore the reasons for the lack of insurance

---

* The Triple Aim is the goal of improving the patient care experience (quality and satisfaction), improving the health of populations, and reducing the cost of healthcare (Institute for Healthcare Improvement, 2017).

and significant implications of the demographic incidence of uninsurance. We also consider the early evidence of the effects of the PPACA health insurance mandate, Medicaid expansion, and HIXs. We follow the discussion on access with a look at healthcare costs in Chapter 2. It is common knowledge that healthcare costs are rising faster than the rate of inflation, and these cost increases are creating stress on private and public insurance systems (the government pays for more than half of all healthcare through Medicaid, Medicare, the Veterans Administration, military treatment facilities, and other programs). Finally, we explore the issues related to healthcare quality in Chapter 3. Media stories continue to highlight the failure of the U.S. healthcare system, and in this chapter, we look at the evidence that our current quality is inadequate, analyses of the underlying issues, and strategies to increase quality of care.

By the time you have finished reading Section I, you will have gained a sense of the complexity of the issues facing our healthcare system. You will see that it is impossible to solve any one of these problems in isolation. Instead, a complex web of interactions links the three problems:

- Poor access often means poor-quality treatment. (The rural health provider is necessarily a generalist, but often the best care is provided by specialists, or episodic treatment at an emergency room does not generate the coordination needed to ensure a good outcome.)
- Low quality can generate unnecessary costs.
- High costs often spur efforts to contain cost—which frequently limit access.

Because we focus on evidence-based analysis, each chapter utilizes standard problem-solving procedures: (1) organize background information, (2) diagnose the problem, and then (3) examine solution options—past and present.

Chapter 1

Access

Introduction

The term *access* to healthcare focuses on the ability of individuals, groups, and communities to obtain needed medical services. While problems with accessing healthcare can be attributed to many factors, such as the availability of providers in a geographic area, language barriers, or cultural differences, it is most often associated with low household income or lack of citizenship or documented immigration status. Low-income people have difficulty paying for health insurance, and—if they are uninsured—they have difficulty paying for healthcare out-of-pocket. Despite the availability of publicly provided coverage through Medicaid and subsidies to help low-income people purchase insurance in the state health insurance exchanges (HIXs), 8.8 million non-elderly people who are eligible for these programs remain uninsured. Of these, 3.2 million are children (Rudowitz et al., 2016). In addition, undocumented individuals are not eligible for public assistance. Lack of insurance coverage is a serious issue, because it is associated with lower healthcare utilization. This in turn can be associated with poorer health and subsequent high costs.

In addition, insured people worry that they could become uninsured due to regulatory changes, changes in employment status, or escalation in the cost of health insurance premiums.

Ongoing debates about state and federal health policy address a wide array of issues. Issues that specifically impact financial access to health insurance include

◼ The concept of "affordable" expenditures for health insurance is currently defined as any amount up to 10% of income for middle- and upper-income individuals, and 7% for low-income individuals (Collins et al., 2015). Policy analysts debate the merit and details of this definition.

◼ Disparities in access to healthcare pose salient issues because some aspects of healthcare are lifesaving (e.g., appendectomies) and life extending (e.g., insulin for diabetics), while others increase comfort or reduce pain (e.g., analgesics for arthritis). As a progressive society, we also worry about equitable access to housing, computers, and education, but access to these goods does not raise the same level of passion as access to healthcare, because the potential impact of healthcare on our quantity and quality of life is uniquely direct and personal. This idea generates important but sometimes acrimonious debates about strategies for accomplishing this goal.

◼ The cost shifting necessary to finance uncompensated care provided to uninsured individuals still poses significant challenges. Under the Patient Protection and Affordable Care Act (PPACA), undocumented individuals are not eligible to purchase subsidized health insurance through a state-run health insurance exchange (HIX). The PPACA reduced hospital expenditures for uncompensated care in states that elected to expand Medicaid from 16.7 billion in 2013 to 11 billion in 2014 (vs. a decrease from 18.1 billion to 17.9 billion in nonexpansion states) (Cunningham et al., 2016). This reform reduced—but did not eliminate—the role of uncompensated care in the U.S. healthcare system and the challenges posed by uncompensated care.

Health insurance coverage patterns reflect decisions made by individuals, employers, insurers, and government agencies. These decisions are influenced by an array of demographic and economic factors. To understand the issues that shape health insurance coverage patterns, and the impacts of alternate solution strategies, we examine the logic of these decisions and empirical evidence on the impacts of government policies.

Sources of Insurance and Characteristics of People Who Are Uninsured

Insurance Sources and Trends

The majority of Americans have traditionally been covered with insurance purchased in the private market, often by their employers (Figure 1.1).

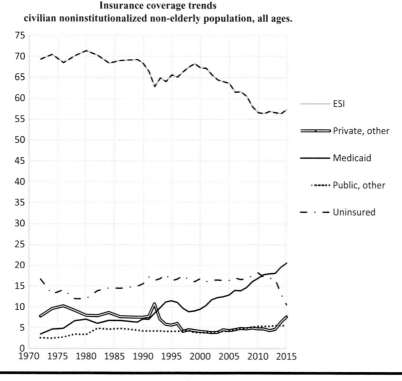

Insurance coverage trends
civilian noninstitutionalized non-elderly population, all ages.

ESI
Private, other
Medicaid
Public, other
Uninsured

Figure 1.1   Public and private insurance coverage trends. (From Center for Disease Control. 2017. Long-term trends in health insurance: Estimates from the National Health Interview Survey, United States, 1968–2015, table 1. Percentages of persons under 65 years. https://www.cdc.gov/nchs/data/nhis/earlyrelease/trendshealthinsurance1968_2015.pdf.)

During the year preceding passage of the Affordable Care Act (ACA) (2009), 63% of the noninstitutionalized U.S. population was covered by insurance purchased through the private sector, 21.3% of these individuals were covered by publicly provided insurance, and 17.5% were uninsured. From 1996 to 2006, the proportion of the non-elderly U.S. population covered by private-sector insurance decreased by 3.2 percentage points, while the proportion covered by private-sector insurance increased by approximately the same amount, and the proportion who were uninsured remained steady.

Unemployment increased during the recent Great Recession* (2008–2010), which led to decreased coverage through employers and increased enrollments in state Medicaid programs. The economic recovery

---

* The Great Recession impacted health insurance patterns, due to the unusual increase in the proportion of individuals who were unemployed. This is an important issue; however, it complicates the task of considering longer-term trends.

continued through 2014, when major components of the PPACA were implemented. Hence, univariate information about changes in insurance coverage rates from 2008 to 2014 must be interpreted cautiously.

Most individuals who were covered by private-sector insurance obtained this insurance through their employers. This type of insurance is known as employer-sponsored insurance (ESI). The distinction between ESI and individually purchased insurance is important because health insurance companies and health insurance regulators segment the health insurance market into three components:

1. The large group market, in which large employers purchase health insurance for large groups of employees.
2. The small group market, in which small employers purchase insurance for groups of 50 or fewer employees (the definition varies across states).
3. The individual market, in which individuals purchase insurance directly from insurance companies. In 2009, fewer than 10% of privately insured individuals purchased health insurance directly from insurance companies.

The majority of individuals who are covered by publicly provided insurance are enrolled in either Medicaid/State Children's Health Insurance Program (SCHIP) or Medicare. Medicaid provides coverage for low-income individuals, SCHIP provides additional coverage for children, and Medicare provides coverage for elderly and disabled individuals. Almost all (96%) individuals who are age 65 or older are covered by Medicare.

Due to near-universal coverage of individuals who are age 65 or older, two methods are commonly used to report information about the proportion of individuals who are uninsured: some report information about the civilian non-institutionalized population (all ages), while others report information about the non-elderly subset of this population. Both methods are correct; however, it is useful to note the definition of the denominator used to compute proportions of individuals who are uninsured when analyzing these numbers.

Who Is Uninsured and Why?

Who Is Uninsured?

To understand policy options for increasing the proportions of Americans with insurance coverage, we examine the demographic characteristics associated with uninsurance, and we consider a study that estimated the likely impacts of three policy strategies for helping those individuals gain coverage. We examine associations between demographic characteristics and lack of health insurance from two perspectives.

Table 1.1 reports the prevalence of uninsurance among specific demographic characteristics in 2015. Three points are salient:

1. The probability of being uninsured was highest among working-age individuals (age 18–64): 13.1% of individuals in this age group were uninsured in 2015. Fewer than 1% of individuals age 65 or older were uninsured. The probability of being uninsured was 4.8% for individuals younger than 18.
2. The proportion of U.S. citizens who were uninsured was 7.5%, compared with 34.8% of noncitizens.
3. While 6% of individuals living in households with an income of at least 200% of the federal poverty level (FPL) were uninsured, 17.7% of individuals living in households with an income below FPL were not covered by health insurance.

Table 1.2 presents profiles of the uninsured in 2 years, 2012 and 2015. The difference between the types of information presented in Tables 1.1 and 1.2 can be seen clearly by looking at the information presented in Table 1.2 on U.S. citizenship status. While Table 1.1 reports that the uninsurance rate is substantially higher among noncitizens than among citizens, Table 1.2 reports that 77.5% of the uninsured are citizens. The difference between these two statistics reflects the additional fact that most people living in the United States are citizens (a small proportion of a large number can outweigh a larger proportion of a much smaller number).

From the perspective of identifying characteristics of the uninsured population, Table 1.2 presents four additional salient points about uninsured individuals in 2012, prior to implementation of the state Medicaid expansions and the HIXs:

1. Most (88%) of the uninsured were working-age adults.
2. One-third of the uninsured adults (age 16–64) worked full-time and year-round. (Note, however, that this information does not specify whether these individuals worked for an employer or were self-employed.)

Table 1.1   Prevalence of Uninsurance by Demographic Group, 2015

	Proportion Uninsured in Each Demographic Group (%)
AGE	
Civilian Noninstitutionalized Population	
Under 18 years	4.8
18–64 years	13.1
65 years and older	0.8
GENDER	
Civilian Noninstitutionalized Population	
Male	10.6
Female	8.3
U.S. CITIZENSHIP STATUS	
Civilian Noninstitutionalized Population	
Native-born or naturalized citizen	7.5
Not a citizen	34.8
WORK EXPERIENCE	
Civilian Noninstitutionalized Population, 16–64 Years	
Worked full-time, year-round in the past 12 months	7.2
Worked less than full-time, year-round in the past 12 months or did not work	11.1
RATIO OF INCOME TO POVERTY LEVEL IN THE PAST 12 MONTHS	
Civilian Noninstitutionalized Population for Whom Poverty Status Is Determined	
Below 99% of the poverty level	17.7
100%–149% of the poverty level	16.0
150%–199% of the poverty level	14.6
At or above 200% of the poverty level	6.0

Source: U.S. Census Bureau, American Community Survey 2015, table S2701. Selected characteristics of health insurance coverage in the United States. 2015 American Community Survey 1-Year Estimates. https://factfinder.census.gov/faces/tableservices/jsf/pages/productview.xhtml?pid=ACS_15_1YR_S2701&prodType=table

Table 1.2   Profiles of the Uninsured, 2012 and 2015

	Percent of Uninsured Who Are in Each Demographic Category	
	2012	*2015*
Percent Uninsured (Civilian Noninstitutionalized Population)	14.77	9.40
AGE		
Civilian Noninstitutionalized Population		
Under 18 years	11.50	11.90
18–64 years	87.60	86.80
65 years and older	0.90	1.30
GENDER		
Civilian Noninstitutionalized Population		
Male	53.50	54.80
Female	46.50	45.20
U.S. CITIZENSHIP STATUS		
Civilian Noninstitutionalized Population		
Native born or naturalized citizen	77.50	73.80
Not a citizen	22.50	26.30
WORK EXPERIENCE		
Civilian Noninstitutionalized Population, 16–64 Years		
Worked full-time, year-round in the past 12 months	33.40	37.70
Worked less than full-time, year-round in the past 12 months or did not work	66.70	62.30
RATIO OF INCOME TO POVERTY LEVEL IN THE PAST 12 MONTHS		
Civilian Noninstitutionalized Population for Whom Poverty Status Is Determined		
Below 99% of the poverty level	28.30	28.00
100%–149% of the poverty level	17.10	15.60
150%–199% of the poverty level	14.50	14.10
At or above 200% of the poverty level	40.10	42.70

Source: U.S. Census Bureau, American Community Survey 2012 and 2015, table S2702: Selected characteristics of the uninsured in the United States; more information 2015 American Community Survey 1-Year Estimates. https://factfinder.census.gov/faces/tableservices/jsf/pages/productview.xhtml?pid=ACS_15_1YR_S2702&prodType=table and Selected characteristics of the uninsured in the United States more information 2012 American Community Survey 1-Year Estimates. https://factfinder.census.gov/faces/tableservices/jsf/pages/productview.xhtml?pid=ACS_15_1YR_S2702&prodType=table

3. Sixty percent of the uninsured lived in households with an income of less than 200% of the FPL.
4. Two and half percent of the uninsured were not U.S. citizens.

Why Are Some People Uninsured?

The profile of uninsured individuals provides a starting point for considering the question, why are some individuals uninsured? A non-elderly adult may not be covered by health insurance for three broad reasons:

1. Some individuals are not eligible for insurance offered by an employer:
   a. Some employers do not offer insurance.
   b. Some individuals do not work enough hours to qualify for insurance offered by the employer.
   c. Some individuals do not work for employers.
2. Some individuals do not accept or "take up" offers of insurance:
   a. Some individuals do not accept insurance offered by employers.
   b. Some individuals who are eligible for public insurance do not enroll.
3. Insurance companies use "restrictive practices" to avoid selling insurance to people with serious health conditions.

We examine key factors that shape these decisions. We begin by examining basic insurance principles. This will equip us to examine employer decisions to offer insurance, individual decisions to accept or decline this offer, and insurance company decisions on restrictive practices.

Private Insurance Markets

Private insurance markets continue to play an important role, even post-ACA, because most non-elderly people are expected to continue to obtain health insurance through employers. Indeed, most employers are mandated to either offer group health insurance or pay a fine.

In this section, we examine key economics concepts about insurance and insurance markets. Because we assume that most of you did not major in economics, we walk through the economics analyses step-by-step. Your investment of time and effort will pay off in a deeper understanding of the trade-offs that must be considered to design workable and equitable policies to facilitate access to health insurance.

Insurance Principles: Insurance Is a Mechanism for Managing Risk

When we purchase insurance, we essentially shift the risk to the insurance company. The insurance company can bear the risk efficiently, because it pools the risk of many participants. To understand how this works—and then explore the implications for health policy—consider a simple example from the perspective of one individual who faces risk, and from the viewpoint of the insurance company that determines the premium for the policy.

How Will the Insurance Company Compute the Premium for a Specific Type of Insurance?

Suppose Bill owns a house in an area that is at high risk for earthquakes. Bill is considering purchasing insurance. His options are summarized Table 1.3.

If Bill buys the insurance and then his house incurs significant earthquake damage, he will pay the deductible, and the insurance company will cover most of the cost of the structural repairs. On the other hand, if he buys the insurance and the house is not damaged by an earthquake, he will have simply purchased "peace of mind."

Table 1.3   Bill's Insurance Purchasing Options

	Bill Does Not Purchase Insurance	*Bill Purchases Insurance*
No earthquake	No damage.	No damage. Bill pays monthly premium to purchase insurance.
Earthquake occurs	Bill spends $100,000 to repair structural damage.	Structural damage requires extensive $100,000 repairs. Bill pays monthly premium to purchase insurance, and he also pays the deductible specified in the policy.

If Bill buys insurance, he will purchase a policy from a company that sells earthquake insurance to thousands of homeowners—in many areas of the country. Some of the houses will experience earthquakes—and the insurance company will cover the cost of the structural repairs. Others will not sustain any damage. The insurer will collect premiums from each home-owner, and these pooled funds must be sufficient to pay for

- The claims filed by homeowners who sustain earthquake damage
- The insurance company's administrative expenses
- The return on the company's invested capital (that is expected by the investors).

This means that—on average—each homeowner must pay his or her fair share of the cost of the earthquake damage plus administrative expenses, which include expenses associated with operating a com-pany, such as rent and salaries, and activities such as preventing fraud and complying with government regulations. An insurance company that does not charge sufficient premiums to cover the cost of paying claims plus these business and administrative expenses will go out of busi-ness. This means that insurance will not "make earthquake repairs more affordable." Instead, it adds to the cost of paying for earthquake dam-age, because the insurance company cannot operate without employees, computers, and office space. Some homeowners are willing to incur these extra costs, because the insurance also spreads the cost of earth-quake repairs across a large group of homeowners. Premiums paid by lucky homeowners who do not experience earthquakes help cover the costs of damage incurred by unlucky homeowners who experience earthquakes.

When Will an Individual Decide to Purchase Insurance?

Bill faces a diverse array of risks: his house could be damaged in an earth-quake, his television could be damaged if his house is hit by lightning, his car may need oil changes, his new household appliance may be defective, and his daughter might lose a library book. Each of these events has two important characteristics: the probability that the event will occur, and the cost that Bill will face *if* the event occurs. Some of these bad events have low probability (lightning could hit the house—but this is a very rare event), while other events are routine and predictable, such as automobile oil changes. In addition, some bad events are very costly (repairing structural damage after an earthquake), and some are inexpensive (changing the oil in a car). Bill is faced with the question, how should I manage these risks? Should I buy the earthquake insurance? Should I buy the extended warranty next time I purchase a household appliance? Should I search for "car oil change insurance"? Bill could create a chart to help him sort-out these issues, as illustrated in Table 1.4.

As Bill considers his options, he will not buy insurance for oil changes for his new car. Think about his logic. Based on the number of miles he typically drives each year, Bill expects that his new car will need four oil changes next year. Each oil change will cost $30, so Bill expects to spend $120. If Bill buys oil change insurance, the premium will have to cover this expected cost *plus* Bill's share of the company's administrative expenses and profit. This implies that the premium would be higher than $120. Bill will not buy this insurance, because the oil change expenditure is highly predictable and financially manageable for him. It doesn't make sense to pay the insurance company to pool the "risk," when there is very little risk because the expenditure can be predicted, with minimal uncertainty.

If Bill buys the extended warranty for his new dishwasher, he will pay a premium that will cover "his share" of claims for all defective dishwashers *plus* his share of the insurance company's administrative expenses and profit. Bill will only be willing to pay this premium if he values the peace of mind associated with shifting the risk that the dishwasher might be defective. This is unlikely, because Bill could wash the dishes by hand if he had to live without a dishwasher for a while.

While Bill can afford to manage these relatively small risks on his own, the possibility of earthquake damage involves genuine risk of a substantial

Table 1.4   Insurance Purchasing Decisions

Event	Probability	Cost	Decision to Purchase Insurance
Bill's car will need regular oil changes	Very high	Low	No
Household appliance might be defective	Medium	Medium	Maybe the decision will depend on the price
Earthquake mightcause structural damage	Low	Very high	Maybe the decision will depend on the price

financial loss, as his home could be completely destroyed. Buying insurance could make sense, if Bill believes that the extra peace of mind is "worth" the price embedded in the premium. Typically, this means that people buy insurance for events that are

■ Risky in the sense that the events cannot be predicted with a high degree of certainty but still represent a significant probability of occurrence
■ Potentially expensive, which implies that peace of mind is an important issue for these events

Application of Insurance Principles in Markets for Health Insurance

Healthcare expenditures—as a whole— meet the criteria for purchasing insurance coverage:

■ Medical care expenditures involve substantial risk, in the sense that expenses vary significantly from year to year (even if we know what Bill spent last year, it would be difficult to predict his expenses for next year).
■ Medical care expenses can be substantial (tens of thousands of dollars for some chronic diseases or even hundreds of thousands of dollars for serious illnesses or injuries).

However, the Nobel Prize–winning economist Milton Friedman (2001) cautioned that we should look more closely before we conclude that we should insure *all* types of healthcare expenditures. Some expenditures (routine dental cleanings) are highly predictable and relatively low cost, while others have a low probability and high financial impact (heart surgery). Friedman argued that insurance policies should cover events in the second category, but they should not cover events in the first category. In fact, catastrophic insurance coverage implements this idea—by only providing insurance coverage for high-cost healthcare expenditures.

Some argue that it makes sense for health insurance policies to cover preventive services, even though they are highly predictable, because these episodes of care may save money in the long run. This logic essentially argues that preventive services constitute a special category of healthcare services that should be included in health insurance policies because they will generate net savings. This argument is based on the assumption that these will generate net savings, and this assumption could be tested using healthcare claims data.

Health Insurance for Preexisting Conditions: Risk versus Subsidy

The issue of insurance coverage for preexisting conditions is complex, but it becomes clearer if we apply the principles of insurance that we just discussed. Let's begin by considering the issue from Bill's perspective. Suppose Bill is currently uninsured. He generally incurs $10,000 in medical expenses each year to treat and manage a chronic condition. Suppose he learns that his neighbor pays $6000 for a health insurance policy that would cover all his medical expenses. Bill will immediately attempt to purchase this insurance coverage, so he can save $4000. It makes financial sense from his perspective. If the insurance company refuses to sell him that policy, he will complain that they are denying him the opportunity to save $4000.

But does it make sense from the insurance company's perspective? If the insurance company sells a policy to Bill for $6000, it will definitely lose money on that policy. If the company consistently engaged in similar money-losing transactions, the company would be forced to close. Instead, the company will note that this individual's healthcare expenditures are highly predictable—and the company will want to charge a premium that will cover the predicted expenditures. These expenditures are equal to $10,000 plus the associated administrative expenses and profits. (The company's shareholders expect to earn profits—otherwise, they will shift their invested funds to a company that will give them a better return on their money.)

Insuring Risk versus Subsidizing an Expenditure

The concept of buying insurance to spread the risk of unknown future events doesn't make sense in this situation. If Bill tried to buy a car insurance policy after he damaged the car by hitting a tree, Bill's car would have a preexisting condition. We would not expect the car insurance company to cover the repair costs for this condition.

Many people view healthcare as more important than car repair. The general notion of fairness suggests that the population of healthy people should help cover the costs incurred by the unlucky individual who has a preexisting high-cost condition. It also suggests that individuals with moderate or high incomes should help to provide healthcare for low-income individuals who could not reasonably afford to buy health insurance policies. If we are developing a system to implement this notion of fairness, we should be discussing the concept of *subsidy* to provide assistance to low-income or high-cost individuals.

This distinction between the function of insurance to spread risk and the equity argument (for subsidies to help people who are dealing with difficult health problems) plays an important role in health policy debates. The distinction between insuring risk and subsidizing expenditures suggests that public passion about "universal coverage" does not focus on access to health insurance. Instead, this debate is really focused on universal subsidized access to healthcare, and health insurance is viewed as a good strategy for financing this subsidy.

The debate about catastrophic insurance illustrates the distinction between the risk management function of insurance and the subsidy function of a public program (Box 1.1). If health insurance is simply a tool that allows us to reduce exposure to risk, the public discussion of access to health insurance would focus on catastrophic insurance. However, the debate about mini-med policies suggests that most advocates of increased access to health insurance are advocating for subsidies to help low-income and high-cost individuals purchase health insurance. This important point helps explain why the access problem has been so intractable, why the PPACA debate was so contentious, and why the debate continues.

This point has important implications: there will not be any short-cut solutions to the access issue. Subsidies will be needed. The key policy question focuses on designing a strategy to pay for the subsidy. You might be thinking, "That's easy—government, employers, hospitals, insurance companies, and/or pharmaceutical companies can provide the subsidy." We will see below that the answer will not be that simple. The challenge of developing a strategy to finance universal access to a good or service is not unique to healthcare. We have traditionally assumed that it is important to ensure universal access to services such as telephone, electricity, and Internet. Analyses of strategies for financing universal access to health insurance echo the issues raised by the telephone service subsidy. (Box 1.2 provides some perspective on this issue.)

**BOX 1.1 MCDONALD'S AND MINI-MED POLICIES:
SHOULD THIS "COUNT" AS PROVIDING INSURANCE?**

A recent story reported by the *Wall Street Journal* brings this debate into the public discourse by highlighting two issues with limited benefits plans (commonly referred to as mini-med plans) that the healthcare reform regulations raise. These plans are typically offered by companies with a high turnover of employees (like McDonald's) whose typical employees are young and earn a low income. These employees would not be able to afford high-premium health insurance.

First, mandates in the healthcare reform law require insurers to spend 80%–85% of the premiums on payments for healthcare. Advocates of the mini-med health insurance plans find this regulation problematic, as the overhead to administer these types of policies for companies with a high turnover of employees is higher than that for other types of policies.

Additionally, these plans impose annual expenditure caps that are not compatible with PPACA requirements. For example, McDonald's employees in Montana pay $56 per month for basic coverage that provides up to $2000 in benefits per year. Under the PPACA, catastrophic plans can be purchased on the HIXs by individuals who meet specified requirements; however these plans constitute a small segment of this market.

Source: Healthamburglar. 2010. *Wall Street Journal*, October 2–3. Fuhrmans, V. 2006. More employers try limited health plans: Cheap "mini-medical" policies cover drugs and doctor visits, but little hospitalization. *Wall Street Journal*, January 17.Kaiser Family Foundation. 2011. What is a mini-med plan? Menlo Park, CA: Kaiser Family Foundation, July 5. Retrieved from http://healthreform.kff.org/notes-on-health-insurance-and-reform/2011/july/what-is-a-mini-med-plan.aspx.

Summary of Explanation of Insurance Premiums and When to Buy Insurance

We pay an insurance premium that is higher than the average cost in order to avoid the risk that we might incur a very large expense. Shifting the risk

BOX 1.2   THIS PROBLEM IS NOT UNIQUE TO HEALTHCARE

Consider the following to further illustrate some of the key issues and constraints: What if we had the social goal of ensuring universal access to telephone service (to make sure everyone could dial 911 in an emergency)? For many decades, this goal was accomplished via a cross-subsidy system. When AT&T provided regulated monopoly telephone service, regulators set prices to ensure that business customers subsidized residential customers, and urban customers subsidized rural customers. This permitted regulators to set relatively low residential rates, which permitted a large proportion of households to purchase telephone service. When MCI applied for permission to compete with AT&T, by providing microwave transmission of business telephone service between St. Louis and Chicago, the regulators faced a dilemma. The new competitor offered lower prices for those business customers. The application was initially denied, however, because the new competition threatened the profits generated when AT&T served business customers, and these profits were needed to subsidize the low rates charged to residential customers. It was clear that the telephone industry could not enjoy the benefits of competitive innovation and—at the same time—maintain the cross-subsidy pricing system. If we want to support the social goal of universal telephone service, while also enjoying the benefits of competitive innovation, we must utilize a more direct and transparent strategy to finance that social goal (Reference for Business, 1999).

to the insurance company allows us to plan and manage our household budgets and assets. The difference between the premium and the expected cost of claims is the price we pay in order to shift the risk to the insurance company. (We explain expected value in Box 1.3.) The premium must cover this expected cost of claims plus the cost of the company's overhead plus the profit on the firm's invested capital.

This leads to six important conclusions about insurance:

1. The price of insurance is equal to the difference between the premium and the expected cost of claims, and the price is always greater than zero.
2. It makes sense to buy insurance for high-cost events that do not occur frequently. It does not make sense to buy insurance and pay to shift risk for events that are relatively low cost.

BOX 1.3 EXPECTED VALUE

This is a useful concept for thinking about situations that involve risk. To illustrate the concept, let's think about a lottery. Suppose we have a lottery ticket. If our ticket is a "winning" one, we will win $50. If we don't have a winning ticket, we will not receive anything. Suppose the total number of tickets sold was 100, so our chance of winning is 1/100 (and our chance of going home empty-handed is 99/100). The expected value of the ticket is equal to $1. Here is the detailed computation:

Amount We Might Receive	Probability	Amount * Probability
0	99/100	0
100	1/100	1
	Sum	1

How should we interpret this expected value? We don't expect to receive $1 on any one lottery; instead, we will receive either $100 or zero. However, if we bought individual tickets in 1000 similar lotteries, then we expect that—on average—we would win $1 per lottery.

The concept of expected value allows us to think about average results—if we consider events that may be repeated numerous times. This idea is useful for thinking about insurance premiums because the insurance company does not know how much it will spend to provide care for any one individual. However, the company will insure thousands of individuals, so it can focus on the average expenditure per individual.

3. Insurance is a mechanism to manage risk by paying to shift risk. It does not "make healthcare more affordable." In fact, the opposite is true—it makes healthcare more expensive—because we pay a premium to cover the expected cost of claims *plus* the "price" to shift risk to the insurance company.

4. In a typical employee group, the expected cost of claims is higher for older employees than for younger employees. If we do not adjust the premium to account for this, then the younger (typically lower-wage) employees subsidize the older (typically higher-wage) employees. This

raises a concern, because young employees with a given level of education typically have lower incomes than older employees with the same level of education. This implies that employee group health insurance has a regressive component: on average, lower-income people cross-subsidize higher-income people. Some argue that the intergenerational transfer is fair, because the young workers will gradually grow older. Our current demographic situation demonstrates, however, that this logic is *only* correct if the ratio of younger-to-older workers remains constant. It is clear—instead—that this ratio changes substantially over time. As the baby boomers retire, fewer younger workers will support more and more older retirees. This process raises questions about intergenerational equity.

5. Suppose two employees in an employer group pay the same premium. One has a known health condition that will require expensive treatment this year. The other does not have any known health conditions. In this scenario, the more healthy employee subsidizes the less healthy employee. You might be thinking, yes, that is the purpose of insurance. However, this predictable cross-subsidy from healthy people to less healthy people generates debates about the fair treatment of individual behaviors, such as diet, exercise, and smoking status, that impact health and healthcare expenditures.

6. Health insurance is expensive. In 2017, the average cost of a policy for an individual adult was approximately $6000 (Kaiser Family Foundation, 2017). The annual income for a single adult who works full-time, year-round and earns the federal minimum wage of $7.25 per hour is $15,080. For this individual, the average cost of a health insurance policy is 40% of his annual income. Clearly, this is not affordable.

We've discussed the concepts of risk and price as they relate to health insurance. Next, we'll explore the issues with ESI.

Why Do Some Employers Offer Health Insurance While Others Do Not?

We begin by examining economic analyses of ESI. These ideas are abstract, but they will help us understand why analysts have shifted from using the term *employer-provided insurance* to *employer-sponsored insurance*, they will provide a foundation for analyzing the proposal to mandate that all employers offer insurance, and they will help us predict some of the outcomes of the PPACA employer play-or-pay policy.

Employers Don't Actually Pay for Employer-Sponsored Healthcare

ESI *appears* to reduce the workers' cost of healthcare, because it *appears* to shift the cost from the individual to his or her employer. Unfortunately, however, the empirical evidence is clear: workers actually pay for employer-sponsored insurance, and this indirect payment occurs in the form of reduced wages. The Congressional Budget Office issued a report summarizing the available evidence: "employees, as a group, ultimately bear the costs of any payments an employer makes for health insurance" (Congressional Budget Office, 2008, p. 5). Therefore, analysts have shifted from using the old term *employer-provided healthcare* to the more accurate term, *employer-sponsored healthcare* (see, e.g., Emanuel and Fuchs, 2009).

This conclusion that workers bear the financial impact of ESI may seem surprising: we do not typically observe employers cutting wages in order to pay for rising health insurance premiums. Instead, the process is more subtle. In unionized industries, the trade-off between wages and health insurance may occur during bargaining sessions. Representatives of the autoworkers' union pointed to this trade-off when they protested cuts in retiree health insurance benefits:

The retirees can claim ownership to this benefit legitimately; when they were working, their union accepted lower wages at the bargaining table in return for retiree healthcare benefits. (216Editors, 2009)

In other industries, wages may remain flat, instead of increasing when productivity increases, because the benefits of the productivity increases are used to fund rising health insurance premiums. While this may seem innocuous in the short run, it has important long-run consequences. *When the costs of so-called employer-provided insurance increase faster than the general rate of inflation, the spending power of workers' take-home pay is likely to stagnate or decrea se.**

---

* Inflation means that the purchasing power of a dollar decreases over time. Suppose I have $1000 to spend in Year 1 and another $1000 to spend in Year 2. If inflation is 5%, my Year 2 dollars will not stretch as far as my Year 1 dollars. In Year 2, I can only buy 95% of what I could in Year 1, even though I still have the same number of dollars. Inflation varies tremendously, but it tends to be 3%–4% per year, over long periods of time.

The evidence that workers pay completely for health insurance—in the form of reduced wages—is widely accepted. In response to this evidence, analysts have dropped the term *employer-provided insurance* in favor of the more accurate term *employer-sponsored insurance.*

What Forces Shift the Cost of Employer-Sponsored Health Insurance onto Workers?

Economists use abstract logic to understand the reasons that this process occurs, and we can illustrate that logic with a graph of supply and demand. (Be patient—this picture *is* worth 1000 words!) We start by discussing the basic concepts of supply and demand, and then we use these ideas to examine the relationships among worker decisions, employer decisions, and wages.

Basic Economic Tools: Supply and Demand

Figure 1.2a and b illustrates a supply curve and a demand curve for a specific type of labor service, such as unskilled labor, or nursing services, or behavioral health services. Notice that the vertical axes are labeled "hourly wage" and the horizontal axes are labeled "Quantity=hours of labor services." The workers supply these services and employers "demand" or purchase these services.

The supply curve describes the workers' willingness to offer these services. Consider Point A on the supply curve illustrated in Figure 1.2a. Economists offer two equivalent ways to describe the workers' opinions. Consider, for example, Point A.

First, when the wage is W_A, workers are willing to offer exactly Q_A hours of labor services. If you want to purchase more labor services Q_B, for example, you will have to offer a higher wage; if you offer W_B, then workers would be willing to supply Q_B hours of labor services.

Alternately, we could describe the same information by reversing our perspective. If you want to employ Q_A hours of labor services, then W_A is the lowest wage at which workers will be willing to contract with you. They would, of course, be delighted to provide Q_A hours of labor services for a higher wage, but you do not need to offer more than W_A.

The demand curve illustrated in Figure 1.2b summarizes the views of employers. When the wage is equal to W_A, then employers will want to purchase Q_A hours of labor services. If the wage increases to W_B, then employers will reduce their purchases of labor to Q_B. At the higher wage, W_B, the

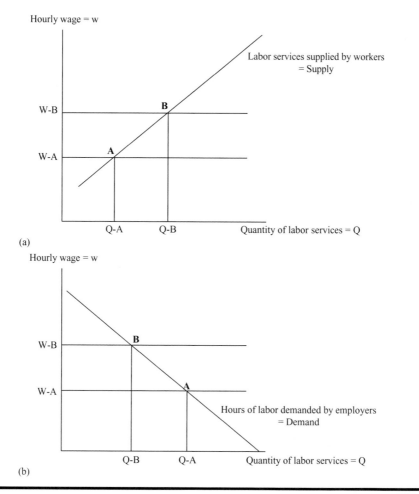

Figure 1.2 (a)   Supply of labor. (b) Demand for labor.

employer might find that it is beneficial to invest in labor-saving equipment that was not cost-effective when wages were lower. We can also describe the same information from the reverse perspective. If an employer is considering purchasing Q_A hours of labor services, W_A is the highest wage the employer will be willing to pay.

Basic Economic Tools: At the Equilibrium Wage, Quantity Supplied Is Equal to Quantity Demanded

Because the supply and demand curves are drawn against the same pair of axes (wage on the vertical axis, quantity on the horizontal axis), we can overlay the two graphs to examine the interaction between workers' views summarized by the supply curve and employers' views summarized by the demand curve. Figure 1.3a illustrates the equilibrium wage, which occurs at the intersection of the supply and demand curves. At this wage, there is no pressure for wage to change—either upward or downward. Firms want to purchase Q_E hours of labor services, and workers want to supply that quantity. Both groups are able to complete their desired transactions.[*]

What Happens When the Actual Wage Is above (or below) the Equilibrium Wage?

When the wage is above (or below) the equilibrium level, suppliers and demanders begin taking actions that push the wage toward equilibrium. In Figure 1.3b, the solid wage line representing the actual wage is below the dashed equilibrium level. Notice that workers want to supply Q_S hours of labor services at this wage, while firms want to buy Q_D hours. The gap between these two quantities represents a shortage of willing workers: firms are not able to purchase all the labor that they would like to buy at the current wage W_A. As firms try to fill these unfilled positions, they will begin offering higher wages. As this bidding process pushes wages up, the number of unfilled positions will shrink: workers will offer more of their services as the wage increases, and firms will reduce their demand for services. The upward pressure on wage will continue until the wage reaches the equilibrium level.

In Figure 1.3c, the solid wage line is above the dashed equilibrium level. At this high wage, workers want to supply Q_S hours of labor services while firms want to buy Q_D hours. The gap between these two quantities represents unemployment: workers who want to work at the going wage face a game of musical chairs, where there are not enough "chairs" for all the hopeful workers. As the unemployed workers realize that they cannot find jobs at the going wage, they will offer to work for slightly lower wages or fewer benefits. As firms realize that they can hire qualified workers at these lower wages, the "going" wage will fall. When it reaches the equilibrium wage, all interested workers will have jobs and there will be no further downward pressure on wages.

---

[*] Despite the plethora of jokes about economists who disagree with each other, economists largely agree on core ideas. One of these core ideas is that price ceilings create shortages, and price floors create surpluses. Impacts of price ceilings have been widely documented in the housing market. To read more, go to http://www.fee.org/library/books/roofs-or-ceilings-the-current-housing-problem/. This article discusses the California housing issue at two critical time periods within the context of price controls.

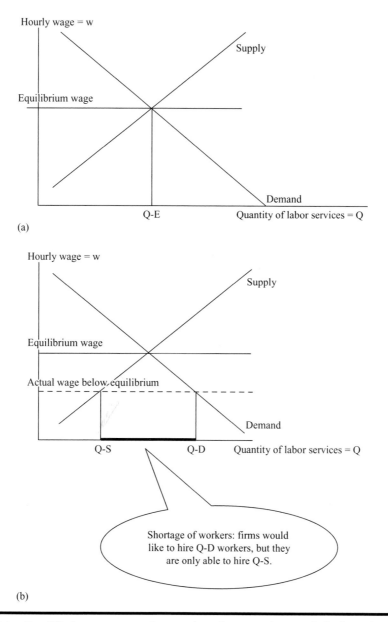

Figure 1.3 (a)   Equilibrium wage and quantity, (b) Actual wage is below the equilibrium wage.

Why Is the Equilibrium Concept Useful?

Even though real-world markets are obviously not always in equilibrium, the concept of the equilibrium wage is useful. By helping us understand the wage pressures that accompany surpluses and shortages, this concept also helps us understand the likely impacts of employer-sponsored

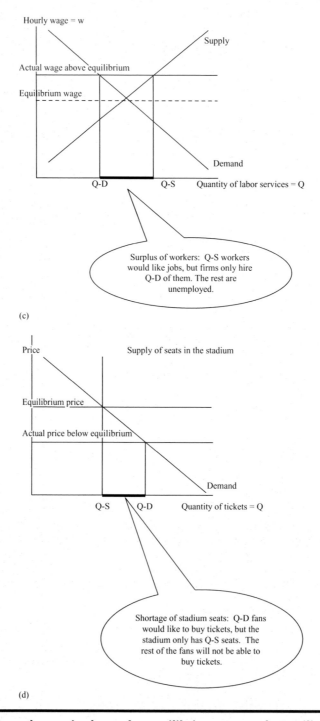

Figure 1.3 (c) Actual wage is above the equilibrium wage, (d) Familiar example: stadium seats.

health insurance. To illustrate the equilibrium concept, consider a familiar example: the market for concert (or sports) tickets. Prices for major events are frequently set below the equilibrium level illustrated in Figure 1.3d. In this case, the supply of seats is simply equal to the number of seats in the stadium, so the supply curve is a vertical line. Fans are the buyers in this market, so the demand curve represents their willingness to pay for tickets. If fans anticipate that the price will be set below the equilibrium level, they know that they will face the musical chairs game: the number of interested buyers will exceed the number of seats. The shortage at the official price is labeled on Figure 1.3d. The result is predictable: fans line up early in an attempt to buy tickets.

This process can be summarized using the wisdom of Goldilocks. If the price or wage is too high, adjustments will occur. If the price or wage is too low, adjustments will occur. If the wage is *just right*, the market is in equilibrium—in the sense that buyers do not have any reason to bid the price up and sellers do not have any reason to bid the price down.

How Does Employer-Sponsored Health Insurance Affect the Equilibrium Wage?

The decision to provide health insurance will impact both the workers and firms; hence, it will impact both the supply curve and the demand curve. The demand curve shows the maximum wage that firms are willing to pay for each quantity of labor services. If firms are currently hiring Q_E labor services as shown in Figure 1.4a, then W_E is the maximum amount the firms are willing to pay to hire this quantity of labor services. When firms begin providing health insurance, they split this amount, W_E, into two buckets: some of the payment will be called "wage," while the other component will be called "health insurance." Firms are indifferent about this split, because the total amount they pay remains unchanged, and it is this total amount that affects their bottom line. This means that the demand curve, which represents the amount the firm is willing to pay as wage, shifts down—as illustrated in Figure 1.4a. The vertical distance between the original demand curve (no insurance) and the new demand curve (with insurance) is equal to the amount the firm pays for health insurance.

Most workers value health insurance, so the employer's decision to provide health insurance will also impact the supply curve shown in Figure 1.4b. This supply curve shows the lowest wage at which workers will be willing to supply their labor. If the wage will be augmented with health

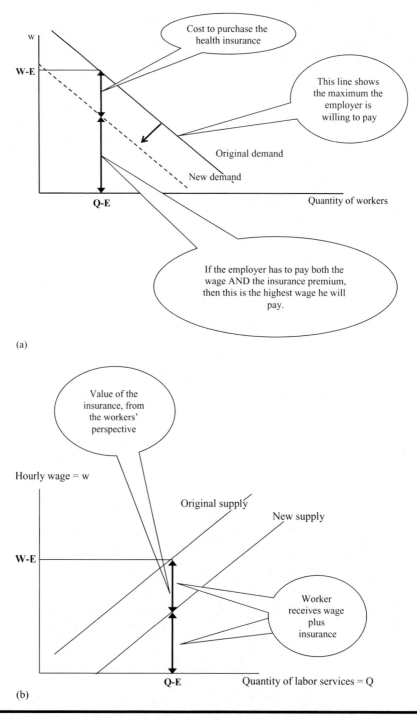

Figure 1.4   (a) When an employer provides health insurance, it makes two types of payments for labor services: wages and health insurance. (b) When the employer provides health insurance, the worker receives two types of payments: wages and health insurance.

insurance, then workers will be willing to supply labor services at lower wages, and the supply curve will shift out. The vertical shift in the supply curve, from the original supply curve to the new supply curve in Figure 1.4b, reflects the wage cut workers are willing to accept in order to obtain health insurance. Economists call this "willingness to pay" for health insurance. Consider, for example, people who specifically choose jobs or stay with a specific employer because the employer offers health insurance. In order to keep their health insurance, these people are giving up opportunities for higher wages, more interesting work, or better possibilities for promotion.

It is important to note that the health insurance cost shift from employers to workers hinges on the relationship between the employers' cost to purchase health insurance and the workers' willingness to pay for health insurance (by accepting lower wages). For any specific quantity of labor services, workers will be willing to accept lower wages if the employer offers health insurance. The key question is, how much do workers value health insurance? This will determine the magnitude of the shift in the supply curve. Two possibilities are illustrated in Figure 1.5a and b.

Scenario 1

We begin with the widespread assumption that workers place a high value on health insurance (Figure 1.5a). In this case, the shift in the supply curve is substantial: workers are willing to accept a significant reduction in wages in exchange for health insurance. To find the impact of health insurance on the equilibrium wage, we show the initial situation (no insurance) with solid supply and demand lines, and a solid line marking the equilibrium wage. We show the new situation (with insurance), using dashed supply and demand lines, and a dashed line marking the new (with insurance) equilibrium wage. Compare the change in the wage (arrow A) with the money spent by the employer to purchase the insurance (arrow B): the drop in the wage is *bigger* than the cost to purchase the insurance! This means that *the employer benefited from providing insurance*! If, for example, the firm spent $3 per hour to purchase health insurance, the firm's decision to purchase health insurance would have reduced the worker's wage by more than $3.

Did the employer gain this benefit at the expense of the workers? No. Compare the magnitudes of the wage reduction with the value of the insurance—as perceived by the workers. The workers obtained insurance at a

Health insurance impacts the equilibrium wage.
Scenario 1: workers place a high value on health insurance
  • Insurance is a bargain for workers: the wage cut A is smaller than the
    workers' perception of the value of the health insurance C
  • Insurance is a bargain for the employer: the wage cut A is bigger than the cost
    to purchase the health insurance B

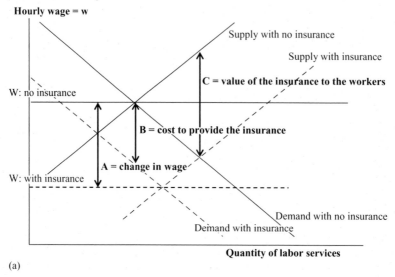

(a)

Health insurance impacts the equilibrium wage.
Scenario 1: workers place a low value on health insurance
  • Workers do not want insurance: the wage cut A is bigger than the workers'
    perception of the value of the health insurance C
  • The employer does not want to offer insurance: the wage cut A is smaller
    than the cost to purchase the health insurance B

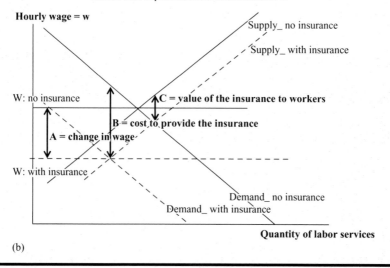

(b)

**Figure 1.5   (a) Health insurance impacts wage: Scenario 1. (b) Health insurance
impacts wage: Scenario 2.**

bargain. The workers' opinion about the value of the insurance (measured by the height of arrow C) is greater than the wage cut needed to obtain the insurance (measured by the height of the shorter arrow A).

This scenario, which is illustrated in Figure 1.5a, is consistent with the statements made by the autoworkers' union—that they explicitly accepted lower wages when they bargained for increased health benefits for the union members. This figure illustrates an important insight: when workers place a high value on health insurance that exceeds the actual employer's cost to purchase the health insurance, the reduction in the equilibrium wage also exceeds the cost to purchase the health insurance. In this case, the employer saves money by providing health insurance. Thus, providing health insurance is a profitable strategy for an employer if the firm's employees place a high value on health insurance.

How did this happen? The key is the relationship between the cost to buy the insurance and the value of the insurance to the workers: arrow A is taller than arrow B. Employer-sponsored health insurance can offer this bargain for three reasons:

1. Large employers (more than 50 employees) purchase insurance in the large group market and they pay substantially lower premiums than the workers would face if they purchased insurance as individuals. We will explore the reasons for this difference in premiums below—when we examine Hypothesis 3.
2. All employers purchase health insurance with pretax dollars, while— until very recently—individuals typically purchased health insurance with after-tax dollars. Consider the tax implications of splitting workers' compensation into two buckets. When the employer labels the compensation as "wages," the worker pays income tax on that amount— and they purchase goods and services with the remaining after-tax dollars.
   - Suppose, for example, a worker receives $100 in wages and pays income tax equal to 20% of this income ($20). Then he has $80 in his pocket, and he can use this money to buy goods and services, such as food, gas, clothing, and health insurance. If he could buy health insurance for $20, he would have $60 to spend on other goods and services.
   - In contrast, if the employer relabels some of this compensation as "health insurance," the employer purchases the health insurance and deducts that cost as a business expense. The worker does not pay

income tax on the value of the health insurance policy. The worker receives taxable income equal to $100−$20=$80, and he pays 20% of this amount in taxes ($16). After he pays this tax, he has $66 to spend on other goods and services.

– The inequity of the historic discrepancy between the tax treatment of ESI and the tax treatment of individual-purchased health insurance has been widely discussed. The 2010 PPACA included measures to attempt to reduce this inequity. However, PPACA does not change the fact that large employers typically purchase health insurance in the large group market, and prices are lower in the large group market than in the market for individually purchased health insurance.

3. Large employers may wield bargaining power to obtain rates that are not available to individuals.

Scenario 2

This scenario focuses on workers who are not willing to accept the wage cuts that would be necessary to pay for health insurance. This attitude could reflect several underlying factors.

1. Low-wage workers might place higher priority on even more basic and urgent needs, such as housing, food, and transportation, than on health insurance. (See Box 1.4 for additional details.)
2. Individuals who are eligible for Medicaid may place low value on private-sector health insurance.
3. Individuals who work for small employers may be likely to fall in this category, since small employers typically pay higher rates for health insurance than large employers. We'll discuss the reasons below; here we are interested in the implication. The downward shift in the demand curve will be larger for small employers than for large employers. Therefore, worker wage cuts will be larger in small firms than in large firms.
4. Young healthy adults typically incur lower average healthcare expenditures than older adults. Thus, young workers are likely to place a lower value on health insurance than older workers and exhibit a lower willingness to pay.

In this case, illustrated in Figure 1.5b, the wage cuts that workers are willing to accept (arrow C) in exchange for health insurance are smaller

BOX 1.4   AVERAGE COST OF HEALTH INSURANCE PER HOUR

A full-time employee works 2080 hours per year (52 weeks × 40 hours per week).

Among large employers, the average premium in 2009 was $4,674 for single coverage and $13,210 for coverage for a family of four. (We use data from 2009 because this year corresponds to analyses used to predict the impacts of the PPACA.)

Thus, the average premium per employee costs between $2.25 and $6.35 per hour, depending on the ratio of employees electing single versus family coverage. The weighted average premium is nearly $5 per hour (using the U.S. Census estimate that the average household size is 2.59 and the Employee Benefit Research Institute estimate that 79 million individuals and 77 million dependents have employer-based coverage). However, employees may pay a portion of this cost—in the form of monthly contributions, copayments, or deductibles—so the employer's average hourly expense is typically lower than the range cited here.

Detailed analysis of the impact of this issue was published in 2007, when the average premium (paid by employers) was approximately $3 per hour; hence, we use that number in our discussion.

The PPACA employer mandate specifies that if an employer does not offer insurance, the penalty is $2000 for every employee (after the first 30) per year. For a large employer, this penalty raises the cost of hiring an employee by $1 per hour. Based on existing evidence, we should anticipate that this penalty will cause the demand curve (for employees) to shift down—and this will put downward pressure on wages. Therefore, employees will bear some (and possibly most) of this cost. However, the penalty will not shift the supply curve—because employees do not directly benefit from the penalty.

Source: Claxton, G., and Damico, A. 2011. Snapshots: Employer health insurance costs and worker compensation. Menlo Park, CA: Kaiser Foundation.

than the employers' cost to purchase health insurance (arrow B). In this case, the change in the equilibrium wage is smaller than the employers' cost to provide health insurance and larger than the value workers receive from health insurance. Employers do not want to provide insurance, and the workers agree with this decision. In this scenario, workers do not want employer-sponsored health insurance—in the sense that they are unwilling to accept the consequent reduction in wages. While the policy discussion of health insurance typically assumes that everyone "wants" employer-sponsored health insurance, this assertion ignores the marketplace reality that workers actually trade wage reductions for health insurance.

Our analysis of Scenario 2 points to a serious concern: mandating that all employers must sponsor health insurance could impose a hardship on low-wage workers. Under PPACA, the low-wage workers' employer must either pay a fine—approximately $1 per hour per employee for a large employer—or purchase health insurance (at least $3 per hour). Either way, the employer faces higher costs per worker; hence, the demand for workers shifts down. This could put downward pressure on the wages (or employment) for these already low-wage workers.

Empirical evidence indicates that these issues are important. A detailed analysis of this issue was conducted by Baicker and Levy (2007) when health insurance premiums averaged $3 per hour. Baicker and Levy (2007) estimated that one-third of uninsured individuals have incomes within $3 of the minimum wage (after adjusting for state-level variations in the minimum wage). The evidence showing that workers essentially pay for ESI indicates that an employer mandate raises equity concerns (Box 1.4).

Implications of Scenarios 1 and 2

An Employer Mandate Only Impacts Workers and Employers Facing Scenario 2

In Scenario 1, the employer offered health insurance pre-PPACA because employers and workers *both* benefit from ESI. The PPACA employer mandate will only impact employers and workers facing Scenario 2. These employers do not offer insurance because neither the employers nor the workers are willing to make the dollars versus insurance trade-off.

An Inefficient Healthcare System Means Lower Wages for Workers

Healthcare expenditures have been increasing faster than the general level of inflation for many years. This implies that healthcare expenditures account for an increasing percent of our national economic output, as illustrated in Figure 1.6. It also implies that the wage–health insurance trade-off cannot, typically, be accomplished by simply foregoing wage increases. Instead, actual wage cuts will be required. This causes strains in labor

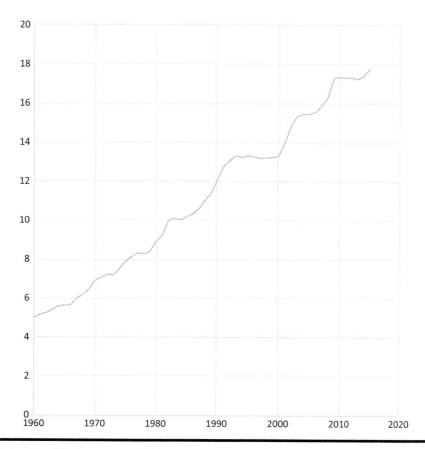

Figure 1.6   Healthcare expenditures as a percent of GDP.

markets because it counters the reasonable expectation that workers should
share in productivity gains by receiving pay increases. Part of the healthcare crisis is exactly this: a costly-inefficient healthcare system means lower
wages for workers.

Healthcare Coverage Mandates Lead to Higher Costs for Health Insurance and Lower Wages for Workers

Our logic and graphs are based on the implicit assumption that the
employer can choose the types of healthcare services that will be included
in the health insurance package—that is, to define the package that maxi-
mizes the net value, the difference between the value generated for the
workers and the cost to purchase the insurance. In recent years, state and
federal coverage mandates have reduced employer flexibility to shape the
package of services that will be covered (Jensen and Morrisey, 1999). For

example, 40 states mandated prior to PPACA that ESI must include coverage for psychologists' services, 39 states mandate coverage for chiropractors' services, and 35 states mandate coverage for dentists' and optometrists' services. While all these professionals provide valuable services, empirical studies indicate that these coverage mandates lead to increased premiums for health insurance.

The typical "news media" discussion of these mandates starts from the implicit assumption that all workers want comprehensive health insurance, and therefore the key issue is a power struggle between employers and workers. Our logic implies that employers want to provide insurance when they have workers who want insurance and vice versa. This implies that mandates to make coverage more comprehensive may harm low-wage workers by pricing them out of the insurance market unless the mandate is accompanied by a subsidy to finance the additional costs. That is, these mandates may trigger reduced health insurance coverage for low-income workers.

Political support for coverage mandates stems from complaints that some employers don't offer enough insurance. Pauly (2001) offers a thought-provoking analysis of complaints about insufficient insurance: a single employer is likely to have employees with a diverse array of preferences. Large firms typically employ a diverse workforce that includes both young healthy workers (with lower healthcare costs) and older workers (with higher healthcare costs). When the typical large employer is considering whether to add a specific benefit to the health insurance package, it probably has some workers with Scenario 2 preferences, and other workers with Scenario 1 preferences. How will the employer decide whether to add the benefit to the firm's health insurance package? If the employer views the health insurance package as a tool to reduce worker turnover, the firm would be most concerned about the preferences of workers who are most likely to quit and seek jobs elsewhere. Because young workers are more likely to seek new jobs than older workers, we expect large employers to place priority on these workers' preferences—and these workers generally prefer less generous benefits. In an employee group, all workers pay the same wage penalty to indirectly purchase insurance, but the older workers incur higher costs. Thus, the young workers subsidize older workers—and therefore they will rationally prefer a less comprehensive package.

The results of the 2013 private exchange that Aon Hewitt operated for 100,000 employees of Sears Holdings Corp. and Darden Restaurants, Inc. indicate that employees within an employee group do have diverse preferences. Each employer offered a fixed amount of money to each employee, and employees were permitted to "spend" that money purchasing insurance in the exchange operated by Aon Hewitt. Some employees (42%) chose plans that were more expensive than their previous plans, while others (26%) chose plans that were less expensive than their previous plans (Mathews, 2013).

States are currently facing this issue directly—as they define the basic benefit packages that will be offered in the state HIXs.

Why Do Some Individuals Remain Uninsured, Even Though They Are Eligible for Public Insurance or ESI?

While it may seem incredible to analyze the proportions of individuals who decline ESI or do not apply for free public coverage, published evidence documents the importance of this issue. For example, Buchmueller et al. (2005) noted that 6 million children who were eligible for public coverage under SCHIP remained uninsured because their parents or guardians did not apply for the coverage. Sommers (2006), Aizer and Grogger (2003), and Aizer (2007) analyzed factors that influence these parental decisions and conclude that information and administrative hurdles, such as asset tests and mandatory waiting periods, exert significant influence on Medicaid take-up rates. (The term *take-up* is used to describe a decision to accept an insurance offer.)

Employees also make decisions to accept or reject employer offers to sponsor insurance: 20% of uninsured workers were eligible for an employer's ESI but were not enrolled. The proportion of workers who decline an employer's offer of ESI is related to income: 29% of workers with income less than the FPL who are eligible for ESI decline the offer. In contrast, 16% of workers with income greater than 400% of the FPL decline ESI offers (Kaiser Family Foundation, 2004). Vistnes and Monheit (2011) investigated whether the decline in ESI coverage stems from a decline in employers offering ESI or a decline in the rate at which individuals take up the offer. They concluded that patterns differ by firm size. They found that both insurance offers and take-up decisions declined at small firms. At large firms, the take-up rate declined, but the proportion of large employers offering insurance remained stable. These authors also make one more important point: the nature of ESI is also changing—fewer firms offer dependent coverage, and the proportion of individuals who take up dependent coverage is declining.

Interactions among these factors add another layer of complexity. Abraham and Feldman (2010) reported that workers are less likely to take up an employer's insurance offer when their children are eligible for Medicaid. In addition, Buchmueller et al. (2005) and Herring (2005) reported that fewer employers offer coverage when charity care is available, and employers raised the worker's contribution for family coverage as SCHIP expanded. These findings suggest that the impacts of PPACA on private insurance markets should be monitored carefully, because they indicate that Medicaid coverage can "crowd out" private coverage—in the sense that individuals will not purchase private coverage and firms may not offer coverage if public coverage is available. Bansak and Raphael's 2006 study of insurance decisions concluded,

> We find that between one-quarter and one-third of the increase in public health insurance coverage for SCHIP-eligible children is offset by a decline in private health coverage.*

This places an additional burden on state Medicaid/SCHIP programs, as some families and employers substitute public for private insurance. The results pose a challenge to states: if a state provides funds to add four children to the SCHIP program, only three of those children were previously uninsured, while one child simply switched from private to public coverage. While the opportunity to switch to public coverage is a boon to that family's budget, it is a burden to the state's budget. Anecdotal evidence indicates that some state Medicaid program analysts assume that some employers will drop coverage when the Medicaid expansion is implemented, and they factor this into their cost estimates.

Similarly, the *Wall Street Journal* reported (Thurm, 2013) that chain restaurants estimate that some of their employees will apply for Medicaid coverage. The concept of *price elasticity* provides a useful tool to measure the sensitivity of purchase decisions—for any good—to changes in price:

$$\text{price elasticity of demand} = \frac{\text{percent change in quantity}}{\text{percent change in price}}.$$

---

* SCHIP is the State Children's Health Insurance Program—sometimes also known as CHIP—Children's Health Insurance Program is a federal and state insurance program designed to provide health insurance to families making too much for Medicaid but whose incomes are still modest.

Okeke et al. (2010), for example, concluded that the probability an employee will decline an employer's offer of insurance increases by 1% for every 10% increase in the out-of-pocket premium. Thus, the price elasticity of the demand for health insurance is equal to

$$\frac{1\% \text{ decrease in quantity}}{10\% \text{ increase in price}} = -0.1.$$

He also finds that married workers are more price sensitive than single workers, presumably because these workers may have the option of enrolling in their spouse's plan, and lower-income workers are more price sensitive than higher-income workers.

The fact that price elasticity is estimated to be low (the magnitude is less than 1) has two implications for health policy:

1. Small premium subsidies may not be an effective strategy for addressing the problem of "the uninsured": a subsidy equal to 10% of the out-of-pocket premium will only increase the take-up rate by 1%.
2. Mandating more generous coverage—such as coverage for mental health conditions—will induce some individuals to drop coverage if the mandate leads to health insurance premium increases. However, the impact of these mandates on insurance take-up decisions is likely to be modest: a 10% increase in out-of-pocket premiums is likely to induce 1% of workers to drop coverage.

Analysis of the high proportion of Hispanic workers who do not have insurance highlights additional issues. Honig and Dushi (2005) and Waidmann et al. (2004) analyzed the key question: Do minorities have lower rates of insurance coverage because

■ They are less likely to receive an ESI offer
■ They are less likely to take up ESI offers

Honig and Dushi (2005) concluded that minorities are less likely to receive an ESI offer, but once an employee receives an offer, the likelihood of accepting the offer is not correlated with race or ethnicity. Waidmann et al. (2004) took this analysis a step further and concluded that subtle details are important to inform policy design and support estimation of the impacts of policy innovations. Waidmann et al. (2004) found that

Hispanic workers are more likely to receive an ESI offer when the analysis controls for job skills, immigrant status and employment characteristics, and take-up rates are lower for immigrant Hispanics compared with non-immigrant non-Hispanics, but—among nonimmigrants—the take-up rates for Hispanics and non-Hispanics are comparable.

Individual attitudes about risk taking and the value of insurance also influence take-up decisions. Vistnes and Monheit (2011) analyzed data from the 2001 Medical Expenditure Panel Survey (MEPS) that provides large-sample data on individual attitudes about insurance and coverage status. These authors used econometric techniques to control statistically for two-way causality issues, and they conclude that worker attitudes about insurance are an important factor influencing job search decisions and insurance take-up decisions. They concluded that adults who do not place a strong value on insurance are more likely to be uninsured, less likely to obtain job offers from employers who offer insurance, and less likely to enroll in insurance when coverage is offered. In addition, Polsky et al. (2005) report that willingness to pay for insurance also depends on the type of coverage: married workers are more likely to decline coverage if the employer offers only an HMO.

Why Do Insurance Companies Utilize Restrictive Practices That Make It Impossible for Some Individuals to Purchase Insurance

Some people argue that we should repeal parts of PPACA, while others argue that the components of this complex plan are inextricably linked. To explore this issue, we will examine the issues posed by restrictive insurance company practices. Several industry practices that have been standard in the market for individual insurance are prohibited by PPACA. In this section, we examine

- Industry reasons for using those practices
- Previous federal law to limit the use of the practices, for example, the 1996 Health Insurance Portability and Accountability Act (HIPAA)
- Issues related to the new limitations in the PPACA

Industry Reasons for Using Restrictive Practices

To streamline the discussion, we focus on one common practice: exclusions for preexisting conditions. (Another widely discussed practice is refusing to renew policies after the policyholder is diagnosed with a high-cost condition. The two practices pose similar issues, from a regulatory perspective. Therefore, we focus on preexisting condition exclusions—as a well-known example.) Preexisting condition clauses in health insurance policies remove the responsibility of the health insurance company to pay for conditions that were in existence (usually within a 12-month period) prior to the policy implementation. A preexisting condition could be evidenced by documentation of symptoms, diagnosis, or treatment of the condition. The 1996 HIPAA limited the types of situations in which insurance companies could impose preexisting condition restrictions, but it did not eliminate these clauses. PPACA further restricts preexisting condition clauses. While this may present good news for patients with these conditions, this policy *only* makes sense if it is coupled with an enforceable health insurance mandate.

You might be thinking that the reasons for preexisting condition exclusions are obvious: profits and greed. However, the health insurance market has specific characteristics that make the situation more complicated. A Stanford economist, George Akerlof, provided a clear analysis of the underlying issues (and subsequently won a Nobel Prize).

The "Lemons Problem"

The lemons problem plays a critical role in health insurance markets and health policy debates, but the problem is not unique to the health insurance market. In fact, Akerlof focused on the used car market as the key example to illustrate the problem—and he used the common term *lemon* to describe a car with persistent repair problems. We'll start by examining Akerlof's description of the used car market, and then apply the concept to the health insurance market (Akerlof, 1970).

Akerlof (1970) provided a logical explanation for the fact that the warning "buyer beware!" (caveat emptor) seems to be particularly important in the market for used cars. The fundamental problem has two components:

1. The quality of used cars varies dramatically.
2. Buyers cannot always directly observe the quality of the car.

A buyer, who is looking at a specific car, say in "good" condition, can research the Kelley Blue Book average market price for this type of car—in good condition. However, even cars in good condition range in quality, and many buyers do not have sufficient mechanical skills to assess where a specific car falls within that range. If the seller tries to assure the buyer that his specific car is at the top of that range, the buyer will not believe the seller's assertions—largely because the buyer cannot verify them. This buyer will not be willing to pay any price above the Blue Book average price.

Suppose further that this particular seller is telling the truth: this car's quality is at the top of the good range, and the seller knows it. He may not be willing to sell at the average price, because he knows the car is worth more. He may decide to withdraw his car from the market and drive it himself for a few more years. If owners of above-average-quality cars decide to keep their cars because the Blue Book price seems too low, then the average quality of cars for sale will fall, and the average Blue Book price will fall. Once again, owners will withdraw cars for which the quality is above the new lower average. In the end, the only used cars that are for sale will be the lemons that no one wants to buy. This process is generally known as a market "death spiral."

Used car buyers and sellers have developed numerous solutions: car title information that specifies whether the car has been in an accident, mechanics offering second opinions, and used car lots that offer warranties.

Lemons Problem in Health Insurance Markets

The lemons problem also occurs in the health insurance market—with a very important twist. In this market, the quality of health insurance buyers varies across individual buyers, and sellers cannot directly observe all aspects of this quality. Healthcare expenditures vary substantially across individuals: in general, 20% of individuals account for 80% of healthcare expenditures (O'Donohue and Cucciare, 2005).

Figure 1.7 illustrates the problem. If all individuals are initially "in" the market, and health insurance firms cannot observe any information about individual health status, the equilibrium premium will be equal to the average health claims plus overhead plus profit. When relatively healthy individuals compare their expected expenditures with the premium, some will drop out of the market because they will think that the insurance premium that they must pay is greater than their future healthcare costs. Thus, the average healthcare expenditures of the people who remain in the market will increase. Therefore, even more individuals will realize that their expected

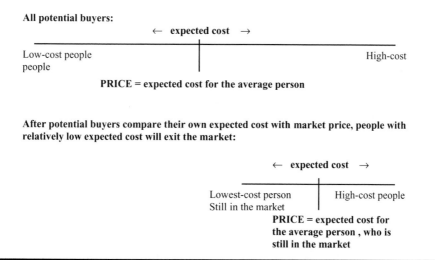

Figure 1.7 The lemon problem.

expenditures are lower than the premium and drop out of the market. In the end, the only people who will remain in the market will be the extremely high-cost people—as the market experiences a market "death spiral."

Firms selling health insurance can discover *some* information about a potential buyer's health by requiring a physical and requiring the buyer to disclose information such as health history and current risky behaviors; however, the individual buying health insurance always has more information about his or her health than the company selling the health insurance. Therefore, health insurance companies worry: Why is this individual buying health insurance *today*? He did not purchase health insurance yesterday. Is this individual buying insurance today *because* he knows about an expensive diagnosis or condition that has not been disclosed?

Employer-Sponsored Health Insurance Mitigates the Lemons Problem

Employer-sponsored group health insurance provides a solution for this problem, particularly in the large group market: individuals are buying coverage today indirectly, through employers, simply because they are employed. Thus, insurance purchases are tied to employment status, rather than health status and expected healthcare expenditures. This solution is not perfect: health status can be correlated with employment status, and some individuals do not accept employer offers of insurance. In addition, employers can attempt to screen applicants on health status as a way to maintain some control over the costs of insurance premiums. However—particularly for large employers—this solution allows the market for employer-sponsored group health insurance to function reasonably well. This is an important explanation for the fact noted above—that premiums for policies offered in the large group market are substantially lower than premiums for policies offered in the individual market. While employer-sponsored group insurance mitigates the lemons problem, it was actually initiated to solve a different problem. See Box 1.5 for details.

The three market segments noted above developed in response to the lemons problem. Prices are lowest in the large group market, because the lemons problem is addressed most effectively in this segment, and because

BOX 1.5   ORIGINS OF EMPLOYER-SPONSORED INSURANCE IN THE UNITED STATES

ESI was not initiated as a strategy to solve the lemons problem. Instead, this inadvertent solution to the lemons problem was developed during World War II as a solution to the problem posed by U.S. government wartime wage and price controls (notice that this is an example of unintended negative effects of government intervention!). During World War II, U.S. firms increased production dramatically to supply weapons, ships, planes, uniforms, and other war materials to the U.S. government. At the same time, a substantial portion of potential young workers were not available to work because they were drafted or enlisted in military units. As a substantial buyer of U.S. manufacturing output, the U.S. government was concerned about upward pressure on wages due to this increased demand and reduced supply. To forestall this problem, the government imposed wage and price controls. The wage controls created a serious problem for firms with large government contracts: they were not able to hire all the workers that were needed to deliver the contracted outputs because workers were not motivated by these artificially low wages; the free market would have provided a much higher wage. These firms wondered:, "What can we do to attract more workers, since we cannot offer higher wages?" Blue Cross and Blue Shield health insurance, developed in New England during the 1930s as a strategy to facilitate payment collection, provided the solution. The 1942 Stabilization Act ruled that firms could offer new health insurance benefits without violating the wage control legislation that prevented the firms from offering wage increases (Wisconsin Policy Research Institute, 2006).

marketing to large employer groups is relatively efficient. Prices are substantially higher in the individual market because the lemons problems is an important issue for individually purchased insurance, and because insurance company efforts to acquire and verify information about the individual's health status generate relatively high marketing costs.

Solution Strategies

The fact that insurance coverage patterns reflect a web of decisions made by employers, individuals, and insurance companies poses a challenge for government policy makers. In this section, we examine

- Legislation passed prior to the PPACA to reduce the proportion of individuals who were uninsured
- Pre-PPACA estimates of the likely impacts of alternate solution strategies
- Strategies implemented as components of the PPACA
- Early estimates of the impacts of these strategies

Pre-PPACA Legislation to Restrict the Use of Preexisting Condition Exclusions

We consider two examples of legislation adopted prior to passage of the PPACA, to reduce the proportion of individuals who were uninsured:

1. Title I of the 1996 federal HIPAA legislation
2. State-level health insurance reforms

Title I of HIPAA: Prohibit Restrictive Practices in the Markets for Small Group and Large Group Health Insurance

Title I of the 1996 HIPAA prohibited restrictive practices in the large group market and in the small group market—but it did not apply the prohibition to the individual market (Table 1.5). These restrictive practices, which are viewed by insurance companies as reasonable efforts to deal with the reality of the lemons problem, are often viewed by consumers as unethical.

Both sides of the 1996 congressional debate agreed that banning the restrictive practices would lead to higher premiums, as people with high-cost conditions obtain coverage, and these higher premiums would

Table 1.5 Overview of HIPPA

	Health Insurance Market		
	Individual	*Small Group*	*Large Group*
Guaranteed renewability	Yes	Yes	Yes
Limit the time period for exclusion of preexisting conditions	No	Yes	Yes
Portability	No	Yes	Yes
Certificate of creditable coverage	Yes	Yes	Yes
Nondiscrimination		Yes	Yes
Special enrollment period		Yes	Yes
Guaranteed access/availability	Only for some individuals leaving group coverage	Yes	No

Source: Scanlon, W. 1998. Health Insurance Standards: New Federal Law Creates Challenges for Consumers, Insurers, Regulators. U.S. General Accounting Office. GAO/HEHS-98-67. p 30–31.

exacerbate the affordability problem. The two sides disagreed about the magnitudes of the impacts. Surprisingly, advocates argued that banning restrictive practices would have minimal direct impact; hence, the unintended cost impact would be small. Opponents argued that the direct impact would be substantially larger—which would produce a larger impact on premiums.

The 2010 PPACA extends the prohibitions to the individual market. Why did the legislators who voted for PPACA feel comfortable extending the ban on these practices to the individual market (when their predecessors who crafted HIPAA did not)? The PPACA includes an essential component: the individual health insurance mandate (or tax). The argument that it was important to combine these two policies was based on evidence from pre-PPACA state-level reforms.

Despite the challenge of implementing employer and individual mandates, continuing advances in genetics highlight the increasing importance of ensuring coverage for high-risk and high-cost people. If advances in genetics make it increasingly possible to predict which specific individuals will develop high-cost conditions, restrictive practices would impact larger numbers of people (Chen, 2002).

State Reforms That Preceded PPACA Reforms

Beginning in the 1990s, several states enacted reforms to expand health insurance coverage that were expected to be successful pilot demonstrations that would guide federal reform—but the results were problematic. Three primary mechanisms for state reform efforts were guaranteed issue, constrained rate setting, and individual coverage mandates.

Guaranteed issue regulations essentially ban restrictive practices, because they require health insurance companies that sell individual health insurance policies to make those plans available for purchase to any individual, regardless of the buyer's health conditions. As of 2011, five states (Vermont, New Jersey, New York, Massachusetts, and Maine) required health insurance companies to guarantee issue to all individual policies in their state. Another seven states implemented modified forms of guaranteed issue policies, which applied to some plans and/or some individuals. Those states were Idaho, Michigan, Ohio, Oregon, Rhode Island, Utah, and West Virginia (Kaiser Family Foundation, 2011).

Constrained rate-setting regulations limit the range of rates that can be charged in the individual health insurance market. Two types of constraints have been imposed by states.

1. Some states mandated "community rating." This rate-setting strategy spreads risk evenly across a group of insured individuals. Rather than calculating the risk for an individual's age, health status, and geographical location, they calculate the risk of the group as a whole. When the PPACA was debated, New York was the only state that mandated pure community rating, while six states mandated adjusted community rating that permitted rates to vary based on demographic characteristics, such as age (Maine, Massachusetts, New Jersey, Oregon, Vermont, and Washington).

2. Other states limited the variation in premiums, under a policy known as "rating bands" (Idaho, Indiana, Kentucky, Louisiana, Minnesota, Nevada, New Hampshire, New Mexico, North Dakota, South Dakota, and Utah). A rating band equal to 3, for example, means that an insurance company's highest premium can only be three times that company's lowest premium.

Finally, several states (California, Maryland, Maine, and Washington) considered individual mandates, but Massachusetts was the only state to enact a mandate. While the Massachusetts initiative did reduce the proportion of individuals who were uninsured, it did not achieve universal coverage (Nardin et al., 2009).

Much can be learned from these state regulatory experiences. Guaranteed issue and constraints on rate setting were implemented with the goal to help individuals who were previously unable to purchase affordable health insurance due to preexisting conditions or age. Without an individual mandate, these policies triggered the lemons problem. As premiums increased, low-risk individuals opted out of the market, leaving high-risk individuals in the pool. This caused subsequent increases in premiums. Insurance companies unable to make a sound business case for staying in the market opted out, leaving some states with few companies willing to sell individual health insurance. The firms that continued to offer policies streamlined benefits and increased premiums (Wachenheim and Leida, 2012).

In 2006, Massachusetts implemented the policy subsequently embedded in the 2010 PPACA that paired the policy of guaranteed issue with a mandate that individuals must have health insurance. The proportion of individuals without insurance decreased significantly, while the cost of the reforms exceeded projections (Tuerck et al., 2011; Nardin et al., 2009; Kaiser Family Foundation, 2012).

Pre-PPACA Estimates of the Impacts of Alternate Strategies for Increasing Access

Meara et al. (2007) provide a concise analysis of the impacts of three proposed strategies for offering coverage to the uninsured. These analysts conclude that no single policy will provide a comprehensive solution. Instead, it may be necessary to deploy a package of policies that offer coverage to overlapping, but slightly different segments of the uninsured population.

Employer Mandate with or without Individual Mandate

An employer mandate will reduce the incidence of uninsurance by 33% if it is accompanied by a mandate that every individual must obtain insurance. The impact will be smaller without the individual mandate because some employees will not take up the employer's offer of ESI. The impact is limited by the fact that this policy will only impact workers. In addition, an employer mandate would reduce the probability of being employed by 1.2 %, and it would reduce the average wage by 2.3%.

Expand Public Programs, Chiefly Medicaid

Expanding Medicaid coverage to individuals with incomes of less than 300% of the FPL would have a smaller impact on the incidence of uninsurance: it would reduce this incidence by 12%. The impact is limited by the facts that

- Some individuals who are eligible for public coverage do not apply.
- The policy would not apply to undocumented workers (aka "illegal aliens").
- Coverage would not be offered to people with incomes above the eligibility threshold.

In addition, 35% of the new Medicaid enrollees would be individuals who were previously covered by private insurance. (This result—typically described as "crowd out"—can occur if some employers respond to the expansion of Medicaid by dropping insurance coverage for their employees.)

Tax Credit

A tax credit for purchasing insurance would have the smallest impact on the incidence of uninsurance: this policy would reduce uninsurance by 3%. Estimates indicate that only 4% of individuals who are eligible and previously uninsured would be induced to purchase coverage in order to obtain the tax credit. The policy would apply to all taxpayers, including undocumented workers and individuals with above-average incomes. Whether it is wise to use public funds to help undocumented workers obtain health insurance depends on the specific policy goal. If the goal of reducing the incidence of uninsurance is to reduce inequity among U.S. citizens and other legal U.S. residents, then these funds are not well targeted. However, we would reach the opposite conclusion if the goals include equity among people living in our communities, or reducing the numerous negative side effects of providing uncompensated care to uninsured individuals.

ACA Solution Strategy for Increasing the Proportion of Individuals Covered by Health Insurance

The version of the ACA printed by the U.S. Government Printing Office includes 906 pages, and led to thousands of pages of regulations (https://www.gpo.gov/fdsys/pkg/PLAW-111publ148/pdf/PLAW-111publ148.pdf). The legislation and the regulations addressed a broad array of issues that impact the Triple Aim of increasing healthcare insurance coverage, strengthening healthcare quality, and reducing cost. In this section, we note key strategies for addressing access to health insurance.

ACA Strategy for Increasing Health Insurance Coverage

The ACA strategy for increasing health insurance coverage included three key elements.

Mandates That Employers Must Offer Group Insurance, Mandates That Individuals Must Obtain Insurance Coverage, and Ban on Provisions in Health Insurance Policies That Exclude Preexisting Conditions from Coverage

The Urban Institute (Blumberg et al., 2011) estimated that most of the non-elderly U.S. population would not be affected by the individual mandate because they already have health insurance, or their income is below the threshold that defines exemption from the mandate. Some individuals will experience a financial impact from the mandate to purchase insurance; however, many will qualify for subsidies to cover part of the cost of purchasing health insurance. Only 3% of the non-elderly population would be impacted by the mandate in the absence of a subsidy to help purchase the required insurance.

Creation of State-Level Health Insurance Exchanges

The exchanges were designed to accomplish two goals:

1. Reduce premiums for plans offered in the individual market by increasing competition among insurance companies offering plans in individual market and decreasing marketing costs
2. Administer a system for providing income-based subsidies for insurance purchased through an HIX

Plans offered in an HIX must meet coverage, actuarial, and premium-setting regulations. Comprehensive plans may be offered in four categories, defined by actuarial requirements. For example, a bronze plan must cover 60% of expected medical expenditures, while a silver plan must cover 70% of these expenditures. Silver plans are the most popular: 70% of HIX plans selected by individuals were silver plans. (See Table 1.6 for additional detail.)

Table 1.6 Characteristics of Plans, by Metal Level

	Bronze	*Silver*	*Gold*	*Platinum*	*Catastrophic*[a]
Proportion of healthcare expenditures paid by the plan, on average	60%	70%	80%	90%	
Can purchaser qualify for cost-sharing assistance?	No	Yes, if income is 100%–250% of the FPL and qualifies for premium tax credit	No	No	No
Market share[b] (March 2016)	22	70	6	2	1

[a] Catastrophic plans can only be purchased by individuals under age 30, with a hardship or affordability exemption.

[b] Data from http://kff.org/health-reform/state-indicator/marketplace-enrollment-by-metal-level/?dataView=1&currentTimeframe=0&sortModel=%7B%22colId%22:%22Location%22,%22sort%22:%22asc%22%7D.

Federal regulations defining subsidies to assist with premium payments, copayments, and deductibles are defined by metal level. For individuals living in households with income between 100% and 133% of the FPL, the subsidy available for premium assistance is equal to the premium for the plan selected by the individual minus 2.03% of the individual's income. If that individual purchases the silver plan with the second-lowest premium, the individual will pay 2.03% of his or her income for the insurance premium. If the individual purchases a more expensive plan, the subsidy available to apply toward the premium will remain the same. This implies that the individual would incur a higher out-of-pocket payment if he or she elects to purchase a more expensive plan (Table 1.7).

Tying the computation of the premium tax credit to the premium of the second-lowest-priced silver plan is a strategy designed to induce price competition among insurers offering plans in a given rating area. Policy makers expect insurers to compete to be the entity offering the cheapest and second-cheapest silver plans, because these plans are likely to enjoy high market shares. Tying the computation of the tax credit to the individual's income insulates low-income individuals from premium increases. As long as the individual with an income between 100% and 133% of the FPL buys the second-lowest-priced silver plan, he or she will only pay

Table 1.7   Premium Cap by Household Income

Household Income (End of Plan Year) (Percent of FPL)	Premium Cap (Final)Maximum Out-of-Pocket Expenditure as Percent of IncomeIf Individual Purchases Silver Plan with Second Lowest Price (Compared withOther Silver Plans),2016
Less than 100	No premium cap
100–133[a]	2.03
133–150	3.05
150–200	4.07
200–250	6.41
250–300	8.18
300–400	9.66
More than 400	No premium cap

Source: Internal Revenue Service. 2014. Internal Revenue Bulletin 2014–50. Rev. Proc. 2014–62. Washington, DC: Internal Revenue Service, December 8. Retrieved from https://www.irs.gov/irb/2014-50_IRB/ar11.html.

[a] The initial definition specified the upper bound of this category as 133% of the FPL. This is equivalent to 138% of the FPL if taxation issues are considered.

2.03% of his income for the premium. The amount that he or she pays will not be affected by premium increases. Instead, the impacts of the premium increases will be offset by increases in the subsidy offered through the premium tax credit.

Individuals with income in the range of 100%–250% of the FPL, who quality for the premium tax credit, can also receive subsidies to reduce out-of-pocket payments for copayments, coinsurance payments, and deductibles if they purchase a silver plan. These subsidies are known as Cost Sharing Reduction (CSR) payments. Individuals who meet the income criteria are not eligible for these subsidies if they purchase plans offered at other metal levels.

Expansion of Medicaid Eligibility for Adults with Incomes up to 100% of the FPL

Prior to PPACA, 26 states did not offer any coverage to childless adults (Kaiser Family Foundation, 2013). The PPACA provides federal funding to cover the cost of expanding Medicaid eligibility for childless adults. The federal funding covered the full cost of expanded eligibility in 2014;

by 2020, the federal funding will cover 90% of the cost and states will have to cover the remaining 10%. Following a Supreme Court ruling, Medicaid expansion is optional for states. As of March 1, 2017, 26 states elected to expand Medicaid, 19 states eschewed the expansion option, and 6 states were expanding Medicaid under federally approved modifications of the traditional Medicaid structure (National Conference of State Legislatures, 2017).

Impacts

The mandates, HIX markets, and Medicaid expansions were implemented by 2014. As shown in Table 1.2, the percentage of individuals without insurance dropped from 14.77 in 2012 to 9.40 in 2015. Figure 1.8 provides a graph showing that implementation of the PPACA provisions is associated with a decrease in the proportion of individuals who were uninsured. At the same time, the previous decline in the proportion with ESI was halted, and we observe increases in the proportions covered by Medicaid and non-employer-based private-sector insurance.

These univariate before- and after-PPACA comparisons do not account for the fact that many parts of the United States were recovering from the high unemployment rates of the Great Recession during 2014. Multivariate

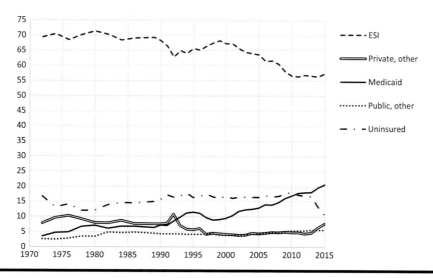

Figure 1.8   Insurance coverage trends of the civilian noninstitutionalized population, all ages. (From Cohen, R. A., *Long-Term Trends in Health Insurance: Estimates from the National Health Interview Survey*, National Center for Health Statistics, Hyattsville, MD, 1968–2015.)

studies are needed to provide a more comprehensive estimate of the impact of PPACA on insurance coverage. Using data from a large nationally representative survey, Frean et al. (2016) estimate that the proportion of individuals without health insurance dropped by 3.5 percentage points, from 14% to 12.6%. Premium subsidies for individual insurance purchased through state HIXs accounted for a 0.85 percentage point increase in coverage. Increased Medicaid coverage accounted for a 1.44 percentage point increase in coverage. Surprisingly, nearly two-thirds of the expansion in Medicaid coverage was generated by increased take-up among individuals who were eligible for Medicaid coverage prior to 2014 but had not enrolled in Medicaid. The remaining portions of the increase in coverage are not explained by the multivariate model.

Conclusion

Insurance is an important tool: people who do not have health insurance get less healthcare than people with insurance, and they have higher mortality risk. However, insurance may not be enough to eliminate health disparities. Evidence indicates that the relationship between socioeconomic status (SES) and health involves a range of factors beyond the connection between SES and health insurance. Some of these factors are well recognized but not well understood, such as the correlation of SES with smoking and obesity, and the impact of gross domestic product (GDP) and education on health. This may reflect an array of factors, such as the ability to choose safer jobs and safer housing locations.

In addition, discussion of universal coverage tends to gloss over the critical issue of defining the package of benefits that will be included in the mandated insurance package. *Health insurance* is an umbrella term with a variety of meanings that differ from person to person. How we ultimately define the components of health insurance has significant cost and access implications:

1. Can we agree on a basic benefits plan? What should be included? What should be excluded?
2. Will we be willing to accept a two-tier system? Medicare already utilizes a two-tier system: some Medicare recipients purchase supplemental insurance policies (Medicare Part C), while others do not. (Payment for Part C is covered by Medicaid or by retiree health plans for some

individuals; others use out-of-pocket dollars to pay the premiums for these plans.)

3. Are we comfortable with health insurance addressing just catastrophic events, or should all insurance plans be required to cover specific types of preventive care—and if so, which ones? Some have suggested that the employer mandate should permit provision of a high-deductible health insurance plan with health savings accounts to cover noncatastrophic health bills. Is this good enough coverage? Who should decide which types of care should be included in all plans?

While the PPACA has made some positive progress toward increasing insurance coverage for some segments of the population, important issues remain. Implementations of HIX and Medicaid expansions have highlighted an array of important issues, such as the degree of competition among insurance companies offering plans in the HIX market areas, network adequacy of plans offered, regulations defining plans that can be offered in these markets, and premiums that can be charged for those plans. Additional debates continue at the state and federal levels over

■ The current federal strategy for subsidizing health insurance for high-risk individuals focuses on mandating that these high-risk individuals be included in the risk pools of all individuals covered by each insurance company. In contrast, some states continue to operate state-level high-risk pools that provide coverage to high-cost individuals. Under the first strategy, relatively healthy individuals insured by a specific plan subsidize the high-cost individuals insured by that plan. Under the second strategy, the subsidy for high-cost individuals is financed by taxpayers as a whole.

■ The PPACA mandates that the ratio of premiums offered to older individuals to premiums offered to young adults cannot exceed 3:1. In contrast, health insurance claims data indicates that the ratio of costs incurred by older individuals to costs incurred by young adults is approximately 5:1. Some argue that the 3:1 limit helps older adults; however, it also mandates that relatively healthy young adults who purchase policies in an HIX must subsidize older adults. This strategy is likely to discourage young adults from purchasing insurance policies.

■ Identifying a "reasonable" premium is difficult, because health insurance is a multifaceted product. It may be more realistic to focus on competition as a strategy for ensuring that premiums will reasonably reflect cost. However, it may be necessary to expand our concept of insurance markets from state-regulated and state-defined markets to a broader national concept—in order to generate effective competition. Some states are now permitting sales of health insurance across state lines.

■ Evidence suggests that insurance companies offering plans on state HIXs compete to offer low prices. One strategy for accomplishing this goal is to offer "narrow" networks of in-plan providers. These narrow networks raise concerns about access to care and provider viability.

This chapter provides an overview of key economic concepts that can be used to analyze ongoing policy issues. As a healthcare provider, this information will equip you to advocate for effective policies that produce the population-based benefits in a fiscally responsible manner, while mitigating as many of the unintended consequences as possible.

Before we move on to exploring possible large-scale solutions, we need to look at the other two pressures for change: cost and quality. In Chapter 2, we build on what we've learned in this chapter to include issues related to healthcare costs.

Chapter 2

Cost

The first lesson of economics is scarcity: There is never enough of anything to satisfy all those who want it. The first lesson of politics is to disregard the first lesson of economics.

Thomas Sowell (1993, p. 131)

Introduction

Healthcare expenditures have been increasing faster than inflation for decades. In this chapter, we explore the question, why is this issue particularly important, urgent, and ominous now?

Americans spent an average of $1172 inflation-adjusted 2015 dollars per capita on healthcare in 1960, we spent $6685 in 2000, and we spent nearly $9986 for every U.S. resident in 2015. After adjusting for inflation, the 2015 per capita expenditures were 8.5 times the 1960 per capita expenditures.

Gross domestic product (GDP) per capita also increased during these years, from $19,027 in 1960 to $57,020 in 2015 (where both numbers are stated in inflation-adjusted 2015 dollars). Per capita GDP measures the total output of goods and services produced in the United States each year. This provides a rough indication of the volume of resources available to support household consumption (including healthcare), business investment (to create jobs and build capacity for future production of goods and services), and government expenditures (to provide services such as education, national defense, environmental protection, and health insurance coverage for low-income and elderly individuals).

While per capita GDP, which measures our standard of living, tripled from 1960 to 2015, our spending on healthcare has multiplied by 8.5. The fact that healthcare expenditures have been increasing faster than GDP per capita means that we are devoting an increasing proportion of our resources to healthcare and a decreasing proportion to other goods and services: healthcare constituted 5% of per capita GDP in 1960, 13.2% in 2000, and 17.7% in 2015 (Table 2.1). This implies reductions in the proportion of these resources that are available to fund nonhealthcare goods and services in the household, business, and government sectors.

This shift in the proportion of resources utilized for a specific consumer item is not necessarily a problem, for two reasons. First, expenditures for electronic devices, including computers and cell phones, also increased more quickly than per capita GDP from 1960 to 2015. Technological advances in both healthcare and electronic devices made both items more useful during

Table 2.1 National Health Expenditures

Year	Per Capita National Health Expenditures Constant 2015 Dollars	National Health Expenditures Percent of GDP
1960	1172	5.0
1970	2169	6.9
1980	3193	8.9
1990	5150	12.0
2000	6685	13.2
2010	9133	17.2
2015	9986	17.7

Source: Centers for Medicare and Medicaid Services (2014) https://www.cms.gov/research-statistics-data-and-systems/statistics-trends-and-reports/nationalhealthexpenddata/nationalhealthaccounts-istorical.html; Federal Reserve Bank of St. Louis Economic Data, Real gross domestic product per capita, https://fred.stlouisfed.org/series/A939RX0Q048SBEA; Federal Reserve Bank of St. Louis Economic Data, Consumer Price Index, https://fred.stlouisfed.org/series/CPALTT01USA661S.

these years. Second, expenditures for basic items, such as food and housing, are not expected to increase as fast as GDP per capita. As food and housing utilize smaller proportions of household expenditures, increases in the standard of living create the flexibility to utilize resources for a broader set of goods and services.

However, it is important to note two critical differences between the increasing expenditures for healthcare services and the increasing expenditures for electronic devices. First, healthcare services play a unique role in extending life, increasing mobility, and reducing pain. Equitable access to these services is widely viewed as an important social goal. Second, households and businesses use their own funds to purchase electronic devices, while public dollars are used to purchase a substantial proportion of healthcare services.

The Centers for Medicare and Medicaid Services (CMS) (2016a) projects that healthcare expenditures will continue to increase more quickly than per capita GDP. If current trends continue, without significant changes in our healthcare system, healthcare expenditures are projected to constitute 19.9% of GDP in 2025. This continued increase in healthcare expenditures is widely viewed as "unsustainable." In this chapter, we examine

- Fiscal pressures caused by continued increases in the proportion of GDP devoted to healthcare expenditures
- Evidence on the causes of increases in healthcare expenditures
- Options for reducing the growth rate of these expenditures

Background Information

Definitions: Cost, Price, and Expenditures

We tend to use the word *cost* in a variety of situations: sometimes we use this word to describe the price per item, while in other situations, we use this word to indicate the amount of our total expenditure. If we were complaining about an increase in the cost of gasoline, for example, we might be referring to increased price per gallon, or—if we just bought a new gas-guzzling vehicle—we might be referring to the increased cost of commuting to work (because we need more gallons of gas). When we say that "healthcare costs are increasing," we are typically referring to total healthcare expenditures. These expenditures could increase as a function of increases in price, increases in quantity, or increases in both price and quantity.

Healthcare Expenditures by Type

Data on U.S. healthcare expenditures is organized and reported in the National Health Accounts. These accounts define several categories of expenditures. National Health Expenditures totaled $3,205,556,000,000 in 2015. With 321 million people living in the United States during that year, per capita expenditures averaged $9986. This total includes four broad categories:

1. Personal healthcare, which accounted for 85% of total National Health Expenditures in 2015, includes expenditures for care delivered to individuals. This expenditure category corresponds to the concept of expected expenditures discussed in the section in Chapter 1 that focused on health insurance premiums. This proportion has remained steady in recent decades (Figure 2.1).
   The largest three subcategories of personal healthcare expenditures are hospital services (38%), physician and clinical services (23%), and prescription drugs (12%). Together, these three types of services account for 73% of healthcare expenditures. Nursing and continuing

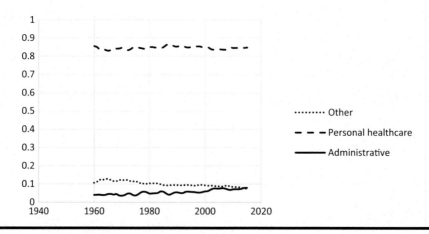

Figure 2.1 Personal healthcare, administrative, and other expenditures as proportions of total National Healthcare Expenditures.

care services, along with other health, residential, and personal care services, and home healthcare services account for 15% of the total; dental and other professional expenditures account for 7%; while medical equipment and products account for the remaining expenditures.

2. Administrative expenditures, which accounted for 10% of the total, include expenditures for administering publicly run programs, such as Medicare and Medicaid. This expenditure category corresponds to the concept of the "price" of health insurance discussed in Chapter 1. Indeed, the full title of this category is "total administration and total net cost of health insurance expenditures." The proportion of total expenditures utilized for administration has increased slightly in recent decades, as investments in health information technology increased (Figure 2.1).

3. Public health activities accounted for 10% of the total. This proportion increased during the years 1960–2000, and it has decreased since then (Figure 2.2).

4. Investment activities accounted for 5% of the total. This category includes two subcategories: expenditures on research and development (R&D) and expenditures for structures and equipment. The research expenditure category includes expenditures by government entities (federal, state, and local) and expenditures by nonprofit organizations. Research expenditures by private pharmaceutical companies are not included in this category.

The proportion of total health expenditures devoted to government-funded research activities has exhibited a downward trend since the early 1960s. Federal expenditures for research were fairly steady, at nearly 2% of total National Health Expenditures during the 1980s and 1990s. The percent declined since 2010, to 1.5% in 2015 (Figure 2.2).

Sources of Funding for Healthcare Expenditures

Most funding for healthcare expenditures comes from three sources: out-of-pocket expenditures by individuals, private-sector health insurance payments, and public-sector funding for health insurance and public programs. In 1960, out-of-pocket payments accounted for more than half of personal healthcare expenditures, and private insurance

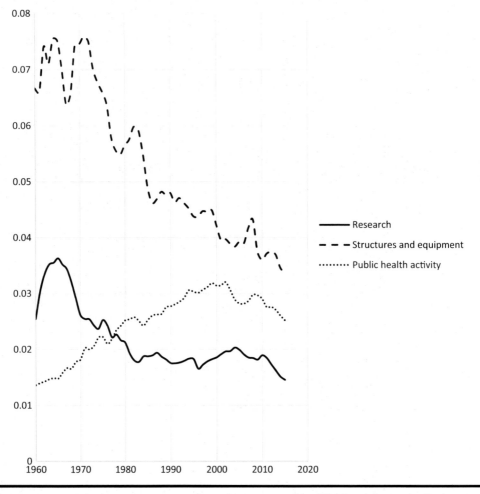

Figure 2.2　Research, structures and equipment, and public health expenditures as proportions of total National Health Expenditures.

payments accounted for approximately 21% of these expenditures. Public health insurance, along with other public programs, accounted for nearly one-fourth of these expenditures. Since then, the role of out-of-pocket payments steadily diminished to 12% of expenditures in 2015. (For comparison, out-of-pocket payments cover 15% of healthcare expenditures in Canada [Canadian Institute for Health Information, 2017]). The role of private health insurance payments increased to cover approximately one-third of expenditures, and the role of public payments (for health insurance and for programs) increased to cover more than half of all expenditures. Substantial increases in the role of public payments occurred in 1963 (with implementation of Medicare and Medicaid) and in 1997 (with implementation of the State Children's Health Insurance Program [SCHIP]). See Figure 2.3.

Sustainability of the Public Expenditures

Continued increases in healthcare expenditures, combined with the aging of the baby boomers, are expected to fuel substantial (and what many see as simply unaffordable) increases in the Medicare budget (Fuchs, 2013).

The Medicare trust fund report (Centers for Medicare and Medicaid Services, 2016a), published annually, presents the trustee's financial projections, along with an actuarial analysis of these projections. Figure 2.4 uses data from that report to illustrate three important points:

1. Current Medicare payroll tax collections and taxes on benefits do not cover current Medicare expenditures. In 1980, Medicare payroll and benefits taxes constituted two-thirds (68%) of Medicare noninterest income; in 2015, they constituted 41% of expenditures, and they are projected to constitute only 32% of Medicare noninterest income by the year 2050.
2. The gap is primarily filled by payments from federal tax revenues: general fund revenues accounted for 23% of Medicare noninterest income in 1980. They currently account for 43% of Medicare noninterest income, and they are projected to account for nearly half (48.6%) of Medicare's noninterest income in 2040.
3. Premiums are also increasing. In 1980, premiums constituted 9% of noninterest income, and they are projected to account for 17% of noninterest income by 2040.

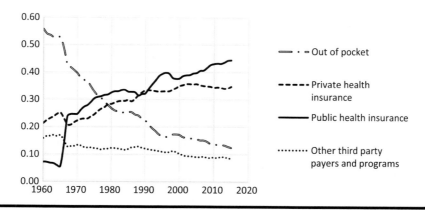

Figure 2.3   Sources of funding proportion of personal healthcare expenditures.

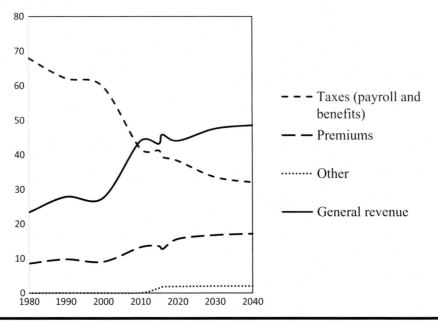

Figure 2.4   Medicare sources of noninterest income and expenditures as a percentage of GDP. (From Medicare trust fund report 2016, Supplemental Appendix A.

The fiscal implications of the Medicare budget projections were described in a report published by the Federal Reserve Bank of San Francisco (2003) and in an analysis prepared by the Congressional Budget Office in 2007:

- The entire federal budget has accounted for 19%–20% of our nation's GDP since 1970.
- If recent trends in healthcare expenditures continue, federal spending on Medicare and Medicaid would increase from 5.5% of GDP in 2017 to 9.2% of GDP by 2047 (Congressional Budget Office, 2017).

Together, these two points imply that maintaining the Medicare and Medicaid programs as they are currently administered would require significant expansion of the federal budget as a share of GDP. If no changes are made, the proportion of GDP utilized to fund Medicare and Medicaid in 2050 would be equal to the proportion of GDP that is currently allocated to cover all federal expenditures. Such a change would necessitate substantial tax increases, substantial increases in the federal deficit, and substantial changes in public attitudes about the appropriate role of government in the U.S. economy.

Together, these reports point to a grim conclusion: these predicted events will impose a substantial burden on younger taxpayers. This can only be prevented by substantial reductions in the rate of growth of healthcare expenditures. Many people wish we could find an easy "magic bullet" solution. However, David Walker, the comptroller general of the United States in 2007, warned in a statement to Congress:

If the American people understand that there is no magic bullet—if they understand that

- We cannot grow our way out this problem;
- Eliminating earmarks will not solve the problem;
- Wiping out fraud, waste and abuse will not solve the problem;
- Ending the "Global War on Terrorism," exiting from Iraq, or cutting way back on defense will not solve the problem; and
- Letting the recent tax cuts expire will not solve this problem;

then they can engage with you in a discussion about what government should do; how it should do it; and how we should pay for it without unduly mortgaging the future of our country, children, and grandchildren. (Walker, 2007)

State and local governments are facing similar issues as they examine the impacts of increasing Medicaid expenditures on state budget options. States, on average, spend 16% of state funds on Medicaid, 38% on education (including elementary, secondary, and higher education), and 44% on corrections, transportation, public assistance, and all other programs and activities (National Association of State Budget Officers, 2016). If Medicaid expenditures continue to grow faster than the general rate of inflation, states will face tough choices: maintaining the current level of Medicaid coverage would require either substantial cuts in funding for education, substantial cuts for other state-funded programs, or substantial tax increases.

Continued growth in healthcare expenditures, as a proportion of GDP, also has serious implications for consumer budgets. The circular flow diagrams in Figure 2.5a and 2.5b illustrate the logic. Members of households go to work every day to produce goods and services. Their employers pay wages and salaries to these workers and then offer the goods and services for sale. Workers use this income to purchase these goods and services. Thus, the average output per person determines the average standard of living per person. *Therefore, this diagram highlights a key point: we cannot be a nation of consumers unless we are first a nation of producers—to produce*

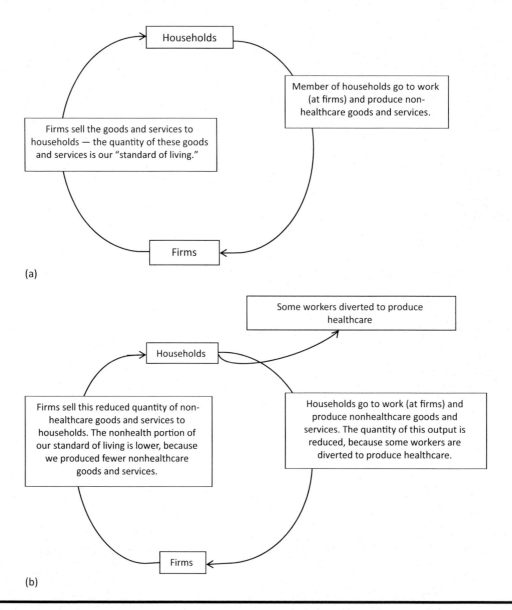

Figure 2.5 (a) Microeconomics circular flow: Minimalist version.
(b) Microeconomics circular flow: Impact of expanding the healthcare sector.

the things we want to consume. If you are thinking, "But we buy our consumer goods from China," remember that we have to produce something to sell in the international market if we want to continue to buy goods in that market. As the healthcare industry expands, the proportion of our nation's productive resources that are employed in the healthcare industry will grow and the proportion employed in other industries will shrink. Unless average worker productivity grows faster than healthcare expenditures, we will produce fewer nonhealthcare goods and services per capita. The nonhealthcare portion of our standard of living will fall. The concern that individuals may view this as a decline in real wages generates political pressure for healthcare "cost containment."

In order to consider strategies to accomplish cost containment, we must (1) understand the forces that are currently causing the cost increases and (2) assess the implications of cost containment. While the idea of cost containment sounds good in the abstract, implementation of serious cost containment measures will impose other types of costs. We must consider our options carefully, and this means that we must start with a correct diagnosis of the underlying causes of the upward trend in healthcare expenditures.

Diagnosing the Problem: What Is Fueling the Cost Increases?

Numerous factors contribute to healthcare cost increases, including

- Aging of the population (older folks use more healthcare than younger ones)
- Lifestyle factors (obesity, smoking, and sedentary lifestyle)
- Medical malpractice claims (must be added to fees as a cost of doing business)
- Profits earned by insurance companies, pharmaceutical companies, and healthcare providers
- Healthcare billing fraud
- Advances in technology (new treatments and more effective pharmaceuticals, such as hip replacements and improved cancer treatments)

Detailed multivariate econometric analyses conclude that the primary cause of the long-term trend of increasing healthcare costs has been technological advancements. These technological advancements include a wide array of treatment innovations, such as medical equipment (e.g., cardiac shunts), software (e.g., electronic health records), drug therapies for cancer, hospice care, new pain medications, and intensive therapeutic treatments for autism. The second most important contributing factor is the aging of the population. Older folks use more medical resources than younger people, and the proportion of people who are over age 65 is growing. Other issues, such as malpractice claims or pharmaceutical company profits, may contribute to the high level of healthcare costs, but they cannot explain the long-term upward trend (because they have not been increasing at a rate that could explain the rapid *increase* in healthcare expenditures). Analysts conclude that the major driver of the escalation in healthcare expenditures has been new technology; hence, we will focus our discussion on technology in healthcare.

Technology Is a Key Driver of Healthcare Expenditure Increases

Okunade and Murthy (2002) provided a big-picture overview of the impact of new technology on our healthcare system, as illustrated in Figure 2.6. There is no sinister plot here. Instead, it is reasonable to say that all the characters in this story wear white hats: private and government entities funded successful R&D that increased the supply of effective—and usually expensive—treatments. No one wants to return to less advanced healthcare—we can more effectively treat many

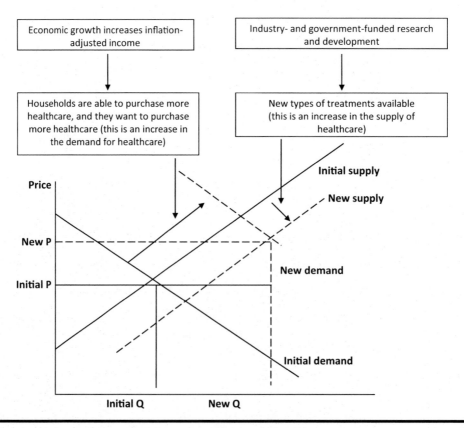

Figure 2.6   Increased healthcare expenditures reflect increases in both supply and demand.

illnesses than we could, say, 40 years ago—but all this comes at a cost. During the same years, U.S. economic growth provided increased per capita income, and this increase in income spurred increased demand for the new treatments. The simultaneous increase in the average cost of new treatments, along with the increase in demand for these treatments, generated increases in both the price and quantity of healthcare services.

While Okunade and Murthy (2002) concluded that healthcare cost increases are driven by increases in both supply (due to increased technology) and demand (due to increased income and population aging), policy discussions focus on the role of technology for a pragmatic reason. Federal policy can influence R&D spending through changes that are politically realistic (i.e., changes in tax policy and patent policy). The variables shaping demand for healthcare are more immutable.

International experience offers an opportunity to check our conclusion that technological progress is the primary force that is generating the steady increase in healthcare expenditures. The technological advances are available worldwide. If technology is the primary cause of increases in U.S. healthcare expenditures, we expect to see a similar *rate* of increase in European countries, even though European countries have different *levels* of healthcare expenditures per capita. Figure 2.7 shows that this has occurred. Per capita spending in the United States is higher than per capita spending in other developed nations (Jones, 2005). However, the real per

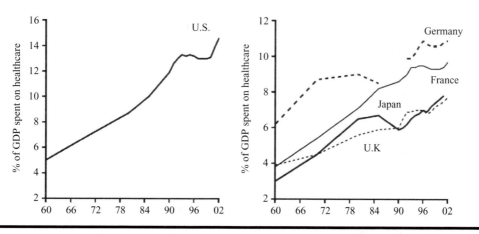

Figure 2.7   Rising health expenditures in the United States and other industrialized countries. (From Jones, C. I., More life versus more goods, explaining rising health expenditures, Federal Reserve Bank San Francisco Economic letter, Federal Reserve Bank San Francisco, May 27, 2005.)

person spending on medical care increased at similar rates in Canada, France, Italy, Japan, the United Kingdom, and the United States from 1960 to 1990 (Cutler et al., 1998).

Other nations are also developing strategies to address the resulting financial pressures. Great Britain announced major reforms in 2010 (Timmins, 2010). Under the new system, general practitioners control most of the healthcare budget, and they are responsible for purchasing healthcare (including hospital care) for their patients. This reform has sparked concern that the general practitioners will become the agents who must ration limited dollars among patients. Some European countries are trimming the range of services covered under the public health insurance plans and increasing the role of privately purchased supplemental insurance (Gechert, 2010).

Value Produced by the New Technologies Compared with the Costs of the Treatments

The fact that technological innovation is a major driver of escalating healthcare expenditures raises two fundamental questions:

1. Do the new treatments improve health?
2. Are the new treatments a good investment as measured by cost per life saved (or cost per additional life-year)?

Do the New Treatments Improve Health?

Americans benefited from both increased life expectancy and increased consumption of (nonhealthcare) goods during the twentieth century. Life expectancy of white males increased 60% from 50 to 77 years during the twentieth century, while our annual consumption of nonhealthcare goods quintupled from $4,000 per person to $20,000 per person (Nordhaus, 2003).

Increases in life expectancy during the first half of this century are largely attributed to increased availability of clean water and sanitation, and increases in per capita GDP that facilitated improvements in nutrition and housing. Cutler and McClellan (2001) examined the increase in healthcare expenditures and the increase in life expectancy during the second half of this century, when it is expected that healthcare technology may have played a larger role. These authors report that life expectancy increased by 7 years, while the present value of expected lifetime healthcare expenditures increased by $35,000 per person. This implies that we paid, on average, $5000 per extra life-year.

In addition, economists used a variety of methodologies to estimate the relationship between the impacts of new technologies on health and the costs of those technologies.

■ Cutler and McClellan (2001) also studied the cost and lifesaving impact of new cardiac treatments that were introduced during the 1990s. The average cost of treating a heart attack increased in inflation-adjusted dollars from $12,100 in 1984 to $21,700 in 1998, and the life expectancy of heart attack victims increased from 4 years 11 months to 6 years during that time period. Essentially, the $10,000 cost increase purchased an extra expected year of life for the average patient.

■ A study of claims data for a large sample of Medicare patients concluded that patients who used newer generations of drugs lived longer than patients who used older generations of drugs (Lichtenberg, 2003).

■ Lichtenberg (2009) concluded that life expectancy increased faster in states with more rapid increases in the proportions of diagnostic imaging and prescription drugs that were "newer," and the proportion of physicians who graduated from more highly ranked medical schools.

■ Hall and Jones (2007) estimated that the marginal cost of saving a life (via healthcare) was $1.9 million in the year 2000.

■ During the years 1988–2000, life expectancy among newly diagnosed cancer patients increased by nearly 4 years. Sun et al. (2009) estimate that the cost of the new pharmaceuticals was approximately $10,000 per life-year saved. In a subsequent study, Lichtenberg (2010) estimated that innovations in pharmaceuticals and imaging reduced the cancer mortality rate by 12% during the years 2000–2009.

■ News stories tend to highlight treatments such as the vaccine Provenge™, developed to treat metastatic castration-resistant prostate cancer. This treatment costs an estimated $50,000–100,000 per patient, and it increases survival by 4–4.5 months (Landau, 2010). This implies a cost up to $300,000 per life-year saved. Similarly, news stories provided extensive coverage for a new drug that cures hepatitis C, at a cost of nearly $100,000 per patient when it was initially introduced.

These studies and news stories suggest that recent healthcare innovations saved and extended lives. The cost of these innovations is estimated to be less than $2 million per life saved, and $10,000–$300,000 per life-year saved.

These results point to the importance of the second question: Do these expenditures produce good value for the dollars spent?

Are the New Treatments a Good Investment as Measured by Cost per Life Saved (or Cost per Life-Year Saved)?

Several federal agencies face analogous decisions: How much should we spend to save lives by increasing highway safety or drinking water quality? These agencies have developed strategies for answering these questions—and we are beginning to see increased use of these strategies for analyzing healthcare issues. These strategies focus on understanding the decisions made by individuals when we face risk versus dollar trade-offs. (See Box 2.1 for examples of such trade-offs.)

When we make these decisions, we don't seriously believe that we are—personally—shortening our lives. Instead, we are accepting risk. We

BOX 2.1 DO YOU MAKE DECISIONS TO TRADE DOLLARS FOR RISK?

■ Did you drive to work (or school) today in a Hummer? If not, why not? Have you compared the death rate (per million miles driven) in your car with the death rate in a high-curb-weight Hummer?

■ Did you ever hold your toddler on your lap on an airplane, instead of buying a ticket for your child?

■ Have accepted risk in exchange for nonmonetary values by
  – Hang gliding?
  – Riding motorcycles?
  – Riding a bicycle without a helmet—just to feel the wind blowing through your hair?
  – Playing racquetball without goggles?

■ Do you routinely check safety equipment in your home?
  – Fire extinguisher
  – Smoke alarm batteries

■ Have you tested for radon in your home?

■ Do you have a fire extinguisher in your car, within reach from the driver's seat?

understand that out of every 100,000 people who make similar decisions, a small number will have an accident, but we don't know the identity of the future accident victims, and we don't believe that we will necessarily be those victims ourselves. We understand that there is a statistical risk, a statistical life-year lost, or a statistical life lost, but the identity of the victim is not known. Parents make a risk versus money trade-off when they decide whether to buy an airline ticket for a child who is under 2 years old (Box 2.2).

BOX 2.2   SHOULD PARENTS BE REQUIRED TO BUY AIRPLANE TICKETS FOR INFANTS AND TODDLERS?

The Federal Aviation Administration considered mandating that each airline passenger be restrained in a separate seat, including children under the age of 2, who are currently permitted to fly on their parents' laps. Newman et al. (2003) analyzed the likely impacts of this policy. They conclude that requiring young children to sit in seats with appropriate restraints would prevent 0.4 deaths (from air crashes) per year. However, mandating that parents purchase tickets for young children would make air travel more costly, and some parents may choose to drive, rather than fly. The probability of death per mile of auto travel is higher than the probability of death per mile from air travel; hence, this substitution could lead to a *higher* rate of travel-related deaths for young children. The analysts also considered a scenario in which parents do not switch from air travel to car travel. In this case, the cost per death prevented is estimated to be $6.4 million.

Parents currently have the option to either purchase a ticket for a child under the age of 2 (which allows the child to sit in a seat with appropriate restraints) or allow the child to travel without a ticket (and hold the child on a parent's lap). Some parents buy tickets to maximize the safety afforded for the child, while others choose the riskier (but cheaper) option to hold their children on their laps. When parents make this choice, they reveal information about their preferences for money versus safety. Economists refer to this type of information as "revealed preference" information.

By studying revealed preference information from an array of types of decisions, economists infer the average amount of money the public is willing to pay in order to obtain increased safety.

Federal regulatory agencies, such as the U.S. Environmental Protection Agency (EPA) and the U.S. Department of Transportation, make numerous regulatory decisions that involve trade-offs between dollars and lives. Are these dollars best spent to

■ Install a stoplight to make an intersection safer?
■ Require side airbags in cars?
■ Tighten the limit for permissible exposure to a chemical?
■ Require infants to have a seat on an airplane (instead of allowing them to ride on their parents' laps)?

These agencies make decisions that affect all of us and they use the evidence summarized above to guide these decisions. Essentially, they look at thousands of decisions made by individuals in order to estimate what "we" would decide in a specific situation. Studies cited by the EPA examine routine decisions that involve trade-offs of money versus risk, such as decisions to accept the risk of driving a small car (because the small car is cheaper) or working at a more dangerous job (to obtain the hazard pay differential).) Based on these analyses, the EPA website states that measures should be adopted if a statistical life can be saved for less than $7.4 million (in 2006 dollars), or a statistical life-year can be saved for less than $360,000 (EPA website). If a proposed policy would save statistical lives (or statistical life-years) for less than these stated amounts, the policy is considered to be cost-effective. Policies with substantially higher costs per statistical life (or statistical life-year) saved are not considered to be cost-effective.

If you are thinking that this statement sounds overly precise, you are right. The criteria establish a reasonable rough order of magnitude, rather than a precise dollar cutoff. If we are considering a policy that will reduce risk for $8 million per life saved, we will not feel comfortable opposing the policy simply because the cost per life saved is slightly above the cutoff level. Indeed, we might advocate further study before making the decision. However, we will feel comfortable supporting a policy that increases safety at $50,000 per life saved or opposing a policy that will require $400 million per life saved.

It is important to be clear about the term *statistical life-year* or *statistical life saved*. No one is suggesting that people offer to be killed 1 year early in exchange for money. Instead, analysts observe that people make numerous decisions to save money by accepting a slight increase in risk or to spend a little more money in order to reduce risk. For example, we save money by accepting risk when we take a riskier job (because the pay is better), buy a small car (which increases our risk of dying in an accident), or decide to drive an extra year on those somewhat worn tires.

You may still be thinking that this type of cost–risk trade-off should not be applied to healthcare decisions. If so, you have identified an important issue: the trade-offs cannot be avoided completely, but there is controversy about the appropriate strategy for addressing this issue. We will examine the implications of this issue for the development of treatment guidelines in Chapter 3.

Solution Options

Solution options can be grouped into five categories:

1. Continue to spend more on healthcare every year, and accommodate this by spending less on other goods.
2. Restrain the quantities of healthcare services that are utilized annually in the United States. This would require a system for rationing the set of available services based on
   a. Price
   b. Wait time
   c. A system of priorities
3. Reduce the rate of technological innovation by reducing the incentive for firms to invest in R&D.
4. Reduce the cost of delivering specific types of care by regulating prices and/or profits of healthcare providers and pharmaceutical companies.
5. Implement measures to increase the *efficiency* of our healthcare system.

Each of these strategies poses costs and benefits. None can be implemented easily, cheaply, or painlessly. Even the last strategy (develop a more cost-effective healthcare system) will require substantial adjustments by healthcare providers, consumers, and regulators. It may also require significant paradigm shifts regarding conceptualizations of "healthcare quality," consumer and patient protection, and the responsibilities of healthcare consumers.

Option 1: Continue to Spend More on Healthcare Every Year, and Accommodate This by Spending Less on Other Goods

It might be wise to reduce spending on nonessentials such as entertainment (or more housing square footage than our grandparents enjoyed), in order to increase spending on healthcare. This is the classic "guns or butter" trade-off economists talk about. The evidence summarized above indicates that the cost per statistical life (or statistical life-year) saved by recent healthcare advances is substantially below the decision threshold used by the EPA (and other federal agencies). This suggests that sacrificing nonhealthcare consumption to purchase expanded amounts of healthcare could be a wise choice.

In this scenario, taxes would be increased to finance the increase of federal spending on healthcare. Households would respond to the reduction in after-tax household incomes by reducing expenditures on other (nonhealthcare) goods and services.

The scenario would be dramatically different if we continue to spend more on healthcare every year *without* raising taxes to fund the increased federal expenditures. In this case, the federal deficit would increase substantially. This would have significant macroeconomic implications. It would also ask our children and grandchildren to shoulder the future burden of repaying the debt. Many consider this irresponsible and even unethical.

Option 2: Restrain the Quantities of Healthcare Services That Are Utilized Annually in the United States

The generic term for efforts to "restrain the quantity utilized" is *rationing*. Three basic strategies have been discussed:

1. We could ration by price.
2. We could ration by wait time.
3. We could set priorities by either
   a. Creating and enforcing treatment guidelines
   b. Asking healthcare professionals to adopt a population health perspective and allocate scarce resources to patients

Ration by Price

Yachts and luxury vehicles are rationed by price—and consequently, most of us do not purchase these items. Their high price is an effective rationing mechanism. While we accept price rationing for most goods, this approach is often viewed as unacceptable for healthcare. However, when we don't have universal health insurance coverage for *all* types of healthcare (e.g., all the physical therapy visits that produce value for the patient), we are implicitly rationing by price. Rationing by price means that people who are not willing or able to pay the price are not able to purchase the good. If some types of healthcare increase life expectancy, price rationing would imply that life expectancy would be correlated with income: people with more income and assets would be able to purchase greater life expectancy, while low-income people would have shorter life expectancy. Evidence clearly indicates that health status and life expectancy are correlated with income in the United States: Singh and Siahpush (2006) found an additional 2.8 years of life for those people in the most affluent group compared with those categorized into the most deprived group in 1980–1982. By 1998–2000, that number increased to 4.5 years of additional life.

While this correlation generates concern when one examines rich versus poor nations, it generates more controversy and concern when it is examined *within* one country. In addition, the idea of rationing healthcare by price raises concerns. We *do* currently allow rationing by price on other products and services, including food, housing, and some aspects of education. The implications of these policies for population health are receiving increased attention.

Ration by Wait Time

Concert and sports tickets are frequently rationed by wait time: individuals who are willing to wait in long lines, perhaps camping overnight, are able to purchase tickets, while others do not get tickets. We hear that Canadian patients may wait weeks or months for some procedures—and that some Canadians seek care in the United States to avoid this wait time—but the idea of adopting this mechanism as a cost control strategy has not been seriously considered in the United States (O'Neill and O'Neill, 2008; Gravalle and Siciliani, 2009).

Ration by Setting Priorities

Defining a basic benefit package that should be available to everyone sounds like a commonsense solution to the cost problem. Oregon implemented this strategy for its Medicaid program during the 1990s to determine which services would be covered and which would not be. The state prioritized treatments and provided Medicaid coverage for high-priority treatments (and denied coverage for low-priority treatments). While this sounds straight-forward, the system encountered legal and political challenges. Given the fact that the new technology saves lives, a system that provides basic care to everyone (while denying high-tech care to all Medicaid enrollees) will not solve the fairness and access issue. If high-tech care is not available to everyone, then we can still expect that people with higher ability to pay for healthcare will have longer life expectancy (Tengs, 1996).

Similarly, managed care in the 1990s denied coverage for some "low-priority" treatments as a cost containment strategy. However, these coverage limitations created a backlash of support for legislation that tempered the use of these cost containment efforts.

Option 3: Reduce the Rate of Technological Innovation by Reducing the Incentive for Firms to Invest in R&D

The federal government could implement policies that would reduce the rate of technological innovation in healthcare. It could do this directly by reducing government funding for healthcare research. Alternately, the federal government could modify tax and patent policies to make industry-funded research investments less attractive. However, analysis of the benefits generated per dollar spent on new treatments, discussed above, indicates that this would not be a wise strategy. Compared with money spent on other strategies for saving lives, such as vehicle safety, money spent on recent health-care advances appears to have been well spent.

Option 4: Reduce the Cost of Delivering Care by Regulating Prices and/or Profits of Healthcare Providers and Pharmaceutical Companies

Regulate Prices and/or Profits of Healthcare Providers and Pharmaceutical Companies

Price and profit regulations are blunt instruments that have caused unintended consequences. Organizations tend to respond to price and profit regulations by reducing production of goods and services when price does not cover production cost or potential profits are not sufficient to warrant taking the risks associated with developing and producing new products. Concern about these potential consequences makes it difficult to design and enforce these policies.

Recent price increases for prescription drugs have generated pressure for lawmakers to address concerns about pharmaceutical prices. For example, a provision in Nevada SB265 (that was considered but not passed by the 2017 Nevada legislature) would have essentially limited annual increases in the wholesale price of insulin to the rate of increase in the medical care component of the Consumer Price Index. While these actions are typically described as straightforward, estimating the consequences of these actions is not straightforward.

Price regulation of drugs poses two concerns:

■ Price regulation could have adverse impacts on the availability of prescription drugs, if manufacturing costs increase faster than the regulated prices.
■ Price regulation systems have difficulty accommodating rapid changes in technology.

Price regulation has been used, in the past, for transportation prices (railroads and trucks) and for utility prices (electricity, telephones, and natural gas). Many of these industries were deregulated during the 1980s and 1990s as it became clear that the adverse impacts of these regulatory systems had begun to outweigh the beneficial impacts.

Proposals to create more competition among pharmaceutical companies by modifying the patent system also raise concerns. The patent system, which applies to all industries, is designed to provide incentives for innovation by giving innovators a right to operate as a monopoly for a limited number of years. During the period in which the new product enjoys patent protection, the producer can charge relatively high monopoly prices. When the patent expires, competitors enter the market and consumers are able to buy the product at lower prices. Thus, consumers who buy the product in the early high-price years make it possible for the innovator to recover the R&D expenditures.

The patent system is important for pharmaceutical innovation because drug development costs are high. The cost of developing a new drug and completing the testing process required for Food and Drug Administration (FDA) approval was estimated to average $2.6 billion for 106 randomly selected drugs for which human testing was initiated during the years 1995–2007 (Mullin, 2014). Companies invest resources on this scale because they expect to earn sufficient profits on successful drugs to recover this development cost. During the period before the patent expires, the price of a drug will be substantially higher than the cost to manufacture and distribute the drug. Changes in patent policy for the pharmaceutical industry therefore require careful examination of the trade-off between reductions in current prices for drugs that produce significant health benefits for current patients and reduced incentives for innovators to develop new drugs that will benefit future patients.

Other types of changes have also been suggested, but all of them involve trade-offs.

■ Accelerating the FDA approval process could reduce drug development costs (or accelerate market entry by competitors), but reduced testing could increase the risk of adverse drug effects.

■ Allowing Medicare to bargain over drug prices could increase the degree of competition in the market for prescription drugs, but it would not change the fact that innovation incentives hinge on the ability of firms to recover the costs of initial R&D.

■ Additional subsidies for prescription drug insurance could be created to assist individuals who rely on high-cost drugs to improve access, but subsidies must be financed with taxpayer dollars.

Option 5: Implement Strategies to Make Our Healthcare System More Efficient

The PPACA included a provision that highlights the importance of this strategy. The PPACA created an Independent Payment Advisory Board (IPAB). This 15-member board will be responsible for designing and implementing policies to constrain the growth of Medicare expenditures. This provision of the PPACA, includes the following statement:

> The proposal shall not include any recommendation to ration health care, raise revenues or Medicare beneficiary premiums under section 1818, 1818A, or 1839, increase Medicare beneficiary cost sharing (including deductibles, coinsurance, and copayments), or otherwise restrict benefits or modify eligibility criteria.

Thus, the new board would be responsible for constraining the growth of Medicare expenditures, but it would not be permitted to implement any of the first three strategies discussed above. The ACA prohibits the new board from

■ Funding continued spending growth by raising revenues (through increased Medicare premiums or cost sharing)
■ Implementing rationing by any criteria, or otherwise restraining health-care utilization

In addition, the board does not have authority to reduce incentives for innovation by modifying patent policies.

The new board's policy levers focus on Options 4 and 5. The board could focus on reducing payments for healthcare services and prescription drugs (Option 4) given the constraints imposed by the potential impacts on the quantities of services provided. The board could only avoid the political pressures inherent in Option 4 if it could devise sufficient strategies for implementing Option 5 (deploy healthcare resources more effectively). Increasing the efficiency of the process for delivering healthcare services would create the flexibility needed to increase access, strengthen quality, and contain cost.

Conclusion

Implementing strategies to increase the efficiency of the U.S. healthcare system will require significant changes. Based on experience with innovations that generated dramatic efficiency gains in other industries, increasing efficiency in the healthcare industry may require new approaches for defining *healthcare quality* and *consumer and patient protection*. Healthcare providers may face new types of competition. Consumers and patients may assume new responsibilities. Regulators may face challenges that will require developing new types of consumer and patient protection strategies.

When analogous efficiency improvements occurred in other industries, they generated substantial controversies. While consumers benefited from lower prices, established firms struggled to compete against the innovators. Some established firms survived by adjusting their business strategies, but others were forced to close. Consumers also faced trade-offs in some instances: to purchase goods at the new low prices, shoppers may have sacrificed some degree of convenience or personal service.

The prospect of experiencing such changes in the healthcare system raises concerns. Adopting the changes needed to increase system efficiencies will generate some stresses and controversies. However, it is widely believed that increased efficiency is essential because our current healthcare system is not financially sustainable. To the extent that technological innovation (i.e., increased supply) and expansion of the retired population (i.e., increased demand) fuel the healthcare expenditure increases, it appears that it will not be possible to constrain the cost increases without a significant increase in efficiency. Former Soviet premier Nikita Khrushchev summarized our predicament: "Economics is a subject that does not greatly respect one's wishes" (Khrushchev, 2011).

Finally, we note that some policy analysts advocate shifting to a "single-payer" system. While this payment system may offer some advantages, it is not clear that a single-payer system—by itself—would generate sufficient efficiencies to constrain the growth of healthcare expenditures.

While analysts on both sides of the political spectrum advocate increased healthcare system efficiency, there is wide disagreement on the feasibility and desirability of various strategies for achieving this objective. Two sets of innovations are occurring. CMS is implementing payment strategies designed to increase efficiency, and private-sector innovators are employing radically different strategies for increasing efficiency. (We discuss both types of strategies in Section II of this book.)

In Chapter 3, we explore the third source of pressure for change: concerns about inadequate quality of care. It is our concluding chapter in Section I, which focuses on the pressures for change.

Chapter 3

Quality

Introduction

The Institute of Medicine's (IOM) classic study, *To Err Is Human: Building a Safer Health System* (Kohn et al., 2000), set off a chain reaction across the U.S. healthcare system (this study is available free on the web—we recommend that you at least skim it). The study concluded that avoidable medical errors occurring in U.S. hospitals cause approximately 44,000–98,000 deaths annually. The follow-up report 10 years later, *To Err Is Human—To Delay Is Deadly* (Jewell and McGiffert, 2009), found little had changed in improving patient safety and that preventable medical errors were still causing significant numbers of deaths each year (Jewell and McGiffert, 2009). This report concluded that systemic change would be necessary to improve a healthcare system that is plagued with quality issues, while we spend more on healthcare than any other industrialized nation (Committee on Quality of Health Care in America and Institute of Medicine, 2001). These earlier estimates of medical errors may be much lower than the actual numbers. Newer estimates (James, 2013) put the number of medical errors leading to preventable deaths at 210,000–440,000 patients per year in the United States. Americans might tolerate healthcare cost escalation if they believed that these dollars were deployed efficiently and effectively, but news stories continue to document healthcare quality issues as frequently as they document access and cost issues. Stories of wrong site surgeries, diagnostic test results not reaching the patient or provider, providers ordering unneeded tests because they are worried about litigation, and medication errors remain recurring themes on the nightly news and in daily newspapers. Medical errors drive the cost of healthcare up, with estimates of $17.1 billion annually spent on medical errors that harm patients (Van Den Bos et al., 2011). Additionally, too little treatment is evidence based. This leads to variations in patterns of care and inconsistent quality. Finally, comparisons with other industrialized nations seem to indicate that these other nations have better health outcomes while spending less on healthcare.

If we are not getting value for our dollars, the critical question is, why not? Some argue that the fundamental problem is that our system is built on the diagnosis and treatment model rather than prevention and wellness model. Public health and healthcare professionals have long argued that chronic diseases such as diabetes are the most costly, yet the most preventable. "Despite the evidence that prevention works, the focus in our healthcare system over the past century has not been on prevention of chronic disease, but on treatment of short-term, acute health problems. As a nation, we have emphasized expensive cures for disease rather than cost-effective prevention" (U.S. Department of Health and Human Services, 2003, p. 7).

Nearly half of Americans have one or more chronic conditions. These conditions are the leading cause of illness, disability, and death in the United States, and they account for more than 75% of the healthcare expenditures (Gerteis et al., 2014; Anderson, 2004). An often overlooked chronic illness is mental illness. Approximately 1 in 5 adults in the United States experience mental illness each year, and 1 in 25 adults experience a serious mental illness, such as depression, that substantially interferes with their ability to function in one or more major life activities and costs an estimated $193.1 billion in lost earnings per year (U.S. Department of Health and Human Services, National Institute of Mental Health, 2015; Insel, 2008). Untreated or overdiagnosed mental health issues continue to pose intractable problems in the U.S. healthcare system. Depression is often missed, and other disorders, such as attention deficit disorder and bipolar disorder, are overdiagnosed. When conditions are diagnosed, behavioral health interventions are not consistently evidence based (Fisher and O'Donohue, 2006).

Economists describe the same issue from a different perspective. Rather than focusing on the difference between the treatment–cure and wellness–prevention paradigms, economists note that individuals and healthcare systems can use a diverse array of tools or "inputs" to produce health. Healthcare is one set of tools; other "inputs" that contribute to health include public health measures, such as sanitation and vaccination; environmental protection; and individual behaviors, such as healthy eating and exercise. Some inputs that produce health are clearly outside our traditional notion of the healthcare system, including traffic safety, education, and anti–gang violence programs. (Education may contribute to health through several pathways. On a detailed level, education is associated with the ability of individuals to understand and implement healthcare instructions [Smith, 2007]. On a more general level, education may equip individuals to earn sufficient income to obtain stable housing and nutritious food [Johnson, 2011]). The diversity of factors that influence health makes it difficult to define, and then to assess, the quality of our healthcare system.

In this chapter, we explore the evidence that the U.S. healthcare system often does not provide quality care and examine the solutions that have been implemented to address these issues, as well as some of the controversies these solutions have created.

Background Information: Three Types of Evidence Indicate That Quality Is Not Consistently High

Three types of evidence indicate that quality is not consistently high:

1. International comparisons indicate that other countries are "doing more with less."
2. Published studies document the occurrence of preventable medical errors.
3. The Dartmouth Atlas documents significant variations in treatment patterns across geographic areas.

We examine each type of evidence.

International Comparisons Indicate That Other Countries Are Doing More With Less

The United States has the highest healthcare cost per capita, while countries with lower expenditure levels have better infant mortality statistics, lower proportions of elderly individuals with two or more chronic diseases, and longer life expectancies (Organization for Economic Cooperation and Development, 2015). On the surface, this evidence seems to point to a clear conclusion: our healthcare system is not delivering value for the dollar. Measures such as infant mortality and life expectancy are "summary statistics," in the sense that these statistics provide a quick overview of population health; therefore, the problematic U.S. performance on these measures could signal fundamental problems. We focus here on a study that compared U.S. and Canadian data, conducted by the U.S. National Center for Health Statistics and Statistics Canada (O'Neill and O'Neill, 2008). Garber and Skinner (2008) placed the issues in a larger context, in their interesting comparison of the United States with Canada, France, Germany, Japan, and the United Kingdom.

The detailed comparison of U.S. and Canadian data indicated that these types of summary statistics should be viewed with caution—for two reasons (O'Neill and O'Neill, 2008). First, healthcare is only one factor that influences population health. The authors of this study present cancer incidence and mortality data that highlight three key points:

1. Cancer-related mortality is higher in the United States than in Canada.
   - In the United States, 163 women died from cancer each year (for every 100,000 women), but the comparable number in Canada is only 149.
   - The situation is similar for males. For every 100,000 males, 239 die from cancer each year in the United States, but only 220 die from cancer in Canada.
2. The probability of getting cancer is higher in the United States than in Canada.
   - For every 100,000 women, 415 are diagnosed with cancer each year in the United States, compared with 350 in Canada.
   - For every 100,000 men, 562 are diagnosed with cancer each year in the United States, compared with 464 in Canada.
   The authors of the study point to a possible explanation: the obesity rate is higher in the United States than in Canada. If the obesity rate is, indeed, the primary explanation for the higher U.S. cancer-related mortality rate, then we should reconsider our interpretation of the two countries' mortality rates. Instead of providing a measure of the quality of the two health systems, the comparison of the cancer-related mortality rates may be signaling the importance of lifestyle issues that lie outside the healthcare system.
3. The probability of surviving a diagnosis of cancer is higher if you receive the more aggressive (and expensive) U.S.-style treatment.
   - For women, the U.S. mortality per case is 0.39, while the Canadian mortality rate is higher: 0.42.

■ For men, the U.S. mortality rate is 0.42, while the Canadian mortality rate is higher: 0.47.

The authors of the study conclude that you are more likely to contract cancer if you live in the United States, but the relatively aggressive and more expensive treatment provided in the United States offers a higher probability of survival for cancer patients. These conclusions offer a relevant comparison of the impacts of the treatments offered by the two countries' healthcare systems. They also point to the importance of careful thinking about the definition of the healthcare system, and roles of multiple systems (outside the healthcare system) in producing health. While life expectancy is an important measure of population health, we must be cautious about using life expectancy as a measure of healthcare quality. Healthcare is only one of a large set of factors that influence health, and these factors can vary systematically across populations and nations.

Violence also causes more deaths in the United States than in Canada. Data from the Centers for Disease Control and Prevention shows that homicide accounted for 3.3% of deaths in the United States in 2008. Similarly, Lemaire (2005) reported that the U.S. firearm homicide rate is 5.5 times higher than that of the country with the next highest rate, Italy. Homicide and suicide rates due to firearms account for a loss of 103.6 days of life for the average American. While these statistics have been updated since this study was published, the key point remains relevant. Firearm possession and use is a social factor that is clearly outside the scope of the healthcare system, yet it influences the summary statistic of life expectancy. For example, life expectancy of males between the ages of 20 and 24 in the United States is much lower than that of males in Canada, and the gap is largely due to differences in the accident and homicide rates. The study authors conclude, "Although the overall mortality rate is higher in the U.S. at all age groups, the importance of non-disease related factors (accidents and homicides) is much greater in the U.S." (O'Neill and O'Neill, 2008).

Second, international comparisons of summary statistics, such as infant mortality, can be impacted by differences in treatment options available to residents of the two countries and differences in the definitions that are used to create this data. Infant mortality is an important issue in the United States. Racial disparities, teen pregnancy, and gaps in prenatal care access and utilization pose troubling issues. Nonetheless, the O'Neill and O'Neill comparison of U.S. and Canadian data raises important points about international comparisons of infant mortality statistics.

- Compared with Canada, the infant mortality rate is lower in the United States for single births.
- Compared with Canada, the infant mortality rate is also lower in the United States for multiple births.
- Infant mortality rates are higher in both countries for multiple births than for single births.

The authors conclude that the overall infant mortality is higher in the United States *because* the rate of multiple births is higher in the United States. One contributing factor to the higher rates of multiple births in the United States is greater access to elective fertility treatments among insured individuals. Access to fertility treatments indicates greater wealth and is certainly important to those would-be parents who value having children. However, treatments that stimulate ovaries to produce eggs and treatments that involve the implantation of embryos increase the likelihood of multiple births—which are in turn associated with lower birth weight and prematurity. Although premature babies are more likely to survive if born in the United States, prematurity increases the risk for infant death (Kramer et al., 2005).

In addition, definitions for infant mortality rely on the reporting country's measure of "live birth." Many European countries and Japan record a live birth only if the baby takes a breath upon delivery or is at a certain gestational age or weight. This definition differs significantly from that used by the World Health Organization and the United States. International differences in definitions of *live birth* make it difficult to compare infant mortality rates (defined as deaths per live birth) across nations (Grady, 2009).

What Can We Conclude about This Evidence?

All this does not prove that the U.S. system is efficiently and effectively producing high-quality healthcare. Instead, it demonstrates that international comparisons must be approached with caution. And these data do not, by themselves, provide the evidence needed to diagnose and solve our problems. More detailed work is needed to understand the issues. However, examination of the international evidence does raise an important question: How do we define the boundaries and responsibilities of the healthcare system? Does the healthcare system encompass everything that produces health (anti–gang violence programs, and vegetable selection and prices in grocery stores to remove "food desserts")? Or, should we define *healthcare* to be confined to steps to produce health that are implemented by a well-defined set of healthcare providers? What about cosmetic plastic surgery? This activity is implemented by those healthcare providers, but is it healthcare? Do we consider fertility treatment for the first child to be healthcare? What about the third child? Are elementary school smoking prevention programs examples of healthcare or education? What about redesigning bridges to reduce highway deaths? Where should one draw these lines?

Diagnosing the Root Cause of the Quality Problem

Two major efforts to document, analyze, and diagnose quality problems point to a clear conclusion: the root cause of our quality problem is our failure to implement systematic procedures. Let's take a closer look at this evidence.

Evidence Documents the Occurrence of Preventable Medical Errors

Reports issued by the IOM provide the second type of evidence that the U.S. healthcare system "needs improvement" (Box 3.1). These reports document the magnitude of the problem, estimate the numbers of resulting deaths, and analyze the underlying causes. They also present a clear diagnosis: medical errors do not simply result from greed, laziness, incompetence, or gaps in medical science. This is good news, because it is difficult to solve problems that require eliminating greed and laziness. Instead, these reports point to a clear solution strategy: the reports argue that a substantial portion of medical errors could be prevented by developing stronger systems for implementing and monitoring systematic care processes.

These IOM reports argue that examples of medical errors arise when

- Pharmacists misread handwritten prescriptions
- Test results are lost or misdirected
- Critical information is not shared accurately among members of the healthcare team
- Patients are not given proper treatment, as defined by evidence-based protocols

BOX 3.1   INSTITUTE OF MEDICINE'S QUALITY INITIATIVES

Phase I of the IOM's quality initiative produced the report "America's Health in Transition: Protecting and Improving Quality" (Institute of Medicine, 1994). This report emphasized that quality must be monitored and improved. Phase II produced two widely publicized reports: *To Err Is Human: Building a Safer Health System* (Kohn et al., 2000) and *Crossing the Quality Chasm: A New Health System for the 21st Century* (Committee on Quality of Health Care in America and Institute of Medicine, 2011). These reports highlighted the importance of quality issues, and generated widespread public discussions of the failures of the current healthcare system. Phase III of this initiative encompasses efforts to operationalize the recommendations made in these reports—to increase safety and quality while also being effective, equitable, timely, efficient, and patient centered. A summary of the key priorities from these reports can be found on the website http://www.acmq.org/education/iomsummary.pdf.

Electronic information systems, decision support tools, and other strategies for building systematic processes can be designed to mitigate these problems. Healthcare leaders have looked to other fields where significant quality improvement gains have been made. One such field is automobile manufacturing. Toyota focused on systematic processes to minimize automobile manufacturing defects (Lean manufacturing), and healthcare organizations have been adapting these methods to strengthen healthcare processes using adaptations of Toyota's process for improvement, called Lean Six Sigma or Six Sigma.

Following the IOM reports of medical errors and patient safety issues in U.S. hospitals, the Joint Commission on Accreditation of Healthcare Organizations (JCAHO) strengthened requirements for systematic processes to improve the quality of care provided in U.S. hospitals, including

- Patient identification that included two means to identify patients, such as name and birth date
- Medication safety that included mandates for medication labeling, patient education regarding their medications, and reconciling a patient's medication at the time of admission and discharge with that patient's list of prehospitalization medications

■ Infection control methods that prevented and identified postoperative infections and prevented central line and urinary catheter infections

■ Elimination of surgical mistakes that resulted from misidentification of the patient and/or surgical site

The JCAHO also requires hospitals to report "sentinel" events, including patient safety events that result in "death, permanent harm or severe temporary harm and intervention required to sustain life" (Joint Commission on Accreditation of Healthcare Organizations, 2017). In addition to reporting, immediate investigation and action to prevent further events is required. This system is designed to identify and learn from past mistakes, instead of ignoring or hiding these errors. This is a central orientation of quality improvement. The Japanese have a saying, "Each mistake is a treasure." From its initial focus on sentinel events, the JCAHO policy has expanded to include all patient safety events that include adverse events, no-harm events, close calls, and hazardous conditions. Hospitals are required to establish processes to respond to patient safety events that do not meet the requirements for classification as sentinel events. Box 3.2 lists the National Patient Safety Goals announced by JCAHO in 2017.

BOX 3.2   JCAHO NATIONAL PATIENT SAFETY GOALS

■ Improve the accuracy of patient identification
■ Improve the effectiveness of communication among caregivers
■ Improve the safety of using medications
■ Reduce the harm associated with clinical alarm systems
■ Reduce the risk of healthcare-associated infections
■ Reduce the risk of patient harm resulting from falls
■ Prevent healthcare-associated pressure ulcers (decubitus ulcers)
■ Identify safety risks inherent in an organization's patient population
  – Identify patients at risk for suicide

Source: Joint Commission on Accreditation of Healthcare Organizations, Introduction to the Universal Protocol for Preventing Wrong Site, Wrong Procedure, and Wrong Person Surgery™ JCAHO Patient Safety Goals, Oakbrook Terrace, IL, Joint Commission on Accreditation of Healthcare Organizations, https://www.jointcommission.org/standards_information/npsgs.aspx.

Evidence Documents Variations in Regional Treatment Patterns

Beginning in 1973, a group of researchers have been documenting a startling fact: the composition of healthcare varies dramatically across U.S. cities, states, and regions. Medicare patients in high-spending regions are receiving more diagnostic tests and are being diagnosed with more diseases. According to the researchers (Song et al., 2010), the typical patient in a high-spending region is "in fact, less sick than average" (p. 1). The likelihood of having hip, shoulder, or knee replacement surgery varies by a factor of 10, depending on where a Medicare patient resides (Fisher and Bell, 2010). The variation is notable even within states; for example, hip replacement surgery rates ranged from 2.7 per 1000 in Los Angeles, California, to 6.7 in San Luis Obispo, California (during 2005–2006). In addition to these diagnosis and treatment variations, healthcare spending differs markedly across the United States. Spending ranged from 13.1% of GDP in Utah to 21.7% in Massachusetts in 2011 (Savings and Goodman, 2013). A comparison of similar Medicare patients in low-spending and high-spending regions estimates that those living in high-spending areas receive 60% more services, equating to nearly 29% more healthcare spending (Fisher et al., 2003). The Dartmouth Atlas website provides maps that illustrate county-level variations in practice patterns, expenditures, and utilization rates across the United States (www.dartmouthatlas.org/).

Multivariate statistical analysis indicates that these variations are not explained by observable differences in demographic or health system variables; hence, the Dartmouth Atlas evidence raises fundamental questions:

- What is influencing physician decisions?
- Does higher healthcare spending produce better outcomes?
- Are the regional differences large enough to be important?

What Is Influencing Physician Decisions?

Researchers at RAND reviewed 50 published studies of specific types of care, and concluded that patients, on average, only receive half of the recommended and appropriate care. (Think about what would happen to total healthcare expenditures if this problem were corrected. Providing additional care would—by itself—push healthcare costs up, but providing more appropriate care could generate net savings.) This gap between scientific evidence and actual practice probably leads to more than 19,600 additional deaths each year when we just look at two preventive diseases, pneumonia and colorectal cancer (McGlynn et al., 2003). There is great variability in the quality of care provided, whether the care is preventative, acute, or for chronic conditions. These authors concluded that we should define, measure, and monitor quality of healthcare in the same ways that we measure the quality of products such as automobiles, and these measures should be made publicly available on a national level (McGlynn et al., 2003). This would allow consumers to make more informed decisions.

Doyle et al. (2008) offer a different perspective. These analysts analyzed outcomes for 30,000 patients who were randomly assigned to clinical teams. Patients treated by physicians at the higher-ranked institution spent fewer days in the hospital and incurred lower costs than patients treated at the lower-ranked institution—but the health outcomes were not significantly different. The analysts suggest that the physicians trained at top-ranked institutions had superior ability to apply judgment in clinical situations, but the other physicians substituted more time and diagnostic tests—to reach a similar outcome.

Does Higher Healthcare Spending Produce Better Outcomes?

A study conducted by Tsugawa and Jena (2017) looked at healthcare spending of physicians within the same hospital and across different hospitals and found that variations in healthcare spending could be primarily attributed to individual physicians (8.4%) and, to a lesser degree, differences across hospitals (7.0%). Those patients treated by the higher-spending physicians did not have lower mortality or readmission rates than those treated by the lower-spending physicians. These results suggest that spending more on healthcare does not equate to better patient outcomes, and that efficiencies can be gained by reducing physician practice variability.

Are the Regional Differences Large Enough to Be Important?

Fisher et al. (2009) estimated a cumulative savings of $1.42 trillion by 2023 if annual growth in per capita Medicare spending were reduced from the 3.5% annual average (from 1992 to 2006) to 2.4% (the rate in San Francisco). This is a rough computation, of course, and the details are controversial. However, it suggests that the magnitude of the geographic variation—that is not currently explained by differences in population, socioeconomic status, or health characteristics—is substantial. This suggests that patterns of care are influenced by a variety of factors that are not related to scientific evidence. This leads to a much broader conceptualization of the problem: improving healthcare system quality requires more than reducing errors related to bad judgment or negligence. To ensure that healthcare decisions are evidence based, it will be necessary to develop more systematic processes of care, and new types of research to ensure that strong evidence is available to support provider decisions.

Solution Options: How Can We Make Our Healthcare System More Systematic?

This set of evidence spurred substantive efforts to utilize Total Quality Management (TQM), clinical pathways, and clinical guidelines to strengthen quality by institutionalizing systematic processes.

Applying Total Quality Management Principals to Healthcare

Dr. Donald Berwick (President and CEO, Institute for Healthcare Improvement, Boston, Massachusetts) and Dr. Brent James (Executive Director, Intermountain Health Care Institute for Health Care Delivery Research, Salt Lake City, Utah) established research and training programs to develop strategies for applying industry TQM methods to strengthen systematic processes in healthcare. Both argued that investing time and effort to develop and maintain systematic processes would address two critical goals: (1) by reducing medical errors, the processes would increase quality, and (2) at the same time, these processes would reduce cost. These processes would reduce medical errors in individual cases, as documented by the IOM reports, and also reduce medical errors in the larger sense, as documented by the Dartmouth Atlas. In addition to the effort required to apply TQM principles in specific healthcare settings, this effort would require two additional inputs. A well-developed set of evidence-based guidelines is needed to define the "right" processes, and health information technology (HIT) is essential for managing the information needed to support and monitor care coordination, guideline compliance, and systematic quality reporting. This evidence is creating pressure to develop strategies to ensure that healthcare decisions are evidence based. We discuss TQM principals and evidence-based guidelines here; we will examine strategies to gain efficiencies through HIT in Section II of this book.

Brief History

TQM principles were initially developed by W. Edwards Deming to improve quality in manufacturing industries. These principles were embraced by Japanese industrial leaders after World War II, and are widely credited with providing the foundation for the high-quality levels achieved by firms such as Toyota. The TQM principles articulate a philosophical approach and a pragmatic strategy for achieving high-quality output by focusing on:

1. Systematic processes designed to minimize random variation and control systematic variation.
2. Evidence-based decision making ("In God we trust; all others bring data"; Hastie et al., 2009, p. 3).
3. A customer-focused definition of quality.

Drs. Berwick and James have demonstrated the value of applying these ideas in healthcare, to develop the systems needed to reduce medical error. Both contributed to the IOM quality chasm report (Committee on Quality Health Care in America, Institute of Medicine, 2001), along with individuals from other industries (e.g., Henry Ford Health System, Delta Airlines, and General Electric Company). It is also notable that Dr. Berwick headed the Centers for Medicare and Medicaid Services (CMS) from 2010 to 2011.

The quality improvement philosophy focuses on the importance of systematically collecting data on processes, outcomes, and customer viewpoints, and using this data to proactively improve the processes involved in producing the good or service. Deming (1993) emphasized that data should be used to support analysis; it should never be used as a weapon for punishment of individuals. (One of his 14 key principles is "drive out fear.") In this view, customer complaints provide useful data—that supports the analysis needed to identify opportunities for improvement. Data is also used to diagnose the root causes of process variation, to test the success of solutions designed to reduce variation, and to track outcomes.

The pragmatic strategies for achieving TQM goals focus on the importance of a team approach. The problem-solving team is essential, because evidence-based diagnosis of the root causes of process problems requires detailed frontline knowledge of the process. A broad-based team that includes individuals with specific knowledge of every process component is essential to provide this information. Teams are typically trained to use a series of "quality tools," which provide specific strategies to help the team build a base of shared knowledge about the process, diagnose critical process issues, analyze sources of process variation, target specific issues for improvement, diagnose problems, and design possible solutions. Teams are advised to implement a series of steps, summarized by an acronym, such as FOCUS:*

- **F**ind an opportunity for improvement (i.e., specify the problem to be solved).
- **O**rganize a team that has frontline knowledge of the process components.
- **C**larify existing information—to provide a foundation for evidence-based decisions.
- **U**nderstand the sources of variation and the root causes.
- **S**olve the problem.

Notably, the team is not invited to discuss solution options until it has completed the previous steps of collecting and analyzing data to diagnose the source of the problem.

The JCAHO embraced the TQM approach to strengthening healthcare quality in the early 1990s, and produced materials to help organizations implement quality improvement programs based on TQM concepts, such as:

- Quality improvement in ambulatory care (1994).
- The measurement mandate, on the road to performance improvement in healthcare (1993).
- Forms, charts, and other tools for performance improvement (1994).

Recognizing that the application of manufacturing-based principles to the delivery of healthcare would require careful thought (and new types of thinking by healthcare professionals), advocates of this strategy renamed the set of ideas, using the terms *quality improvement* or *continuous quality improvement* (CQI). The term *quality improvement* was intended to denote a significant change in strategy from the previous quality assurance programs. JCAHO began inspecting for CQI implementation in the 1995 accreditation process: hospitals were expected to demonstrate (1) implementation of CQI teams and training, and (2) use of quality tools.

---

* FOCUS is one of several acronyms that summarize this series of steps. While the summarizing acronyms vary, the underlying ideas do not.

While TQM programs can provide clear benefits for specific process improvement applications, they can also support the increased use of systematic evidence-based processes that are essential for strengthening healthcare quality (particularly when combined with HIT). Current federal policy is focused on the premise that TQM's emphasis on strengthening processes can radically transform the way we think about doing our jobs and the meaning of being a skilled professional. Well-designed processes supported by HIT can potentially make it possible to systematize care for a large proportion of patients, and it is widely believed that this systematic approach can dramatically reduce medical errors. Consider, for example, the treatment of a hip surgery patient that has just entered the hospital. If the physician's job is to manage every detail of this patient's care, then the physician must be alert to ensure that no detail is forgotten. If, instead, the physician logs onto a computer that is programmed with standing orders for "typical hip surgery" patients, then the physician's job is to determine whether this particular patient is typical or whether this patient requires a customized treatment plan. In this process-oriented setting, it is expected that fewer medical errors will occur due to neglected details, and the physician will be able to devote a larger proportion of his or her time to the more difficult cases. To realize these benefits of HIT and TQM, it will be necessary to have clear treatment guidelines for a broad array of diagnoses and conditions.

This of course raises questions about who will develop and update those guidelines and what constitutes scientific evidence. Large entities, such as Kaiser and Cleveland Clinic, have been active in developing and implementing systematic protocols. They have also been active in analyzing their electronic data, and using the results to update and improve their protocols. For example, Kaiser published a press release on April 14, 2009, stating that analysis of their data on diabetic patients indicated that too tight control of blood sugar was associated with a higher incidence of subsequent Alzheimer's (Kaiser Permanente Division of Research, 2009). This type of data analysis raises the question of whether healthcare providers should utilize this type of result to modify treatment protocols. Kaiser intended to alter its treatment of certain diabetic patients with slightly less tightly controlled blood sugar. TQM's emphasis on data-driven decision making and process analysis indicates that this is the type of response that healthcare organizations and providers should be making. On the other hand, it raises questions about the role of scientific bodies and scientific consensus in developing and updating treatment guidelines (Box 3.3), and the amount of evidence needed before treatment protocols should be revised.

> **BOX 3.3   CONTRAST THE PACE OF TECHNOLOGY DEVELOPMENT AND IMPLEMENTATION IN THE HEALTH INDUSTRY AND IN THE MICROCHIP INDUSTRY**
>
> Andy Grove, the CEO of Intel from 1987 to 1998, asserts, "There are important differences between healthcare and microchip industries in terms of research efficiency" (2005). During the 40 years from 1965 to 2005, the microchip industry produced remarkable technical advances, while the "war on cancer" proceeded slowly. Grove (2005) identifies several critical differences in the research processes that support these two industries: the microchip industry has more advanced techniques for early evaluation of new technology, and for adopting new technology in the workplace.

Implement Systematic Protocols: Clinical Pathways and Guidelines

Efforts to implement systematic care processes proceeded on two levels. Clinical pathways were used at the healthcare provider level, to ensure the systematic quality of care delivery. Clinical guidelines were developed by organizations, such as medical associations and managed care organizations, to translate research results into operational guidelines for healthcare providers.

Clinical Pathways

Clinical pathways (also known as critical pathways, integrated care pathways, or care maps) became prevalent in the acute care and home health settings beginning in the early 1980s. As an established management tool in the airline and construction industries, clinical pathways were adopted and developed by interdisciplinary health team members. Their purpose was to standardize care processes based on established guidelines and evidence, thus improving the quality and coordination of care among the healthcare team. Specific interventions were time sequenced to optimize healing and control lengths of stay based on standards of care.

Expected patient outcomes were assessed along a sequenced time continuum to evaluate whether important milestones in the healing process had been achieved. These pathways or maps could be tailored to focus on individual patient conditions. For instance, if a postsurgical patient had complications with blood pressure control, ambulation within the first 8 postoperative hours may not be clinically appropriate, and therefore the pathway or map could be modified to reflect the specific patient issue. Several studies have identified improved quality of care and positive financial outcomes with the implementation of these pathways for specific patient populations (i.e., total knee and hip replacement surgeries, heart failure, pneumonia, etc.); however, resistance from physicians who object to the development of "cookbook medicine" and the perceived erosion of their professional autonomy limited the overall effectiveness of this quality and cost improvement strategy (Every et al., 2000; Rotter et al., 2010). These attitudes are slowly changing as the emphasis on outcomes and outcomes-based reimbursement grows.

Clinical Guidelines

Clinical guidelines summarize research results and identify best practices. While guidelines were initially developed to support provider decision making and help patients understand treatment options, these may also be relevant to malpractice cases and health insurance coverage decisions. Acceptance of the concept of clinical guidelines has increased since the Agency for Healthcare Research and Quality (AHRQ) (previously the Agency for Health Care Policy and Research) announced a program to develop evidence-based guidelines in 1993. Later, they established Evidence-based Practice Centers (EPCs) to "synthesize scientific evidence to improve quality and effectiveness in health care." In addition, AHRQ partnered with the American Medical Association (AMA) and the American Association of Health Plans (now America's Health Insurance Plans) to create the *National Guideline Clearinghouse.*

Advocates argued that this effort to summarize and synthesize research results and articulate the implications for clinical practice is important due to the complexity and annual volume of research results. If guidelines succeed in helping physicians identify and implement best practices, they will significantly impact the healthcare provided to individual patients.

While the concept of using guidelines to summarize and synthesize available scientific evidence sounds good, the controversy over new mammogram guidelines that sparked consumer outrage illustrates the complexity and difficulty of this task. The federally funded U.S. Preventative Services Task Force announced new and revised mammogram guidelines in

November 2009 (U.S. Preventive Services Task Force, 2009a). This touched off a storm of controversy that resulted in passage of the Vitter amendment, which requires health insurers to cover mammograms for women ages 40–49 without a copayment (Herszenhorn, 2009).

We will examine two underlying issues in this controversy that illustrate the issues that face the guidelines effort in general. First, the guidelines were based on the scientific evidence that was available to the panel, but that evidence was not high quality; in fact, the panel did not rate any of the available evidence as having a quality better than fair. Second, creating the guidelines required the panel to weigh the benefits of screening for breast cancer against the potential harms—and this trade-off raised serious ethical, pragmatic, and analytical issues. A set of articles (DeAngelis and Fontanarosa, 2010; Berg, 2010; Murphy, 2010; Woloshin and Schwartz, 2010; Woolf, 2010) published in the *Journal of the American Medical Association* (JAMA) details these issues.

Quality of the Evidence

We begin by examining the quality of the science that was available to the mammogram panel, the options for dealing with this problem, and the resulting controversy. The panel made a decision to use only studies that were based on randomized clinical trials, even though this meant that the panel relied on older studies that were conducted in the 1960s and 1970s. No clinical trials of mammogram effectiveness have been undertaken since that time (due to ethical questions about assigning women to control groups that would not receive mammograms). Now that screening is widely recommended, it is no longer feasible (or perhaps ethical) to have unscreened control groups. Numerous studies therefore rely on observation rather than randomized experimental designs, despite the fact that randomized clinical trial studies are often viewed as the gold standard for medical research. The panel's decision to consider only randomized controlled trial (RCT) studies is controversial because these studies have two serious disadvantages. First, because the studies were relatively old, the accuracy of the screening technology may have been lower than the accuracy of more recent mammogram screenings, and that accuracy rate plays a key role in the comparison of the costs and potential harms of screening.

Second, the RCT studies divided women into two groups: those invited to participate in the screening, and those who were in the control group and were not invited to participate in the screening. Compliance with the study instructions was only 70%–80%, which means that some of the women who were invited did not actually obtain screenings, and some of the women in the (unscreened) control group obtained mammogram screenings outside of the study. However a woman who was initially included in the treatment (screened) group remained in the "screened" group even if she did not actually have a mammogram. Similarly, a woman who was randomly assigned to the control group remained in the "unscreened" control group even if that woman did obtain a mammogram outside the study. The researchers used this strategy to avoid self-selection bias.

Opponents of the panel's methodology argued that the panel should have considered studies using other research designs, such as nonexperimental observational studies that looked at populations of women who actually did and did not obtain screenings. These studies indicated that mammography is more effective than the results presented by the RCT studies. It is possible that this reflects the fact that the observational studies are more recent, and therefore rely on more accurate mammography technology. It is also possible that the observational studies show a higher effectiveness for mammography if women who are at higher risk are more likely to seek screening. In fact, one research study shows that women with higher risks, such as those with relatives who had breast cancer, are more likely to obtain mammography screenings (McCaul et al., 1996).

The panel attempted to maximize the value of information that was available by using meta-analysis and statistical and mathematical modeling. We explore one aspect of these models below—to provide an illustration of the type of thinking that is used in these models. Here we should note the high degree of uncertainty about the estimates. The panel argued that routine screening should begin at age 50 rather than age 40 because 1904 screenings are required to avert one death for women in their forties, but only 1339 screenings are required to avert one death among women in their fifties. The U.S. Preventative Services Task Force (2009b) recommendations published in the *Annals of Internal Medicine* state, however, that the ranges of these estimates are wide (for women ages 40–49, a relative risk of 0.85 for breast cancer death, with a screening of 1904 to prevent 1 death [C.I. 929-6378], and for women ages 50–59, a relative risk of 0.86, with a screening of 1339 [C.I. 322-7455]). Given these wide ranges, it's not clear that the difference between 1904 and 1339 is meaningful.

Weighing the Costs and Benefits

The second controversial aspect of the panel's work focused on the methods used by the panel to weigh the benefits of screening against the potential harm. These potential harms include overdiagnosis and overtreatment, such as unnecessary biopsies that are triggered by a false-positive result. The full set of costs associated with screening mammography includes the cost of the screening, along with costs for associated physician visits and follow-up care triggered by false positives. The 2017 monetary cost of a screening mammogram is approximately $100 (cost helper). The costs of care triggered by each false positive are more substantial. This aspect of the panel's work generated controversy about two issues.

First, questions were raised about who should make these trade-offs: Is this a scientific trade-off that should be made by a scientific body that is removed from political debate and discussion, or is this fundamentally a policy issue that should be debated in the political arena? While the panel argued that it was not considering or making any recommendation about insurance coverage, others viewed this position as naïve. It seems unrealistic to expect that insurers will not base coverage decisions on federally funded panel guideline recommendations. In fact, one reaction to the panel's recommendation for reduced mammography screening was passage of a bill that requires insurers to cover mammograms on the former, more frequent, schedule.

Second, the appropriate role of cost considerations in healthcare guidelines is a long-standing hot-button issue. Dr. David Eddy has been a long-time vigorous advocate of the importance of explicitly considering cost trade-offs (Eddy et al., 1988). Similarly, the British National Institute for Health and Care Excellence (NICE) utilized quality-adjusted life-years (QALYs) to determine the cost-effectiveness of new treatments. The NICE website states, "With the rapid advances in modern medicine, most people accept that no publicly funded healthcare system … can possibly pay for every new medical treatment which becomes available. The enormous costs involved mean that choices have to be made. It makes sense to focus on treatments that improve the quality and/or length of someone's life." To maximize the benefits that can be achieved with available resources, the NICE website states that treatment impact on QALYs will be compared with treatment costs. Treatments that cost less than £20,000–£30,000 ($26,000–$39,000) per QALY will be categorized as cost-effective. This policy, of course, generated controversy.

Example of the Statistical and Math Modeling

To further examine the substance of the mammogram screening debate, we must consider a critical issue. Analysis of the value of testing and screening programs inevitably faces the substantive question, what is the value of the information produced by the test? A test may have a high degree of scientific accuracy and still produce information that is of limited value. In order to understand the underlying mechanism that causes this problem, we need to examine Bayesian statistics. We examine the statistical concept using a straightforward example that was published in the journal *Decision Sciences*, on the issue of whether we should do random drug testing of college athletes, and then we apply the ideas to the mammography issue (Feinstein, 1990).

The *Decision Sciences* article focused on the question, if we do random drug testing of athletes, how much information will the test results give us? Let's assume that the test has a lab accuracy of 95%. This means that the test result will accurately reflect reality 95% of the time:

■ If an athlete is actually using drugs, the test will correctly identify the athlete as a drug user with a probability of 0.95 (this is usually called the *sensitivity* of the test).
■ If an athlete is not using drugs, the test will correctly identify the athlete as a nonuser with a probability of 0.95 (this is usually called the *specificity* of the test).

However, if we do this testing on a population in which a very low proportion of athletes use drugs, the test results may not give us any information at all. To understand the problem, consider Table 3.1.

Suppose we administer this test to 1000 athletes, of which 50 actually use drugs and 950 do not. Then the incidence of drug use in our sample is 5%. (This is the base rate of drug use in this student population. It is also known as the Bayesian prior probability). These numbers are shown in the last row of Table 3.1, labeled "number of students." When the 50 students who actually use drugs take the test, it will provide an accurate result for 95% of these students. This implies that the test results will show that there are 45 students who use drugs (and who actually do), but it will also miss 5 who do use the drug by indicating that these 5 do not. When the 950 students who do not use drugs take the test, it will correctly identify 905 of the students as non-drug users, and it will incorrectly identify 45 of the students as drug users. (These 45 students will be falsely accused of drug use because the test has produced false-positive results for the students.)

Taken as a whole, the test results for the 1000 students will indicate that 90 of the students use drugs and 910 of the students do not (as shown in the last column of Table 3.1). If we look at the 90 positive results, shown in the

Table 3.1 Test Results vs. Reality for Hypothetical Set of Student Athletes: Only 5% Actually Use Drugs

	Reality: The student does *use drugs*	*Reality:* The student does not *use drugs*	*Total number of students in each row*
Test result: The student *does* use drugs	45: Test result is *accurate* for 95% of the 5 students who use drugs	45: Test result is incorrect (false positive) for 5% of the 95 students who do not use drugs	90: Students receive test results that indicate drug use
Test result: The student *does not* use drugs	5: Test result is incorrect (false negative) for 5% of the 5 students who do not use drugs	905: Test result is accurate for 95% of the 95 students who do not use drugs	910: Students receive test results that indicate *no* drug use
Number of students	50: Students who really *do* use drugs	950: Students who really *do not* use drugs	1000: Students tested

first row of the table, we will see that half of them are accurate and half of them are false positives. This is shocking. We administered a test that, from a scientific point of view, is 95% accurate, and yet when we look at the test results that indicate drug use, only half of them are correct. The problem is that we administered the drug test in a population in which actual drug use is very low. We only have false-positive results for 5% of the non-drug-using students, but the number of non-drug-using students is high compared with the number of drug users.

If we administer the same test to a different group of 1000 students in which the rate of drug use is high—perhaps 50% of students use drugs in the second population—the test results yield significantly more information. In this case, 95% of the positive drug test results are accurate and only 5% of them are wrong (Table 3.2).

Clearly, test results provide valuable information when the lab test has a high scientific accuracy rate *and* the test is performed on a population in which the incidence (or base rate) is high. This implies that screening tests, such as mammography, make sense in populations with a relatively high expected incidence, and they do not make sense in younger populations,

Table 3.2   Test Results vs. Reality for Hypothetical Set of 1000 Student Athletes: 50% of the Students Use Drugs

	Reality: *The student* does *use drugs*	**Reality:** *The student* does not *use drugs*	*Total number of students in each row*
Test result: The student *does* use drugs	475: Test result is *accurate* for 95% of the 5 students who use drugs	25: Test result is incorrect (false positive) for 5% of the 95 students who do not use drugs	500: Students receive test results that indicate drug use
Test result: The student *does not* use drugs	25: Test result is incorrect (false negative) for 5% of the 5 students who do not use drugs	475: Test result is accurate for 95% of the 95 students who do not use drugs	500: Students receive test results that indicate *no* drug use
Numbers of students	500: Students who really *do* use drugs	500: Students who really *do not* use drugs	1000: Students tested

where the incidence of cancer is much lower. The idea that we should apply this logic to analyze screening tests is not new: Louise Russell wrote an interesting book in 1994, *Educated Guesses,* that examined these issues for a series of tests, such as mammography and prostate cancer. Despite this long-standing discussion, the mammogram screening guidelines announced by the U.S. Preventive Services Task Force (2009a) generated vigorous controversy—that focused on the details of the decisions that are needed to apply this logic to a specific situation.

The panel used this Bayesian logic as it examined trade-offs for women ages 40–49 and those for women ages 50–59. The panel concluded that the harm outweighed the benefits for the younger group of women, while the benefits outweighed the harm for the older group of women. Opponents reject this conclusion for three reasons. First, the criteria for weighing deaths against the harm of unnecessary treatment are not clear. Second, opponents do not believe that the panel gave sufficient consideration to the probability that mammogram screening permits women with cancer to be treated at an earlier stage, with less of a burden on the patient. Third, opponents of the revised guidelines argue that dividing the population into age groups 40–49 and 50–59 was arbitrary. The opponents argue that the number of deaths averted by mammogram screening is similar in the two groups. The panel reported that 0.5 deaths would be prevented per 1000 screenings for women ages 40–49, and 0.7 deaths would be prevented per 1000 screenings for women ages 50–59. Given the uncertainty intrinsic to these estimates, opponents of the panel's conclusion argue that it is not clear that these groups are significantly different. Similarly, the estimated numbers of women who would be overtreated are similar for the two groups: for every 1000 women screened, the panel estimated that the number of women overtreated would lie between 1 and 5 for women ages 40–49 and between 1 and 7 for women ages 50–59 (Woloshin and Schwartz, 2010).

Dr. David Eddy has argued that we should address the first issue raised by the opponents, by quantifying both the benefits and the harms in terms of dollars. This approach would permit a more straightforward and transparent comparison of benefits against harms. He developed a model in 1988 (with coauthors) that indicates that screening frequency should be considered carefully (Eddy et al., 1988). The information reported by Eddy et al. in 1988 indicates that annual screening is probably not cost-effective, while benefits would outweigh costs if we screen every other year or every third year.

Mammography screening technology has advanced since 1988; however, the question of *whether* we should use this type of analysis during the guidelines development process is still a hot-button issue. The U.S. Preventive Services Task Force (2016) now recommends that average-risk women age 50 to 74 years be screened once every two years, and that women age 40–49 weigh the potential benefits and potential harms. The evidence and logic underlying this recommendation focus on directly weighing costs and benefits, instead of comparing estimated dollar values for the costs with life-years saved (Mandelblatt, et al. 2016).

Advocates of comparisons on costs with benefits argue that treatment guidelines should provide recommendations that are grounded in the reality that resource allocation issues cannot be ignored. Others shy away from this analysis, citing concerns about the social impact of explicit decisions to accept increased risk of some deaths—to save money. (The book *Tragic Choices* [1978] offers a thoughtful discussion of this view.) Note also that this involves a classic trade-off in economics—the so-called guns and butter decision. One could take the (naïve) view that any expenditure is justified even if it saves one life. This view is economically naïve because dollars and healthcare resources are scarce—spending these on mammograms necessarily means that there are fewer resources to spend on other good causes, such as HIV/AIDs treatment or prenatal care. The question then becomes where one gains the most "bang for the buck."

This controversy is not confined to the United States. In 2005, a headline in the *Wall Street Journal* described the controversy: "Britain Stirs Outcry by Weighing Benefits of Drugs versus Price" (Whalen, 2005). This issue is also not unique to healthcare decisions. Significant controversies, in the 1980s, focused on the question of whether cost–benefit trade-offs should be considered when the Occupational Safety and Health Administration (OSHA) specifies occupational safety regulations. Two contentious cases reached the Supreme Court, focused on regulations limiting worker exposure to benzene and cotton dust.

Implications of "Not Enough" Science

One analyst summarized the controversy at its most fundamental level. When we do not have enough science to draw a clear conclusion about benefits and harms of a specific screening program or treatment, how should we proceed? We have two options. We could implement the screening program or treatment until sufficient evidence becomes available to make a determination of whether we should continue or discontinue the treatment. Alternately, we could follow a policy that we will never begin widespread use of the treatment or test until we have sufficient evidence to conclude definitively that the benefits outweigh the harms. As we move toward increased emphasis on evidence-based decision making, the debate between these two approaches will become increasingly salient.

One reason this debate is so contentious is that the stakes are high. If we adopt a strategy of prioritizing resources on the basis of maximizing the benefits per dollar, we will face some implications that are clear but uncomfortable. This discomfort with cost–benefit analysis underlies support for the policy that cost cannot be used to develop guidelines, elderly life-years saved cannot be valued less than those of others, and disabled people's life-years saved cannot be valued less than those of others.

Conclusion: Some Strategies for Strengthening Quality Are Clear, but the Concept of Healthcare Quality Is Complex and Multidimensional

In this concluding chapter of the "Pressures for Change" section of this book, we explored issues related to quality of care in the United Sates. We examined the evidence that supports the perception that there is room for improvement in delivering high-quality care in the United States. In evaluating the evidence, we learned that international comparisons must be used with caution, as some of the differences in quality measures may not reflect differences in the healthcare systems.

Lifestyle factors contribute to disparities in outcomes:

■ International comparisons of infant mortality rates may not tell the whole story, as differences in definitions and access to life-prolonging technologies impact the statistics.

■ Higher rates of obesity in the United States may lead to the higher reported rates of cancer, when compared with Canadian rates.

■ Greater access to firearms may help explain the decreased life expectancy rates in the United States, which are less than those of other industrialized nations.

We also noted that implementing and monitoring systematic care processes could prevent medical errors. Regional differences in healthcare utilization, expenditures, and outcomes support the necessity of basing healthcare decisions on evidence that will require systematic processes of care and new types of research that would provide support for care providers. The proliferation and adoption of evidence-based systematic processes and guidelines may be accelerated with the support of HIT.

As our society grapples with the issues surrounding access, cost, and quality of healthcare, we will need to define what health means. Is it merely the absence of illness and disease? If that is our definition, what roles do the individual and environment play? What will we decide about prevention activities and screenings?

We also consider the web of relationships between health and socioeconomic factors, such as income, education, and occupational status. The federal Department of Health and Human Services report "Health, United States, 2015" (U.S. Department of Health and Human Services, National Center for Health Statistics, Centers for Disease Control and Prevention, 2016) included a section focused on socioeconomic status (SES) and health. This report noted that the web of interactions between SES and health is complex, and it probably includes multiple causal factors. Income and education may impact the individual's ability to access healthcare resources. These factors are correlated with health-related behaviors, and an individual's health may impact his or her ability to pursue educational opportunities and earn income. Evidence of these relationships is long-standing.

For example, researchers in the 1990s presented evidence that

■ Low SES is associated with increased morbidity and mortality (Adler et al., 1994; Adler and Coriell, 1997).

■ Low-income individuals are two to five times more likely to suffer from a diagnosable mental disorder than those in the top SES bracket (Bourdon et al., 1994; Regier et al., 1993).

We need to more clearly define the boundaries and responsibilities of the healthcare system and develop stronger systems for implementing and monitoring systematic care processes. In Section II, we examine five strategies for strengthening the system:

1. Aligning incentives via payment system design
2. Creating organizations that provide better care coordination
3. Focusing on wellness and preventative care
4. Utilizing new types of providers to gain greater efficiencies
5. Leveraging HIT to become more systematic in healthcare delivery and quality of care monitoring

Conclusion to Section I

Each of the three problems (access, cost, and quality) is complex, and the three problems are inextricably linked. Solutions that focus on just one area will always fail to deliver the results we intend to achieve. This is why health reform is so complex, and why it is not realistic to expect that specific pieces of the Patient Protection and Affordable Care Act (PPACA) can be repealed or replaced, without causing new types of problems. It's a jigsaw puzzle.

While the mandate remains unpopular, universal access reduces distortions that hinder competitive market forces, and these forces are essential to reduce cost and increase quality. At the same time, lower cost would reduce the price tag for universal coverage. Similarly, better coordination (facilitated by continuous insurance coverage) would strengthen quality, and systematic quality would reduce cost.

In addition, examination of the difficult issues posed by the three problems points to a deeper layer of complexity: the boundaries of our healthcare system are not clear. We tend to view the healthcare system as the set of services that are typically provided by licensed medical professionals, and covered by standard health insurance policies. As we explore the access, cost, and quality issues, however, we see that healthcare is simply a tool for producing health. We don't wake up in the morning and think, "This would be a good day to get some healthcare—I would really enjoy that experience!" Instead, we obtain healthcare only as a strategy to increase our health. Further, healthcare is only one of a broad array of strategies for increasing health. One analyst concludes that 40% of early deaths can be attributed to individual behaviors, 30% result from genetic predispositions, 15% reflect social circumstances, and only 10%–15% stem from deficiencies in our healthcare system (Heckman, 2012). This inconvenient truth has three important implications:

1. It is difficult to measure the performance of the healthcare system (or specific healthcare providers), because healthcare outcomes are frequently impacted by factors outside the provider's control.
2. We cannot address the important issue of health inequality simply by offering universal access to insurance coverage. Health inequality is clearly an important issue—that is becoming more salient. Data from the Social Security Administration demonstrates increasing health inequality, based on remaining life expectancy for individuals who reach age 65.
   ■ For individuals born in 1912, the gap between the remaining life expectancy of 65-year-old individuals with high versus low income was less than 1 year.
   ■ For individuals born in 1941, this gap was 5.5 years.
3. Allocating increasing proportions of public funding to healthcare could be counterproductive if we find those funds by decreasing efforts to provide universal access to a reasonably good education, adult literacy and job training, or measures to prevent or alleviate poverty.
4. A recent article written by James Heckman (who won a Nobel Prize in economics) argues that we are seeing increasing evidence that early experiences (in utero and early childhood) shape important elements of the individual's subsequent experience—such as educational attainment and propensity to engage in risky behaviors (Heckman, 2012). If this set of early results turns out to be correct, it has important implications for prioritizing our efforts to build health.

Our healthcare system faces multifactorial problems. The good news is that there are efforts currently underway to try to address and resolve these issues. The bad news is that not all of these efforts will be successful, and political agendas will prolong the debate of how to accomplish the Triple Aim. In Section II of the book, we begin to explore strategies and solutions to the pressures for change that have occurred or are being proposed in order to address the issues of our current healthcare system. Through this exploration, we will have the opportunity to apply the economic principles we've learned in Section I—to identify what works and what doesn't, and examine how these efforts may influence our futures as healthcare professionals.

STRATEGIES TO INCREASE EFFICIENCY

Introduction

In a publication by the Clayton Christensen Institute for Disruptive Innovation (Clayton Christensen is the author of the much quoted and influential book *The Innovator's Prescription*), the authors noted, "It is through leveraging opportunities to innovate and disrupt within the health care industry that we will move closer to the one goal almost everyone agrees upon: making health care more affordable and more accessible to all people" (Wanamaker and Bean, 2013). They also noted that there are some provisions of the Patient Protection and Affordable Care Act (PPACA) that promote or incentivize innovation (e.g., employer and individual insurance mandates, accountable care organizations, and wellness programs) and provisions that may de-incentivize positive changes to our healthcare system (e.g., mandated essential benefits, cost sharing, medical cost ratio, and Medicaid expansion). It is important to understand that each set of changes brings with it new regulatory challenges and new opportunities for innovation. You may find it useful to read this analysis of opportunities and challenges for innovation in the post-PPACA U.S. healthcare system, to enhance your understanding of the implications of key elements of the PPACA.

If we want to understand where the healthcare system is headed and how to advocate for changes that will bring about positive healthcare reform, it will be useful to examine

- Ongoing changes as providers align their healthcare processes and business practices with PPACA requirements and with evolving Medicare payment strategies

- Changes in the healthcare market and their impacts on the healthcare system
- Impacts of these changes that are shaping debates about alternate strategies for working toward the Triple Aim

We begin by assessing the roles of market forces and government regulations in the healthcare industry.

Do Healthcare Markets Operate Efficiently?

Statistical evidence indicates that market forces do operate in the healthcare industry, but this industry has some unique characteristics that create inefficiencies:

- Some healthcare market participants wield market power—including large purchasers (e.g., Medicare and Medicaid), physicians (e.g., the American Medical Association), hospitals, and insurance companies.
- Insurance distorts normal incentives that influence both the amount of healthcare and the types of healthcare that patients want to purchase, and providers want to provide. Milton Friedman's (2001) warning, "Nobody spends somebody else's money as wisely as he spends his own," is important: consumers are more careful about monitoring expenditures when they pay directly out-of-pocket than when they are essentially spending the insurance company's money.
- Healthcare providers (physicians, psychologists, and nurse practitioners) have significantly more information about treatment options and expected treatment outcomes than patients—in fact, it is fair to say that patients "hire" healthcare providers to make decisions and provide advice. In the language of economics, patients are the "principals" and healthcare providers are the "agents"—hired to act in the best interest of the principals. Knowledge in healthcare is asymmetric—the healthcare providers have more information than patients—and this can generate incentives to overprovide care. This problem also occurs when drivers hire auto mechanics to diagnose and repair car problems, when individuals hire attorneys to handle legal matters, and when homeowners hire contractors to address home repair or remodeling issues. The principal faces the same problem in each of these situations: he or she is not sure whether the agent's actions and recommendations are also influenced by the agent's financial self-interest.

Kenneth Arrow, who won a Nobel Prize for his work in economics, wrote a classic paper in 1963 that detailed the plethora of market failures in healthcare. Other analysts, who examined government regulatory behavior, conclude that policy makers and regulators also face limitations. Therefore, it is reasonable to expect that our healthcare sector will continue to be shaped by *both* government policies and market forces and by interactions between the regulatory policies and market forces (Glazer and Rothenberg, 2005).

Two Key "Market Failures" in Healthcare

Principal–Agent Problem: Healthcare Providers and Auto Mechanics

The principal–agent relationship between patients and providers poses significant problems for healthcare interactions. The principal (the patient) usually does not have sufficient information to accurately assess the quality of the agent's work (the healthcare provider) and the veracity of his or her stated opinions. This is in direct contrast to other purchasing decisions, such as buying a gallon of milk or even a car, where the consumer can feel confident that he or she can gain sufficient information to properly access quality and value. Because the agent knows that the principal has limited ability to assess the quality of his or her work, the incentives embedded in the payment system can exert substantial influence on the agent's behavior.

A provider, or an auto mechanic, who is reimbursed on a fee-for-service (FFS) basis has a monetary incentive to overtreat patients or recommend unnecessary auto repair. In fact, Sears was prosecuted some years ago (Anderson, 2011) for implementing a payment incentive system in which employees in the auto repair shops could increase their earnings by increasing the number of repairs completed. The prosecutor charged that the result was predictable: recommendation and completion of unnecessary auto repairs. Sears subsequently redesigned the payment system to eliminate this incentive.

The question of whether empirical evidence supports the hypothesis that healthcare providers systematically generate demand for their services by recommending unnecessary treatments has been controversial in economics. Economists describe this process with the shorthand phrase "supply-induced demand" (SID). Empirical evidence on the magnitude of SID is mixed. The statistical challenges of testing this hypothesis are formidable. However, an interesting analysis of the incentive for unnecessary auto repair provides a useful clue: this incentive is strong when the mechanic does not have enough customers to completely fill his schedule, and this incentive is blunted by the mechanic's concern about the impact on his reputation if unnecessary repairs are discovered (Darby and Karni, 1973). This implies that overtreatment probably varies significantly across physicians, and across time periods, which complicates statistical analysis of this hypothesis. Nonetheless, empirical evidence does support the basic idea that providers respond to payment system incentives (Clemens and Gottlieb, 2014).

Insurance Reduces the Incentive for Patients to Shop Wisely

This problem is compounded by the fact that insurance reduces patient incentives to be cautious about healthcare expenditures. While patients may realize that FFS payment gives providers an incentive to overprovide care, health insurance blunts patient incentives to be skeptical of suggested treatment options, as they may be paying only a small portion of the cost of these unnecessary services.

How Should Government Address These Market Failures?

These market failures are not unique to healthcare; each type of market failure occurs in a broad array of industries. Strategies deployed to address these problems fall into two categories:

1. Government can address market failure problems by developing programs or specifying regulations aimed to supplant the market process.
2. Government can design policies to mitigate the market failure and strengthen the market outcome.

Many of the debates about health policy are, essentially, debates about the optimal balance between these two types of strategies. These debates also occur in other areas; for example, Box 1 provides an overview of the application of these strategies to increase average automobile fuel economy. Many policies combine the two strategies. In this section, we examine the use of these two options to address market failures that impact the efficiency with which healthcare is produced. Specifically, we examine five strategies to increase healthcare system efficiency:

- Better aligning payment incentives
- Managing care
- Preventing and managing chronic conditions

BOX 1 ALTERNATE REGULATORY STRATEGIES TO ACHIEVE A SOCIAL GOAL: FINDING A COST-EFFECTIVE STRATEGY

Consider, for example, our current strategy for increasing average automobile fuel economy. The United States currently uses the first option: regulations mandate that automakers must ensure that their cars meet corporate average fuel economy standards. In 2007, the standard for automobiles was 27.5 mpg, and automakers must achieve an average of 54.5 by the year 2025. In contrast, the second strategy would focus on raising gas taxes to induce consumers to purchase fuel-efficient cars. While this strategy is not popular, a Congressional Budget Office report concluded that consumers would spend less, overall, if we implemented the gas tax strategy. According to this report, the Corporate Average Fuel Economy standards (CAFE) strategy leads to increased costs because consumers and firms respond to the regulation by adjusting their behaviors. As a result, the "straightforward" regulatory approach is not as straightforward as it seems.

Source: Congressional Budget Office, Fuel economy standards versus a gasoline tax, Economic and Budget Issue Brief, March 9, 2004, Congressional Budget Office, Washington, DC, https://www.cbo.gov/sites/default/files/cbofiles/ftpdocs/49xx/doc4917/12-24-03_cafe.pdf.

■ Facilitating competitive innovation
■ Harnessing the potential offered by health information technology

This discussion will help you identify the strengths and limitations of these efforts to generate significant efficiency gains (that may also fundamentally redesign our healthcare system). We will apply "lessons learned" from past experience, and assess new proposals and innovations.

Chapter 4

Align Incentives via Payment System Design

Introduction

Hospitals and physicians treat patients who are covered by public and private insurance policies that utilize an array of payment designs. Healthcare payers vary in both the level of payments provided and the structure of those payments. Some healthcare payers utilize fee-for-service (FFS) payments, while others provide fixed payments for a type of care or an episode of care. Some payers also utilize bonuses or penalties based on quality metrics.

In this chapter, we primarily focus on Medicare payments for hospital services; however, a parallel set of issues is relevant for physician payments. We begin with information on types of payment structures and the incentives intrinsic to those structures. We then consider the evolution of strategies to control cost and strengthen healthcare quality. Finally, we use data from one short-term general hospital to examine the implications of current payment systems for hospital operations and strategy.

Background: Alternate Hospital Payment Designs

While hospitals list charges for each service they provide, actual payments are typically substantially lower than the stated charges. Instead, healthcare payers specify the types of payment structure they will use.

- Some payers utilize FFS payments. In this case, the hospital receives payments that correspond to the supplies and activities detailed on a hospital bill. The payments for each item are typically less than the amount indicated on the hospital bill (which is known as "charges"). Private-sector payers typically negotiate discounted rates with hospitals. Public-sector payers specify the amount they will pay for each item.
- Some payers specify that they will pay a fixed amount (set by the payer) for an inpatient stay. This payment structure is known as DRG payment, because the Diagnostic Related Group (DRG) coding system is used to categorize inpatient admissions and payment amounts are specified for each DRG.
- Some payers agree to pay a fixed amount (set by the payer) for care delivered during a contracted time period. This strategy includes monthly capitated payments made by managed care companies to physicians and monthly Medicare payments to accountable care organizations (ACOs). In each case, the payer agrees to pay a fixed monthly amount to the provider organization for each patient listed on the provider's roster (or panel) of patients.
- Bundled payment refers to contracts in which the payer agrees to provide a specified payment for a bundle of services provided by the hospital, plus services provided by other healthcare providers such as independent physicians or nursing facilities. One entity (typically the hospital) receives the fixed payment from the payer and forwards payments to the other providers.

Each payment structure creates a set of incentives for hospitals. FFS payment generates incentives for lengthy hospital stays that include provision of numerous services. This "cost-plus" payment system raises concerns that hospitals may inflate the cost of healthcare by providing services that are not medically necessary.

DRG payment creates incentives to reduce the length of stay (as the payment would still be the same, but the hospital would provide fewer services and incur fewer expenditures), and it creates incentives to avoid providing unnecessary services (as there would be no incremental payment). This raises concerns that hospitals may skimp on care, although medical guidelines for hospital discharge and the malpractice liability system constrain the degree to which hospitals can respond to this incentive.

Bundled payment creates incentives for the group of healthcare providers to reduce the cost of delivering the bundled set of services by coordinating and integrating their services efficiently. If the group of providers successfully reduces cost, they share the benefits of these cost savings.

This array of payment structures generates a complex array of incentives for an individual hospital. Consider a hospital that provides hip replacement surgery for Mary Smith. Mary is one of numerous patients receiving this surgery during the current fiscal year. The hospital is likely to implement a common set of treatment protocols for all these patients. The hospital will receive FFS payment for some of the hip replacement patients, DRG payment for others, and (possibly) bundled payment for others.

This diversity of payment structures also makes it difficult for hospitals to provide "price transparency" or for states to mandate meaningful disclosure of hospital prices. It would be easy to mandate disclosure of hospital charges, but these charges do not represent the amounts actually paid by most patients. Instead, they represent the starting point for negotiations with private-sector insurance companies. The idea of mandating disclosure of actual payment rates is more complex. Payment rates for Medicaid and Medicare patients are public information, but rates paid by private-sector insurance companies vary widely. Some firms, such as Castlight, aim to fill this information gap, much as travel websites provide convenient access to rates for hotels or airline tickets. These firms provide detailed information about average rates paid for specific services in a local geographic area. Some employers provide this information about paid claims to help employees understand prices paid to specific healthcare providers in their area. This information is relevant to patients who will pay a percentage of the hospital payments (as a copayment) and to patients with high-deductible insurance plans.

Strategies to Control Cost: Rate Design Replaced Certificate of Need Programs

FFS Payments for Hospital Services and Certificate of Need Programs

When the Medicare program was developed in 1963, it was structured to conform to the payment system that was widely used at the time: FFS payment. A 1973 federal law authorized states to create certificate of need (CON) programs to address concerns that the incentives created by FFS payment would spur hospitals to acquire excessive amounts of costly equipment and too much hospital bed capacity. The idea that each hospital would have an incentive to match competing hospitals' acquisition of the latest and best equipment was known as the "medical arms race." Hospitals were required to demonstrate that new facilities were needed to meet community requirements. This concept had a fatal flaw: there were no clear criteria to distinguish hospital stays that were needed to provide high-quality care from those that were simply desired due to the perverse FFS payment system incentives. Statistical evidence indicated that the programs did not effectively reduce capital expenditures or contain cost (Conover and Sloan, 1998). The federal law was repealed and the state-level programs were largely abandoned.

Rate Redesign

Top-down planning efforts, such as CON programs, have largely been replaced with efforts to create incentives to induce providers and patients to make efficient healthcare decisions. As a large buyer, Medicare makes decisions about the structure and the level of rates that will be paid to physicians, hospitals, and other healthcare providers. These rate decisions exert significant influences on the numbers and types of healthcare providers, the healthcare decisions made by these providers, and the competitive relationships among these providers.

As it works to design an effective payment structure, Medicare faces a complex problem. Because Medicare payments constitute 20% of healthcare expenditures, the rates at which Medicare reimburses healthcare providers have far-reaching economic implications: these rates influence the mix of services provided, the numbers of services provided, and the structures of hospital and physician markets (Centers for Medicare and Medicaid Services, 2015). Federal policies also influence the supply of physicians through policies that impact medical and nursing education.

From an economics perspective, the "right" price will induce enough individuals to offer physician services—to see all the patients who are willing to pay that price. (This is the equilibrium price we discussed in Chapter 1 on access.) The right set of prices will help the Centers for Medicare and Medicaid Services (CMS) stretch its dollars while still providing sufficient reimbursement to induce physicians and hospitals to continue to treat Medicare patients.

The task of specifying prices is complex because

1. The CMS is such a large buyer that it cannot simply observe the current price; instead, the prices paid by Medicare and Medicaid exert significant impact on each segment of the healthcare market so that Medicare is the key "market maker." In the language of economists, Medicare has "monopsony" power. (A monopsonist is a single buyer that wields enough purchasing power to significantly impact the market. Instead of simply paying typical prices, a monopsonist has enough bargaining power to set the price.)
2. The healthcare industry is experiencing substantial competitive and technological innovation that creates pressure for frequent price adjustments.
3. Efforts to control healthcare costs exert negative impacts on healthcare provider revenues, and some healthcare provider organizations maintain active lobbying efforts.

DRG Payment for Hospital Services

The first major effort to reengineer the incentive structure occurred in 1983 when Medicare implemented the DRG payment system for hospitals. The DRG system replaced the pre-1983 FFS system that created incentives to keep patients in the hospital for lengthy stays. The DRG system is designed to create incentives to produce care more efficiently by focusing on the diagnoses for which patients are admitted to hospitals. For example, DRG 544 is assigned to each patient admitted to the hospital for hip replacement surgery. Medicare's payment to the hospital for each patient with DRG 544 is set by Medicare payment schedules; it is not determined by the patient's actual length of stay (or cost of care) in the hospital. This system is also known as the prospective payment system (PPS) because the reimbursement amount is estimated prospectively (prior to completion of the patient's care), based on the patient's admitting diagnosis. (We should note that this is a streamlined description of the DRG system. For a few extra details, see Box 4.1).

BOX 4.1   ADDITIONAL FEATURES OF THE DRG SYSTEM

This is a streamlined description of the DRG system. The DRG system includes additional features, such as

- Categories for more complex and less complex patients (e.g., DRG 774 is vaginal delivery with complicating diagnoses, while DRG 775 is vaginal delivery without complicating diagnoses)
- Outlier payments for unusual cases
- Adjustments for geographic location

Consider the impact of the change from FFS payment to DRG/PPS payment, as illustrated by Mary Smith's hypothetical hip surgery.

Pre-1983 FFS system: Suppose the FFS rate schedule specified the rates that would be paid for the surgery and for each day in the hospital. Mary Smith might have been admitted to the hospital the day before the surgery (it is convenient for the hospital to complete preop lab work if the patient is *in* the hospital), and she might have stayed for 8–10 days after the surgery—until Mary and her physician decided that Mary was ready to be discharged.

DRG system: The DRG system introduced a dramatic change. A hospital admitting a patient under a DRG classification of hip surgery would expect to receive $12,257 on average across the United States, regardless of the length of the patient's stay (Kaiser Family Foundation, 2007). This created a new incentive to organize treatment efficiently and coordinate with post–hospital care providers (such as nursing facilities or rehabilitation centers). Today, unless there is a complication, a patient undergoing hip replacement surgery can expect to have a 4- to 5-day hospital stay. Mary will be approved for discharge (regardless of her preferences) once she has met the discharge criteria, which typically include stable clinical condition, ability to walk, and appropriate pain control. If she is unable to meet the discharge criteria within the 4- to 5-day time frame, a referral to a rehabilitation facility would be considered. This payment strategy was pioneered by Medicare, but it is no longer unique to Medicare.

This shift from a cost-plus pricing system to a fixed price per episode radically altered the incentive structure faced by hospitals. Hospitals responded to the DRG system by reducing the average length of stay. Nursing homes provided early evidence of the changes in treatment patterns when they began complaining that hospitals were discharging patients "quicker and sicker." (It is important, however, to note that concurrent development of new technology also contributed to the decrease in average length of stay shown in Figure 4.1.)

Implementation of the DRG payment system raised three additional concerns:

1. Moving care traditionally provided in an acute care setting to a lower-level setting or reducing service intensity could potentially jeopardize patient health (Rock, 1985).
2. Hospitals that treated more severely ill patients (teaching and specialty hospitals) might be financially disadvantaged because they would receive the same reimbursement as those hospitals treating less severely ill patients (Horn and Backofen, 1987).
3. While DRGs were devised to contain the escalating cost of Medicare, there was an unintended loophole: hospital readmissions generated revenue. If a patient was discharged from the hospital and was later readmitted with, for example, a postoperative infection, the hospital received reimbursement for the second hospitalization regardless of the quality of care that had been provided during the first hospital stay (Brown, 1995).

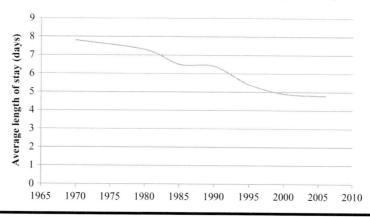

Figure 4.1   Average length of hospital stay: Surgical and nonsurgical procedures.

National hospital discharge survey: 2006 Annual summary. CDC. Dec 2010 http://www.cdc.gov/nchs/data/series/sr_13/sr13_168.pdf

Capitated Payment for Physicians; Accountable Care Organizations for Wider Sets of Providers

Managed care organizations utilize capitated payment for physicians. Under a capitated (prepaid) contract between the physician and an insurance company, the physician commits to provide care for a set of patients and the insurer pays a fixed dollar amount per person per month. Capitated payment contracts raise questions about the amount of risk that should be shouldered by physicians. Insurance companies receive fixed monthly payments (per insured individual), and they are obligated to pay for medical services covered in the insurance policy. Because these organizations assume substantial risk, they are regulated by state insurance commissioners. These regulations typically mandate that the organization must demonstrate that it holds sufficient assets to ensure that it will be able to make payments for covered services. Physicians are not regulated by insurance commissions because physicians receiving capitated payments are not legally defined as "risk-bearing entities."

The question of whether these physicians should be subject to insurance regulations was hotly debated during the 1990s. It appears that this issue may become important again. New Jersey initiated a pilot program in 2016 to provide capitated payments for primary care services for the state health benefits program. This contract is described as direct primary care (DPC) because the state is contracting with the physician practice directly without utilizing a managed care organization as a middleman. New Jersey does not currently specify regulations for DPC; however, some states have already clarified that DPC is not a risk-bearing entity for the purpose of insurance regulation (Glans, 2017).

Medicare ACOs will receive capitated payments from Medicare. The ACO will receive a set monthly amount for each patient listed on its patient panel, and the ACO will be responsible for providing services for the patient, as needed. ACOs are expected to include an array of provider types, such as physicians, hospitals, and nursing facilities. Hence, the set of services included under an ACO capitated payment system will be substantially larger than the set of services included in a physician capitated payment contract.

Bundled Payment: Eliminate Silos

The use of separate payment systems to reimburse specific types of providers creates payment silos with minimal incentives to coordinate care across the silos. For example, Medicare continued to use an FFS system to reimburse nursing facilities after it began using the DRG/PPS system to reimburse hospitals in 1983. This payment system dichotomy does not provide appropriate incentives for the two sets of facilities to coordinate care across their institutional boundaries. Consider, for example, a Medicare transfer patient. By definition, a transfer patient lives at home prior to the episode of care, is hospitalized for treatment, and then requires follow-up treatment at a nursing facility before returning home when the episode of care is complete. The DRG payment system created a financial incentive for hospitals to minimize discretionary services (such as patient teaching or physical therapy) that can be postponed until the nursing facility phase of the patient's treatment and to discharge the patient to the nursing facility as quickly as possible.

Medicare attempted to address this problem by implementing bundled payment for transfer patients. Under bundled payment, one of these institutions (e.g., the hospital or the nursing facility) assumes financial responsibility for the entire episode of care and subcontracts with the other institution. For example, a hospital could assume financial responsibility for the patient's bundle of care and subcontract with a nursing facility for the second phase of the treatment. Under this system, the hospital has a financial incentive to work with nursing facilities to figure out the optimal treatment pattern and implement that pattern. Medicare is currently expanding the use of bundled payment (Miller et al., 2011).

Selective Contracting

The strategy of "selective contracting" offers an alternative to the approach of setting a price. Congress mandated that Medicare begin using the selective contracting strategy for durable medical equipment (DME) beginning in 2007 (Federal Trade Commission and Department of Justice, 2004). Instead of announcing rates that it would pay for DME, Medicare would solicit bids from DME suppliers. Companies with low bids would be selected to provide DME for Medicare recipients. This strategy would induce DME suppliers to reveal the prices at which they are willing to provide DME instead of requiring Medicare to guess at these prices. This contracting strategy was controversial, largely due to concerns about the potential impact on small suppliers. Small business advocates were concerned that large suppliers, who might enjoy economies of scale, might underbid small DME suppliers. In addition, opponents expressed concern about the competitive bidding process, particularly in rural areas, as there may not be sufficient potential bidders to create real competition. Congress responded by delaying the phased implementation until 2011, and legislation has been proposed to terminate the program. (Consider the overall cost implication of this concern that selective contracting might harm small business by reducing the reimbursement rate!)

Both of the two general strategies, DRG-type incentive systems and competitive contracting systems, raise complex issues. The complexity of the DRG-type incentive approach lies in the level of necessary detail, and the complexity of the selective contracting approach lies in performance monitoring. It is essential to monitor service quality because the provider will have a strong incentive to underprovide services once the contract has been signed. Some of the strongest concerns raised by the opponents of selective contracting for DME focused on this issue.

Pay for Performance and Consumer Information to Incentivize Increased Quality

Medicare has been working to address the DRG-based incentives to skimp on quality. The problem occurs because patients and payers cannot readily observe the technical aspects of healthcare quality. While we can easily observe the customer service aspects of healthcare quality, we generally do not have sufficient information to assess the accuracy of a physician's diagnosis and recommendation or the quality of a hospital's infection control program. This asymmetric information (individuals who produce healthcare services know more about quality than the individuals who purchase and receive the services) presents the same "lemons" problem that plagues the health insurance market. Competing by offering high quality is not an effective strategy when buyers cannot observe the quality differential. Instead, the pressure to compete on price leads to cost-cutting efforts—which can lead to reductions in quality, sometimes described as a "race to the bottom."

Medicare is implementing pay-for-performance (P4P) programs for hospitals and other provider entities to create a quality-based "race to the top." For example, hospitals are required to report data on a set of quality measures (such as the incidence of hospital-acquired infections) to a centralized database. This data is used to compute the percentile ranking of each hospital, and then these rankings are used to adjust Medicare payments to each hospital. Initially, high-scoring hospitals (in the top 10%) received a bonus equal to 2% of the Medicare payments for the relevant conditions, and hospitals in the next 10% received a 1% bonus. In contrast, hospitals in the lowest 20% were penalized 1%–2% of the relevant Medicare payments.

Thus, the P4P system rewards providers (hospitals and individual care providers) who meet quality goals. This is essentially a merit-based system that has been implemented in the business sector for nearly a decade. Werner et al. (2011) analyzed the impact of P4P on a group of 260 hospitals. These hospitals participated in a demonstration project undertaken by the CMS in partnership with Premier Inc. The study examined the quality measures reported by these participating hospitals, compared with a control group of 780 hospitals within the same nationwide hospital system. The findings indicated that more than half of the hospitals participating in the demonstration project achieved the quality measures, compared with less than one-third of hospitals in the control group. However, after 5 years, the quality measures were undifferentiated in the two hospital groups. Factors positively affecting quality performance were high incentives, less competitive market, and being in good financial shape. These findings seem to suggest that a "one-size-fits-all" and a "top-down" P4P approach may not generate widespread and continuous quality improvements.

Providers have articulated concerns about P4P:

■ Providers need to purchase expensive computerized data collection systems in order to capture and report quality measures.
■ The relevance and validity of some quality measures are controversial.
■ Providers and consumers may lose autonomy and privacy.
■ Administrative costs may offset any cost savings.
■ Hospitals and providers may develop strategies to avoid providing care to high-risk patients.
■ Most complex patients have multiple care providers; hence, it is difficult to assign responsibility for poor performance. This problem is exacerbated by the fact that 50% of consumers change primary care physicians (PCPs) in a given year.
■ If rural and safety net hospitals are not able to meet P4P standards, their revenues will be reduced. Some commentators suggest that the financial strength of these hospitals should be tracked—as P4P continues to expand its scope.

Current Efforts: Value-Based Purchasing for Hospitals

Efforts are underway to expand the concept of structuring payment rates to create a quality race to the top. Medicare is implementing "value-based purchasing" (VBP). This concept focuses on tying payment rates to measured (and audited) performance on a set of well-defined quality measures. We will see—in Chapter 8 on health information technology—that the Health Information Technology for Economic and Clinical Health (HITECH) Act incentivized providers to adopt electronic medical record systems. To qualify to receive these payments, providers must report data on a substantial list of new quality measures. This data infrastructure is expected to provide the necessary platform for administering this system.

Physician Payment Systems: RBRVS and MACRA

Medicare has traditionally utilized FFS payment for physicians, with the payment rates based on the Resource-Based Relative Value Scale (RBRVS). This system focuses on the cost of producing physician services as the basis for setting physician payment rates. It raised two concerns: First, the system generated high annual earnings for specialists, relative to the earnings for PCPs. The earnings gap is criticized for fueling the relative shortage of medical school students choosing to focus on primary care.

Second, the RBRVS payments are based on the quantities of services provided. This system does not provide incentives to coordinate care, increase the quality of care, or develop new strategies for delivering care more efficiently. Congress and CMS augmented this system with quality incentive systems known as the Physician Quality Reporting System (PQRS) and Meaningful Use (MU). In addition, Congress initiated the Sustainable Growth Rate (SGR) system in 1997, as a strategy to constrain the growth of Medicare beneficiaries. The SGR concept abandoned the idea that the payment rates should cover the cost of producing the services. Instead, the SGR system was designed to ensure that Medicare expenditures (per individual covered by Medicare) would not grow more quickly than per capita gross domestic product (GDP). If expenditures did grow more quickly than per capita GDP, Congress mandated that the physician payment rates would be cut to (artificially) ensure that the two growth rates were equal. Annual Medicare expenditure growth rates routinely exceeded the allowed rate; yet the mandated physician payment cuts were generally not implemented.

Congress abandoned the SGR system in 2015, and replaced it with a budget-neutral quality incentive system known as the Medicare Access and CHIP Reauthorization Act (MACRA). MACRA aims to replace the PQRS and MU incentive systems with a comprehensive set of incentives. MACRA was signed into law in 2015 and scheduled to begin in 2017, with payment bonuses and penalties scheduled for 2019. This system allows physicians to choose one of two tracks.

- Under the Merit-based Incentive Payment System (MIPS), the physician will report data on quality measures similar to PQRS measures (50% of the score initially, reduced to 30% in 2021), measures similar to MU (25% of the score), clinical practice improvement measures (15% of the score), and resource use measures (10% of the score initially, increasing to 30% by 2021). The bonus and penalty system is designed to be budget neutral; penalties paid by low-performing physicians will fund the bonuses earned by high-performing physicians. CMS anticipates that most physicians will work under MIPS initially.
- Under the Alternative Payment Model (APM), physicians will receive fixed monthly payments for patients included on their panels, and they will be financially responsible for all care required by the patients that falls within a specified list of care types.

In addition to care provided by physicians, the MACRA system will encompass care provided by an array of medical professionals, including clinical nurse specialists, nurse anesthetists, physical or occupational therapists, nurse midwives, clinical social workers, and clinical psychologists. This broad inclusion of an array of professionals gives physician practices incentives to develop strategies for efficient coordination of care delivered by all these providers.

The MACRA system aims to (eventually) achieve two related goals:

1. Incentivize physicians to create efficient strategies for producing high-quality care (by creating incentives for physicians move into APMs) without the need for detailed quality metric reporting that is currently required under PQRS and MU
2. Incentivize a dramatic gain in the efficiency of the U.S. healthcare system

These goals are ambitious. It is not clear whether they will be achieved or how quickly the system will progress.

Implications of Public and Private Payment Systems for Hospitals

We will consider the implications of public and private payment systems using one-year of de-identified patient-level information on inpatients from one short-term general acute care hospital located in a small city. This data predates implementation of the ACA provisions regarding accountable care organizations, medicaid expansion, and health information exchanges; hence, it provides a view of the financial challenges that face hospitals that is not complicated by healthcare provider and payer efforts to adjust to ACA-induced changes.

The dataset includes nearly 35,000 inpatient stays. Most of these patients were admitted only once during the data time-period; however some of the inpatient stays represent multiple admissions for individual patients. Five DRGs accounted for 22% of the year's admissions, as detailed in Table 4.1.

Two of these high-volume DRGs involve labor and delivery (766 and 775); one involves caring for the newborns (795), one focuses on digestive tract issues (392), and the last involves orthopedic surgery (470).

The admitted patients were covered by several types of insurance. The three most common insurance types were Medicare, Medicaid, and

Table 4.1 Top 5 DRGs by Volume

DRG	DRG Name	Number of Admissions
392	Esophagitis, gastroenteritis, and miscellaneous digest disorders W/O MCC	671
470	Major joint replacement or reattachment of lower extremity W/O MCC	964
766	Cesarean section W/O CC/MCC	745
775	Vaginal delivery W/O complicating diagnoses	2,337
795	Normal newborn	2,742
Subtotal for the top 5 DRGs		7,459
Total number of admissions in all DRGs included in the dataset		34,690
Percent of admissions in the top 5 DRGs		0.22

Note: Hospital admissions in the dataset, including patients with nearly 700 DRG codes. W/O, without; CC, complication or comorbidity; MCC, major complication or comorbidity.

commercial insurance (which is private-sector insurance that is most commonly purchased by employers as group insurance). The proportions of patients covered by each type of insurance vary by DRG. Medicare, which provides insurance coverage for individuals age 65 or older and for younger individuals with disabilities, covered 0.01% of patients in DRGs involving labor-and-delivery and care of newborns; however it covered nearly 60% of patients admitted for joint replacement or limb reattachment (DRG 470). In contrast, Medicaid provided coverage for almost half of the women admitted for DRGs 766 and 775, but it covered only 0.01% of patients with DRG 470 (see Table 4.2).

The distribution of payer types within each DRG is important because payment rates vary significantly across payer types. The hospital that supplied the data utilizes an activity-based cost accounting system that provides estimates of the fixed and variable cost of treating each patient. Two variables are computed for each patient to provide information about the relationship between payments and costs.

- The *net revenue over cost* for each patient is equal to the payment received minus the total cost (fixed cost plus variable cost) incurred to treat the patient.
- The *margin* for each patient is equal to the payments received minus the variable cost incurred to treat each patient.

The data in Table 4.3 has important implications for hospital business strategy decisions and for public policy. *Net revenue over cost* for patients covered by Medicaid in all five of the high-volume DRGs is negative (see

Table 4.2   Distribution of Admissions for the Top 5 DRGs by Payer-Type

DRG	Medicare	Medicaid	Commercial Insurance	Other
392	0.40	0.13	0.29	0.17
470	0.59	0.01	0.35	0.04
766	0.00	0.46	0.40	0.13
775	0.00	0.45	0.39	0.15
795	0.00	0.27	0.34	0.40

Note: The category "Other" includes uninsured (self-pay), plans that cover work-related injuries, individuals covered under insurance for military personnel, etc.

Table 4.3). *Net revenue over cost* is also negative for commercially insured patients admitted with the three high-volume DRGs associated with labor and delivery and caring for newborns (DRGs 775, 795, and 766). Because Medicaid and commercial insurance are major payers for patients with these DRGs, revenue did not cover fixed and variables costs for the full set of patients admitted with these DRGs. This is important, because these patients accounted for 17% of all inpatient admissions.

In contrast, commercial insurance revenue and Medicare revenue exceeded the cost of providing care for patients in DRGs 392 and 470. In general, revenues for labor and delivery and for care of newborns do not cover the total cost of providing that care, while revenues from cardiac and orthopedic surgery patients exceed the cost of that care. This situation, in which some hospital units generate positive *net revenue over cost* that offsets negative *net revenue over cost* in other units within the same hospital, implies that hospitals must strategically balance the types of care provided, to ensure that total revenues cover total fixed and variable costs. This situation also has important implications for the discussion of single specialty hospitals in the chapter on new types of providers in Section II of this book.

It is also important to note that *net revenue over cost* was negative, on average, for patients covered by Medicaid. For all patients admitted during the data time period, the average *net revenue over cost* was –$3,676 per patient covered by Medicaid. This loss was offset by the fact that *net revenue over cost* was $359 per patient covered by Medicare and $5373 per patient covered by commercial insurance. This situation is not unique to the hospital that provided the data. Hospitals typically break even on patients covered by Medicare and they use positive *net revenue over cost* from commercially insured patients to cover the negative *net revenue over cost*

Table 4.3 Average *Net Revenue over Cost** Per Patient for the Top 5 DRGs by Payer Type

DRG	Medicare	Medicaid	Commercial Insurance
392	509	−614	3747
470	810	−8906	3715
766		−4181	−999
775		−2625	−810
795		−842	−694

*Net revenue over cost is equal to payments received minus total cost.

Table 4.4   Average *Margin* * Per Patient for the Top 5 DRGs by Payer Type

DRG	Medicare	Medicaid	Commercial Insurance
392	2237	1067	5208
470	4118	−4588	6600
766		727	4280
775		416	2278
795		−225	−127

*Margin is equal to payments received minus variable cost.

incurred for patients covered by Medicaid. Hospitals (and physician practices) must, therefore, work to ensure that the ratio of commercially insured patients to patients covered by Medicaid does not fall below the breakeven level. (This ratio is one component of the "payer mix.")

This payment pattern is frequently described as a cross-subsidy. Some analysts debate whether "cross-subsidy" occurs and the extent of this cross-subsidy. These debates reflect discussion of the question of whether the overall *margins* are negative for some types of payers. The answer to this question can vary across hospitals depending on the hospital size, location, service mix, and patient complexity. (In addition, it is important to note that the data presented here summarizes patient-specific revenues. Hospitals receive block grant revenues from other sources that are not directly related to care provided to specific patients.) For the hospital that provided this data, patient-specific revenues constitute 97% of total revenue.

While Medicaid payments are not typically set to cover fixed plus variable costs, they are typically set to cover variable cost. This implies that average *net revenue over cost* per-patient is typically negative, but the average margin per patient is small but positive. This is an important distinction: fixed costs account for approximately 40% of the total cost incurred by the hospital in a year. Revenues for each of the five high-volume DRGs exceeded the variable costs of providing care, except for DRG 795. In addition, revenues from each of the three major payer types (Medicare, Medicaid, and commercial insurance) were sufficient to cover the variable costs incurred for patients covered by these organizations. Compared with Medicare and commercial insurance carriers, however, Medicaid contributed substantially less, on average, to covering the fixed costs. See Table 4.4 for details.

A positive margin—for all patients—may be sufficient to continue operating on a short-term basis, but a positive net revenue over cost is needed for long-term financial viability. The fact that hospitals continue to offer a high-volume service (DRG 795) with negative margins for the major payers signals the complexity of the hospital contracting process. Hospitals must offer a full package of services to sign preferred-provider contracts with commercial insurers.

Conclusions

Designing a payment system to induce an array of providers (including hospitals, physicians, and ancillary providers) to provide optimal patient care in an effective, efficient, least-cost manner is a complex task. Because Medicare pays for a significant share of all healthcare services, the structure and level of Medicare rates impact the numbers and types of services provided, the types of integration and coordination across providers, the degree of competition in the healthcare marketplace, and the strategies providers use to address quality issues. As a result, Medicare rate policies generate substantial controversy.

In the remaining chapters of Section II, we will see other examples of innovations designed to improve efficiency and contain healthcare costs. Chapter 5 focuses on the goals and strategies of managed care organizations and the issues triggered by the growth of managed care. We also explore how our earlier experiences with managed care may influence the development and implementation of new primary care infrastructures, such as ACOs and patient-centered medical homes (PCMHs). These new integrated care models require a team-based focus rather than the traditional provider-centered care delivery.

Chapter 5

Managed Care Organizations, Accountable Care Organizations, and Patient-Centered Medical Homes

Introduction

New forms of managed care organizations, including accountable care organizations (ACOs) and patient-centered medical homes (PCMHs), are expected to provide better coordination of care than our current system of fractionated individual practitioners. According to the American College of Physicians (2012), a PCMH is a team-based model of care led by a personal physician who provides continuous and coordinated care throughout a patient's lifetime to maximize health outcomes.

ACOs differ from PCMHs in that their scope is much broader. (Elliott Fisher, director of the Center for Health Policy Research at Dartmouth Medical School, coined the term *accountable care organization* in a 2006 Medicare Payment Advisory Commission meeting.) These organizations are vertically integrated, to include PCMHs, hospitals, and other providers. The ACO is responsible for comprehensive care of a population of patients; hence, Medicare payment criteria include efficiency and quality standards. There are three widely supported core principles of ACOs:

1. Provider-led organizations with a strong base of primary care are accountable for quality and total per capita costs across the full continuum of care for a population of patients.
2. Payments are linked to quality improvements that also reduce overall costs.
3. Reliable and progressively more sophisticated performance measurements will be used, to support improvements and provide confidence that savings are achieved through improvements in care (McClellan et al., 2010).

These are extensions of some of the strategies employed by managed care organizations; hence, understanding the major controversies surrounding managed care will provide a context for anticipating issues that are likely to arise as we gain experience with ACO and PCMH organizations.

Background: Managed Care Organizations

As employers faced increasingly more expensive health insurance premiums in the 1980s and 1990s, they turned to managed care to help mitigate the overtreatment incentives built into the traditional fee-for-service (FFS) system. The two most common types of managed care organizations are health maintenance organizations (HMOs) and preferred provider organizations (PPOs)—we refer to managed care organizations as HMOs to simplify our discussion. The 1973 Health Maintenance Organization Act specified the legal framework for HMOs and mandated that large employers offer an HMO option.

Managed care plans are health insurance plans that provide care through contracted healthcare providers who provide services at reduced rates. The employer pays a fixed amount per month (per member per month [pmpm]) for each patient enrolled in the managed care plan, and the managed care organization is responsible for providing any healthcare that the enrolled individual utilizes—as long as that healthcare is "covered" by the managed care contract. The managed care company is "at risk" for charges incurred by its enrollees, and it uses an array of strategies to manage that risk. These strategies focus on prevention of illnesses and/or injuries, care coordination, negotiation of favorable provider prices (partly due to the volume of patients the managed care organization can provide), and gatekeeper structures to ensure that patients obtain care at appropriate locations. For example, enrollees may be required to obtain a referral from a primary care physician (the gatekeeper) before seeing a specialist, such as a cardiologist, and they may be required to obtain care only from a specified panel of physicians who are considered in the "network" (and who generally have agreed to charge lower rates). Managed care companies contract with these providers to set reimbursement rates, performance measures, and risk-sharing provisions—to encourage care coordination and compliance with guidelines, particularly with regard to preventive care. In addition, managed care strategies include programs such as disease management and pharmacy management, because the HMO prepayment system incentivizes managed care organizations to prevent illness and promote more efficient healthcare.

Managed care organizations use these strategies to create efficiencies by coordinating and managing care, and this effort is facilitated by the fact that five conditions (heart disease, pulmonary conditions, mental disorders such as depression, cancers, and hypertension) account for a significant share of the increase in health spending that occurred during the years 1987–2000 (Thorpe et al., 2004).

Managed Care: Historical Trends

Three trends occurred concurrently in the late 1990s.

1. The market share of managed care organizations increased from 27% of individuals with employment-based coverage in 1988 to 86% in 1998 (Kaiser Family Foundation, 2006).
2. Healthcare cost inflation slowed, and this decrease was widely attributed to the growth of managed care (Orzag, 2007).
3. Patients worried that clinical decisions were increasingly driven by financial incentives, rather than the clinical assessments of the patient's health status or potential for complications. See Box 5.1 to recall the movie versions of these concerns.

Public concerns about "consumer protection" sparked a wave of state and federal legislation, known as the "managed care backlash." However, the concerns expressed in the backlash were not strongly supported by large-scale studies of the impact of managed care organizations on cost and quality. Instead, these studies produced mixed results. Miller and Luft (1997) reviewed the relevant peer-reviewed literature published during the years 1993–1996. They identified 15 relevant studies, and found that

BOX 5.1 HOLLYWOOD REFLECTED PUBLIC CONCERNS IN A SERIES OF POPULAR MOVIES

Hollywood reflected public concerns with movies such as *Damaged Care*, *As Good as It Gets*, *Rainmaker*, and *John Q*. *Damaged Care*, a Showtime movie starring Laura Dern, was a fact-based drama about a medical reviewer for several HMOs, Linda Peeno, and her conflicts with the dilemma of cost versus care. In this docudrama, she reveals the pressure she was under to deny patients care in order to save money. In *As Good as It Gets*, a child's care is depicted as being inadequate due to the HMO, and the child only gets better after the character played by Jack Nicholson agrees to pay for care out of his pocket. Carol, the mother, has a famous line in which, frustrated by denials of care, she uses a series of angry expletives to describe HMOs. The physician responds, "Actually, I think it's their technical name." *Rainmaker* is a movie adaptation of a book by John Grisham in which a young man with leukemia is denied a lifesaving bone morrow transplant by an insurance company, portrayed as "greedy" in the movie. *John Q*, a movie starring Denzel Washington, is about a father who takes emergency room patients as hostages in order to force medical personnel to place his son's name on the heart transplant list. (His son had just been diagnosed with an enlarged heart and had been denied a heart transplant by their HMO.) These movies typified public fears that managed care organizations restrict access to necessary care in order to make profits.

half concluded that HMO quality was significantly better than FFS quality, while the other half reached the opposite conclusion. Miller and Luft (2002) updated the review to cover the years 1997–2001, and reached a similar conclusion: "Quality-of-care findings for HMO plans were roughly comparable to those for non-HMO plans." It is important to note that many medical errors are caused by overtreatment rather than undertreatment—however, public concern focused mainly on the latter.

Managed Care: The Backlash

States responded to the consumer and provider concerns by passing hundreds of laws: for example, California passed 89 laws reforming managed care organizations during 1990–1997, and a patient bill of rights was proposed (but not passed) at the federal level (Enthoven and Singer, 1998). These laws mandated access, disclosure, and coverage for specific benefits, and addressed patient billing, claims processing, provider contracting, and solvency regulation. These authors concluded that the backlash reflected fundamental problems faced by both consumers and providers:

- Consumers do not have a realistic understanding of the impacts of healthcare costs and insurance premiums on wages.
- Insurance rules (addressing the definition of emergency services, medical necessity, and standard vs. experimental care) are not clear.
- Physicians who contract with multiple plans face a complex set of different and evolving rules.
- Physicians who want to assume the managed care risk must work in large groups, to ensure the high volume needed to spread the risk and cover fixed administrative expenses.
- Pressure for increased productivity generates pressures for job cutbacks for nurses and other healthcare workers—the pressure is to do more with less.

States passed hundreds of laws mandating that specific types of providers be included on managed care panels and specific types of treatments be covered: 1000 coverage mandates were in place in 1999. Empirical research indicated that these mandates led to increased premiums, and these premium increases led, in turn, to lower wages and decisions by some employers and employees to drop coverage. Gruber (1994) estimated that state maternity mandates implemented in Illinois, New Jersey, and New York from 1976 to 1977 depressed wages for healthcare consumers by 4.3%, because the full cost of these mandates was paid by working women ages 20–40.

> The differences in wages of married women ages 20–40, for example, was 4.3% lower in Illinois, New Jersey, and New York after the mandate than they were for similar women and control states over the same period.

Using data for the period 1989–1994, Sloan and Conover (1998) concluded that individuals faced higher probabilities of being uninsured in states with larger numbers of coverage requirements. Similarly, Jensen and Morrisey (1999) concluded that mandates generate significant increases in health insurance premiums that, in turn, generate increases in the proportion of individuals who are uninsured (Jensen and Morrisey, 1999). These results point to a startling implication: eliminating benefit mandates would reduce the proportion of uninsured adults. At that time, 18% of non-elderly adults were uninsured, and Sloan and Conover's results indicated that eliminating mandates would have reduced this incidence to 14%.

The four highest-cost mandated benefits were chemical dependency treatment, psychiatric hospital stay, psychologist visits, and routine dental services (Cubanski and Schauffler, 2002). In 1996, 41 states mandated that psychologists be included as providers and 32 states mandated that insurers offer coverage for mental healthcare—but only 18 of the states mandated that employers purchase this coverage. In the other 14 states, insurers must offer the coverage, but employers can choose whether to purchase it. Federal legislation created additional mandates, including the 1996 Newborns' and Mothers' Health Protection Act and the 1996 Mental Health Parity Act. The federal mandates are significant, even though many states had already passed similar legislation. The federal legislation extends the mandates to self-insured employers, while state legislation does not impact self-insured employers.

Current Issues: Lessons Learned

Defining Consumer Protection Is Complex

Consider, for example, the controversy over maternity care. Prior to the advent of Diagnostic Related Groups (DRGs), new mothers stayed in the hospital for an average of 4 days postdelivery. Once the DRG system was implemented, the average length of stay decreased to 24 hours for an uncomplicated vaginal delivery or 48 hours for an uncomplicated cesarean delivery. Public response was fierce: by 1996, 27 states enacted laws to force insurance companies to pay for a minimum of 48 hours of hospitalization following a delivery. Nationally, legislation (the Newborns' and Mothers' Health Protection Act) mandated insurance coverage for postpartum hospitalization for a minimum of 48 hours after an uncomplicated vaginal delivery and 96 hours for an uncomplicated cesarean section delivery (Feeg, 1996; Temkin, 1999).

One study surveyed 5201 mothers and found that most thought that a 24-hour stay was too short, even though a length of stay less than 48 hours was not statistically associated with maternal or newborn readmission.

However, it is notable that a majority of these mothers said they would be willing to go home within 24 hours if additional services were covered, such as a 24-hour hotline, housekeeping services, and day care for other children. Note that two of these three services do not address clinical issues—hence, the mandate would probably have relatively low marginal health benefits.

In order to clarify this complex issue, we examine an abstract view of this problem. Imagine that we can line up episodes of healthcare on the horizontal axis of the graph shown in Figure 5.1 with the most beneficial (lifesaving) care on the left, with less and less valuable care as we move to the right. The diagonal line represents this idea: it measures the marginal benefit of one more episode of care. The first unit of care (at the left edge of the graph) yields high marginal benefit, but the benefits of additional units decrease as we move to the right. For this abstract representation of the problem, we also assume that the "units" of care have been defined so that each unit has the same cost—which is represented by the upper

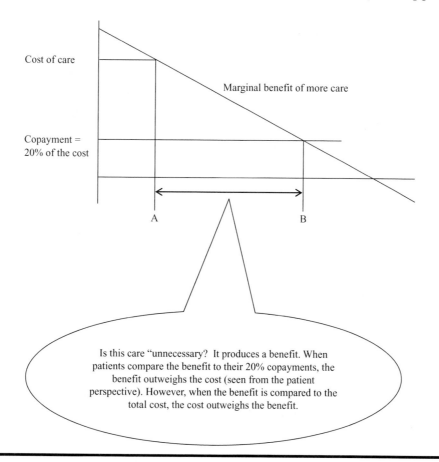

Figure 5.1 How should we define unnecessary care?

horizontal line. The lower horizontal line represents 20% of the cost—which is the amount the insured individual will pay. Now we can see the conflict between the rational payer and the rational consumer:

■ The rational payer will be willing to cover care when the marginal benefit exceeds the cost, and this payer will not cover units of care for which the marginal benefit is less than the cost. Therefore, this payer will view point A as the optimal quantity of care.

■ The consumer will have a different opinion. The consumer will want to obtain all units of care for which the marginal benefit exceeds his copayment; hence, the consumer will think that point B represents the appropriate quantity of care. The managed care organization will view the gap between points A and B as unnecessary or inappropriate care because—from the payer's viewpoint—the benefits do not justify the cost. The managed care organization will—logically—try to prevent the patient from obtaining any care beyond point A, and the rational patient will lobby for all care up to point B.

The survey results noted above suggest that a 24-hour stay (following an uncomplicated vaginal delivery) may be represented by point A, while the longer (nice, but—possibly—not medically essential) stay may be represented at point B.

In addition, Chandra and Skinner (2011) provided a useful framework for conceptualizing the cost containment issue. They suggested that treatments can be categorized into three groups:

1. Treatments that are clearly cost-effective for patients who can benefit, and clearly useless for other patients (such as antiretroviral therapy for HIV)
2. Treatments that are clearly effective for some types of patients, with no clear criteria to identify which patients will benefit
3. "Gray area" treatments with uncertain clinical value (intensive care unit [ICU] days for chronically ill patients)

Cost containment controversies focus on treatments in the second group, for which the central problem is the lack of criteria for predicting whether a specific patient will benefit from a specific treatment. Absent this scientific information, coverage decisions based on expected outcomes will seem arbitrary and unreasonable to patients who believe they might benefit from a specific treatment.

Courts have agreed that it is appropriate for managed care organizations to base decisions on a population perspective (which implies some treatments—with marginal expected benefit—will *not* be covered) to forestall cost increases that could force more people to become uninsured (Rosoff, 2001).

We conclude that the real issue addressed by mandates is not consumer protection against managed care power. Instead, it is equity. Mandates make it impossible for managed care organizations to offer (and consumers/employers to choose among) different "levels" of policies (e.g., comprehensive and expensive vs. barebones, catastrophic, and cheap). This means that employers and employees with low ability or willingness to pay can only choose between two options (high price and high coverage or no insurance). Eliminating mandates would permit an additional option—to purchase a low-price and low-coverage policy. This raises gut-wrenching social questions: Are we willing to pay enough in taxes to subsidize the high-price comprehensive option for everyone? Or, do we prefer to have a multitier system in which some purchase Kia-quality insurance, while others purchase Lamborghini-quality insurance?

Similar issues are raised by other types of consumer protection (or provider protection) initiatives, which were designed to

- Increase malpractice liability for the managed care organization
- Restrict the flexibility of managed care organizations to deny coverage for care that is not consistent with treatment guidelines
- Require managed care organizations to contract with any provider who is willing to accept the reimbursement rate set by that organization*

Managed care organizations clearly face higher costs in states that adopt these consumer protection and provider protection measures, and these additional costs will lead to higher premiums. Therefore, the key question is, how much value do these protections produce? Does the added value outweigh the premium increases?

Analysis of consumer behavior—when faced with a choice between HMO coverage and traditional FFS coverage—provides some evidence to help us think about this question. At this decision point, consumers face a tough

---

* The question of whether these any willing provider laws primarily protect physicians or consumers generated controversy. Managed care organizations argued that these laws blocked their ability to negotiate low provider reimbursement rates, which are essential for cost control. Providers countered that these laws led to more inclusive physician panels that offer consumers an array of options when they are selecting a physician.

choice: you can reduce your out-of-pocket payments (premium, copayments, and deductibles) *if* you are willing to accept additional constraints on your individual healthcare decisions, such as confining your providers to a smaller subset of all possible providers. Analysis of employee health plan choices indicates that consumers are willing to pay additional monthly premiums to avoid these constraints, particularly if the insured individual (or a family member) has a high-cost diagnosis (Bundorf et al., 2008).

In addition, we note that a *New York Times* article (Pear, 2005) demonstrates that the dilemma posed by this issue is not confined to managed care organizations. The article explains that the 2005 law authorizes doctors to prescribe any drug they deem "medically necessary" for their Medicare patients, even if that drug is not included on the insurer's list of preferred drugs. (This list is known as a "formulary.") In addition, companies providing a drug benefit must include, on the formulary, at least two comparable drugs for every treatment category. These two provisions will constrain the companies' ability to negotiate discounts from drug makers. The first provision reduces drug makers' incentives to offer discounts, to ensure that their drugs will be included on formularies. The second provision reduces the threat that a drug might not be included in an insurer's formulary. The *New York Times* article concluded, "Without significant drug discounts, monthly premiums for the benefit could soar above the expected $35 a month." Guaranteeing that patients can access specific drugs imposes a cost: monthly premiums will increase. The critical question is, does the treatment value of this access outweigh the cost? The answer to this question varies across patients, diagnoses, and drugs—and analyzing these details requires balancing health issues and cost issues. As we saw in the Chapter 3 discussion of guidelines, the answers to these questions are important—and these answers are also controversial.

Shifting to Managed Care and/or ACOs Focuses on a Definition of Quality that is New for Many Patients

Prior to the advent of managed care organizations, most consumers might have reasonably assumed that physicians had wide discretion to develop a customized treatment plan for each patient—without constraints imposed by coverage limits or provider networks. During the decade of HMO expansion, physician leaders such as David Eddy, Brent James, and Don Berwick were articulating an expanded concept of quality: that high-quality care occurs when physicians make decisions within a system of care coordination and evidence-based decision guides. Consistent with these views, the HMO concept has evolved from its initial focus on restricting care to the current emphasis on making care more systematic.

Some of the controversy about managed care is really a controversy between two definitions of *quality*. We will describe each model here, and then discuss the implications below.

The first definition of quality focuses on flexibility to tailor treatment plans to accommodate specific patient medical conditions and preferences. This model implies that it would be useful to pass laws to

- Increase physician power, through antigag legislation and "any willing provider" legislation
- Guarantee patient access to providers and treatments through coverage mandates
- Increase managed care malpractice liability and produce "report cards" on managed care quality
- Mandate a consumer bill of rights

In contrast, the second definition focuses on the critical role of evidence-based decision making and systematic processes, to minimize medical errors and ensure that treatment decisions are based on current research results. This model focuses on

- Systematic implementation of guidelines to ensure that physicians recommend treatments that are evidence based.
- Consumer protection efforts focused on clarifying insurance and managed care contracts.
- Developing a strong system for reporting and analyzing data on quality. For example, the Healthcare Effectiveness Data and Information Set (HEDIS) reports performance measures for most health plans, to inform consumers about HMO quality (National Committee for Quality Assurance, 2011).

Growth of Managed Care Organizations Raised Two Types of Market Power Issues

Econometric analyses indicate that managed care can reduce expenditures. The initial impact was blunted by the "managed care backlash," but managed care organizations are currently producing better results. Dafny et al. (2009) present analysis of data on employer-sponsored health plans with 10 million enrollees during the years 1998–2006. These authors analyzed variations across metropolitan areas, and conclude that increased levels of managed care organizations are associated with lower healthcare expenditures for the employers as a whole. Cutler et al. (2000) use a different analytical strategy. They analyzed the treatment of heart attacks and newly diagnosed chest pain in HMOs and traditional plans. The authors argued that focusing on these conditions minimizes the selection bias issue, because most individuals cannot predict these conditions. The authors analyzed 1993–1995 claims data for a large firm that insures 200,000 employees and their dependents. For treatment of these conditions, HMO expenditures are 30%–40% lower than FFS expenditures, and this difference primarily stems from lower prices. A third study analyzed hospital inpatient discharge abstracts for 932 urban counties in 22 states, to identify preventable hospitalizations due to 14 ambulatory care–sensitive conditions (Zhan et al., 2004). These authors concluded that increased HMO market share is significantly associated with lower levels of preventable hospitalizations.

These studies suggest that managed care organizations reduce expenditures through two mechanisms: reduced provider reimbursement rates and improved organization and coordination of care. We focus here on the managed care organization's success in reducing rates paid to providers.

Reducing Healthcare Cost by Reducing Provider Reimbursement Sounds Good, if You Are a Consumer, but Providers See a Different Side of the Issue

Reduced provider reimbursement rates presented a boon to consumers (because this translated into reduced premiums), but they presented a challenge to healthcare providers. To examine the provider response, we must begin by considering the underlying market structure. The fact that managed care organizations were able to use bargaining power to negotiate rate reductions implies that the physician organizations had been successfully wielding market power prior to the advent of managed care.

Managed care organizations initially achieved this result by negotiating to develop provider "panels." If a physician (or other healthcare provider) agreed to the lower managed care reimbursement rate, the physician would be listed as a member of the managed care organization's provider panel and individuals enrolled in that plan would be able to obtain care from that provider. Because managed care organizations tend to enroll large numbers of individuals, the HMO contract offers potential patient volume in exchange for the lower rate. Of course, this offer presents an implicit bargaining threat:

potential loss of volume if the lower rate is not accepted. Thus, managed care organizations viewed the limited provider panel as a key strategic element—that it was essential for inducing providers to agree to accept reimbursement rate reductions.

Providers Responded in Two Ways

1. Physicians lobbied successfully, in many states, for any willing provider laws. These laws mandated that the managed care organizations must reimburse for treatments provided by any physician who was willing to accept the company's rates. This blunted the companies' bargaining power, and some analysts believe that these laws significantly reduced the ability of managed care organizations to impact healthcare cost escalation. One analyst examined state-level data for the years 1983–1997 and concluded that any willing provider laws led to increased per capita healthcare expenditures (Vita, 2001). In a 2004 Federal Trade Commission (FTC) and Department of Justice (DoJ) report on healthcare competition, these agencies recommend that states examine any willing provider laws carefully, to assess whether these laws help or harm consumers and patients.

2. Physician groups joined forces to build "countervailing market power"—as a tool to counter managed care's bargaining power. Physicians used a range of strategies to accomplish this goal: merging small practices to form a larger group practice, allying with other physicians to form an independent practice association, or allying with a hospital to form a physician hospital organization (PHO). Analysis reported by Town and Vistnes (2001) demonstrated the potential value of provider market power (although this analysis focused on hospital reimbursement rates rather than physician rates). This paper showed that a hospital will receive a higher rate from an HMO if the HMO believes that including that hospital on its preferred provider list will help the HMO compete for employer contracts. Mergers that formed larger provider groups raised questions, because efforts to create bargaining power (also known as market power) generally reduce competition. Any merger that focuses primarily on the creation of market power (rather than efficiency) can be challenged by the DoJ, by the FTC, or by private parties as a violation of the antitrust laws. The DoJ issued guidance indicating that it would consider physician group mergers carefully—to assess the relative importance of the two goals of increasing market

power and increasing efficiency. Merging groups of healthcare providers can avoid antitrust litigation by demonstrating that the merger will increase efficiency. This requires demonstrating either financial integration (as evidenced by physician risk sharing) or clinical integration (as evidenced by investment in computer and process improvement infrastructure). Financial and clinical integration are viewed as essential first steps for achieving new efficiencies; hence, failure to take one or both of these steps is viewed as a signal that the merger is primarily focused on enhancing market power.

Managed Care Organizations Also Raised Questions about Physician Risk Taking and Solvency Regulation

"Risk sharing" means that contracted physicians bear some of the risk that a group of enrollees may have higher than expected healthcare costs. In this case, the physician (or a physician group) agrees to both a reimbursement rate and a "withhold." To facilitate explanation of the withhold, assume that a managed care contract specifies a 5% withhold. Each time the provider bills the managed care organization for services rendered, the company would pay 95% of the contracted price and withhold 5%. At the end of the year, the managed care organization would determine whether the physician group had successfully met cost control and/or quality targets, as specified in the contract. If the physician group met the target, the company would pay the withheld 5%; if not, the physician group would only receive a pro-rated share of that 5%. This poses opportunities—if the physician group is able to organize care and control costs. It also raises two types of concerns:

1. We may be concerned about the impact of this incentive structure on patient care decisions. A 1997 federal law addressed this issue, mandating limits to physician risk sharing. No more than 25% of physician compensation can be at risk. This was not a binding constraint at that time—since withholds were typically 10%. The law also capped cost and quality bonuses at 15%. Using data from 1994 to 1997, analysts concluded that the number of physicians in the group impacts the strength of the incentives on individual physician decisions: as the physician group size increases, the incentive impact weakens. In addition, increasing the size of the physician group reduces the probability that the physician group will receive the withhold funds at the end of the year, and it also reduces the average level of quality (as measured by the reported

HEDIS measures). These analysts concluded that physicians do respond to incentives, but increasing the group size diffuses the incentive—and reduces each physician's response. This result is not surprising, but it is problematic: large physician groups are essential for spreading risk, but it is unlikely that individual physicians in these large groups will respond to payment incentives—to increase efficiency.

2. The second concern focuses on the ability of the physician group to bear the risk. Two issues were raised that are likely to reappear as ACOs develop.

First, regulations were implemented to limit the proportion of physician salary that could be at risk. These regulations addressed the concern that this creates a strong incentive for physicians to underprovide care. It is one thing for the managed care organization to be at risk and contract with physicians. There was concern that the incentive to underprovide would be significantly stronger if the physician is also at risk.

Second, state insurance regulations that address insurance company solvency are important. Every state has an insurance commissioner, who regulates insurance companies that do business in the state. Insurance companies must demonstrate that they hold specified amounts of assets—of specific types. These assets provide assurance that the insurance company will be able to pay claims, even if the dollar volume of claims is unusually high. (These are known as solvency requirements.) Insurance commissioners typically enforce solvency regulations—that address the concern that an insurance company, such as an HMO, might collect monthly premiums and then declare bankruptcy and be unable to pay providers for completed care or provide the care for which consumers prepaid at the start of the month.

As physician groups assumed increasing risk (through contracting directly with employers and accepting capitated payment agreements), policy makers considered the question, should risk-bearing physicians be required to meet the same solvency requirements that are imposed on insurance companies? Physicians argued that they did not have sufficient size or capital to meet these requirements, and the issue was resolved in their favor. However, the question of whether physician groups typically have sufficient assets (or reinsurance) to remain solvent and provide contracted care—even during a period of unusually high claims—remains. The consumer protection issue is the same, whether the risk is held by a managed care organization or a physician group. The inability to hold physicians who bear risk to the same solvency requirements that are required of insurance companies clearly raises consumer protection issues.

The importance of the solvency issue posed by physician risk bearing depends on the size of physician groups. Wendel and Paterson (1996) used the Poisson distribution to illustrate the issue. The Poisson distribution is frequently used to compute the probability that a specific number of events will occur. Suppose, for example, that a provider group expects to average five high-cost episodes of care in a typical month. In addition, suppose the physician group might have difficulty providing care during an unlucky month, in which 10 of its patients have high-cost episodes of care (double the expected number). How often will this occur? The Poisson distribution allows us to calculate the answer to that question: the probability that this group will have more than double the typical number of high-cost episodes of care is 0.014. What happens to this probability as the patient population increases? For a larger group, which expects to have 15 high-cost episodes of care per month, the comparable level of risk would focus on the probability that the group will have more than double (30) high-cost episodes of care in a month. The probability that this will occur is only 0.0002. The difference between these numbers (0.014 and 0.0002) represents an important reduction in the level of risk as the size of the provider group grows (because larger groups that see more patients will have higher expected numbers of high-cost episodes of care). This is the essence of the concept of "risk pooling"—and it means that this group's entities are less able to assume risk for the care of a specific patient population. Thus, small providers face a competitive disadvantage, which may have important implications for the concept of forming local ACOs in rural areas. Instead, it may be necessary to form larger ACOs that serve large regions of rural patients.

Mental Health Parity Mandate May Constitute a Special Case

As individuals make choices between HMO and FFS plans, they—wisely—select plans that offer the best coverage for care that is already anticipated. If they anticipate, for example, the need for mental health treatment, they will seek out plans that offer a more generous mental health coverage benefit. Thus, a plan that offers unusually comprehensive care for a high-cost condition is likely to experience "adverse selection." (Adverse selection occurs when a plan has a disproportionate number of high-cost enrollees.) Managed care organizations may therefore design coverage strategically—in an attempt to attract low-cost enrollees and discourage potential enrollees who are likely to incur high costs. Frank et al. (1998) examine the pattern of resulting coverage decisions, and conclude that this strategic behavior leads to systematic underprovision of mental health and substance abuse treatment. Mandating mental health parity is, of course, one regulatory response (Sturm and Pacula, 1999).

Managed care plans that experience higher than expected enrollment by high-cost individuals face a competitive challenge, if it's difficult for these companies to offer competitive monthly premiums (because they face higher costs than their competitors). State Medicaid agencies responded by implementing risk adjustment (RA) systems. RA systems use healthcare encounter data from managed care plans to measure the level of risk shouldered by each plan and adjust payments to a level to increase compensation to plans with higher-risk members. Analysts initially expected that private payers would also adopt this strategy, but RA was primarily used by public payers, such as Medicaid.

The enactment of the Patient Protection and Affordable Care Act (PPACA) heightened market concerns—specifically the mandate placed on insurance companies requiring them to include persons with high-cost (or potentially high-cost) preexisting conditions in the health plan—referred to as guaranteed issue. The insurance companies were also prohibited from charging enrollees with preexisting conditions more for their premiums—referred to as modified community rating. This made RA systems in the private-sector health insurance industry an important issue. Three specific provisions were made to address these market issues for plans offered in the health insurance exchanges: RA, reinsurance, and risk corridors.

Recall our discussion in Chapter 1 on adverse selection (those who have or anticipate high medical care and costs are more likely to purchase insurance) and risk selection (insurance companies want to avoid enrolling people who might be high medical care and cost utilizers) (Table 5.1). RAs were designed to compensate insurers who enrolled sicker patients and to minimize incentives these insurers might have to market their plans to healthier people. This program was designed to remain in place indefinitely for plans offered in the health insurance exchanges, while the other two programs were intended to be temporary stabilizers and timed out by 2017. The reinsurance program was a 2-year program designed to help keep premiums lower by compensating insurers for healthcare costs for high-cost enrollees. The reimbursements were based on actual costs (unlike RA payments that were based on anticipated costs). Given the uncertainty about the cost of providing care to everyone who selected an insurance plan and the associated costs of the care, there

Table 5.1   Summary of Risk and Market Stabilization Programs in the Affordable Care Act

	Risk Adjustment	Reinsurance	Risk Corridors
What the program does	Redistributes funds from plans with lower-risk enrollees to plans with higher-risk enrollees	Provides payment to plans that enroll higher-cost individuals	Limits losses and gains beyond an allowable range
Why it was enacted	Protects against adverse selection and risk selection in the individual and small group markets, inside and outside of the exchanges, by spreading financial risk across the markets	Protects against premium increases in the individual market by offsetting the expenses of high-cost individuals	Stabilizes premiums and protects against inaccurate premium setting during initial years of the reform
Who participates	Nongrandfathered individual and small group market plans, both inside and outside of the exchanges	All health insurance issuers and self-insured plans contribute funds; individual market plans subject to new market rules (both inside and outside of the exchange) are eligible for payment	Qualified health plans (QHPs), which are plans qualified to be offered on a health insurance marketplace (also called exchange)
How it works	Plans' average actuarial risk will be determined based on enrollees' individual risk scores; plans with lower actuarial risk will make payments to higher-risk plans; payments net to zero	If an enrollee's costs exceed a certain threshold (called an attachment point), the plan is eligible for payment (up to the reinsurance cap); payments net to zero	The Department of Health and Human Services collects funds from plans with lower than expected claims and makes payments to plans with higher than expected claims; plans with actual claims less than 97% of target amounts pay into the program, and plans with claims greater than 103% of target amounts receive funds; payments net to zero
When it goes into effect	2014 onward (permanent)	2014–2016 (temporary—3 years)	2014–2016 (temporary—3 years)

Source: Cox, C., et al., Explaining health care reform: Risk adjustment, reinsurance, and risk corridors, Issue Brief, Henry J. Kaiser Family Foundation, Menlo Park, CA, 2016, http://kff.org/health-reform/issue-brief/explaining-health-care-reform-risk-adjustment-reinsurance-and-risk-corridors/.

was a fear (and rightfully so) that premium costs would escalate. The risk corridor program was originally designed to "cushion insurers participating in exchanges and marketplaces from extreme gains and losses" (Cox et al., 2016, p. 10). However, congressional changes to the plan limited its effectiveness. Health insurers in the individual market, which represents approximately 7% of those with insurance, struggled despite these programs (Cox et al., 2017). This raises concerns about companies that choose to leave the exchanges and marketplace and premium costs for those who remain—particularly as two of the market stabilization programs have ended.

Physician Rating Systems Raise Concerns

Physician rating systems are designed to

- Help consumers choose physicians that offer evidence-based care
- Incentivize the provision of high-quality care through a reimbursement mechanism that rewards high performers and penalizes low performers

Advocates of ACOs and PCMHs assert that these delivery systems will improve both coordination of care and patient outcomes. Strategies for measuring these improvements, and reporting these measures, have been controversial. In November 2006, the Washington State Medical Association filed a lawsuit, the first of its kind, against Regence BlueShield alleging that the physician ranking was based on inaccurate and incomplete data. Similar lawsuits followed in Connecticut, Massachusetts, and New York. In 2007, New York's attorney general developed a Doctor Ranking Model Code and garnered support from eight major health insurers in New York. This code requires insurers to

- Identify the degree to which ratings are based on cost, and include additional factors (other than cost) in the rating scores.
- Use established national standards to measure quality, including measures endorsed by the National Quality Forum (NQF).
- Use methods such as RA and valid sampling to permit meaningful comparisons.
- Disclose ranking methods to consumers, and establish a consumer complaint process.
- Disclose ranking methods to physicians, and provide an appeals process.

■ Retain a ratings examiner to audit compliance with the Model Code and report the audit results to the attorney general every 6 months. The audit must be conducted by a national standard-setting organization, such as the National Committee on Quality Assurance (NCQA).

Similarly, Colorado enacted a law in 2008 (Cartwright-Smith and Rosenbaum, 2009) that requires that any public representation of a physician's performance (ranking, grade, or tier) must

■ Include a quality of care component that is endorsed by NQF or a similar organization
■ Use statistically accurate and adjusted data
■ Be attributed to the "right" physician
■ Have a disclaimer about the risk of error

At the national level, the Patient Charter for Physician Performance Measurement, Reporting and Tiering Programs was developed to provide guidelines for quality data reporting (Consumer Purchaser Disclosure Project, 2008). This program, which was supported by consumer, labor, and employer groups, articulates best practices:

■ NQF measures constitute the logical starting point, followed by measures approved by national accrediting bodies, such as NCQA and the Joint Commission.
■ Provider and consumer input should be solicited on supplemental measures (if any are used).
■ The provider rating method should be transparent.
■ Data collection should be coordinated by independent third parties.

These guidelines focus on four key issues: data integrity, disclosure, fair process, and enforcement. The guidelines also delineate common ground between the consumer benefits of physician-quality reporting and the provider interest in avoiding inaccurate reporting. The Model Code and the Patient Charter shift the burden of proving accuracy of data to the health plan, and highlight the importance of sound statistical methods.

Studies are beginning to report positive results and some unanticipated consequences from publicly reporting physician-level data. Smith et al. (2012) examined the impact on physician groups and clinics of public reporting on diabetic care and found that those who reported performance data were more likely to adopt interventions known to improve diabetes care than those who did not publicly report their data. Lamb et al. (2013) compared the performance of a consortium of Wisconsin physicians that elected to report quality metrics with the performance of other physicians. These authors concluded that voluntary reporting was associated with improvement on several quality measures, including cholesterol control and breast cancer screening. Physicians in their study acknowledged that publicly reporting data motivated them to improve their performance on quality measures. George et al. (2012) focused on the fact that prophylactic aspirin is an evidence-based intervention for patients with vascular disease. In a national survey conducted in 2008 (George et al., 2012), these researchers found that prescription of aspirin was 95% in Minnesota (where this quality measure is publicly reported) compared with 35%–47% elsewhere. These studies provide positive support for making physician-level data public. However, one study (Narins et al., 2005) looked at the influence of public reporting mortality rates on interventional cardiologists in New York and found 83% were less likely to recommend angioplasty to critically ill patients even if they believed the intervention would be beneficial. This highlights the potential of physicians to make treatment decisions based on minimizing poor numbers rather than on what may be best for their patients.

Do ACOs and PCMHs Deliver on Improving Quality and Coordination of Care at a Reduced Cost?

Early results point to positive, though modest, results. ACOs in the Medicare Shared Savings Program (MSSP) serve approximately 14% of Medicare beneficiaries and report improvement in most of the quality indicators they track, have better patient satisfaction ratings than those not participating in an MSSP ACO, and have produced overall savings of an estimated $700 million by the summer of 2015 (Cavanaugh, 2014; McWilliams et al., 2014). Pioneer ACOs (high-performing organizations chosen by the Centers for Medicare and Medicaid Services [CMS]) reportedly saved $384 million in the first 2 years of the program. However, 11 of the 32 organizations that started in the program changed over to the MSSP program, and 2 organizations opted out of the program all together (Nyweide et al., 2015). Those moving to the MSSP program did so because they failed to realize the level of savings required to receive their share of the savings, and the two organizations that left the program ended up owing $4 million to Medicare. All pioneer

ACOs improved quality of care within the first year (Gold, 2013). Critics of this program say the program rewards high-spending areas rather than good performers, and that those who generate high savings get very little of that savings ($295 million saved vs. $31.4 million in bonus payments), calling into question the attainability of the Department of Health and Human Services' goal of increasing the number of ACOs so that 50% of the Medicare payments will come through these types of alternative payment methodologies by 2018 (Goldsmith and Kaufman, 2015).

While ACOs are a mechanism to integrate and coordinate care across different types of organizations and care levels, PCMHs were designed to enhance coordination of care and healthcare team communication, and improve quality, while reducing costs in the primary care setting. The Patient-Centered Primary Care Collaborative produces an annual evidence report "evaluating the impact of the PCMH model on cost and utilization measures." In 2016, they synthesized results from 17 peer-reviewed studies and 13 various state and federal government and industry reports and reported that the majority of the peer-reviewed studies found reductions in cost measures (21 of 23 studies) and utilization measures (23 of 25 studies) (https://www.pcpcc.org/results-evidence, 2017). In another systematic review (Zutshi et al., 2013), researchers found that early indicators for success of the new care delivery model PCMHs did exist for quality of care, reduced hospital and emergency services usage, and patient and care provider experience, but also noted a few "unfavorable effects on costs." While PCMHs have been in existence before the PPACA, the increased emphasis on this new care delivery model necessitates ongoing careful analysis of what works, why it works, and what is not working to fully realize significant quality and cost improvements.

Conclusion: Experiences with Managed Care Organizations Provide Significant Lessons Learned, as Providers Begin Forming ACOs and PCMHs

As we conclude the second chapter in our "Strategies to Increase Efficiency" section, we can see that our experiences with managed care organizations provide significant lessons learned for careful consideration as we begin evaluating and modifying ACOs and PCMHs. Consumer and provider protection measures are needed to

- Ensure that consumers know what they are paying for when purchasing health insurance and that they get what they pay for
- Address the controversies surrounding quality measures
- Balance efficiency and market power issues among healthcare providers

In Chapter 6, we explore the efficiency gains we can hope to achieve through wellness, prevention, and disease management programs.

Chapter 6

Wellness, Prevention, and Disease Management

Introduction

The famous saying that "an ounce of prevention is worth a pound of cure" summarizes the strategy that underlies the creation and implementation of wellness, preventive care, and chronic disease management programs. Economists describe this idea by thinking about the inputs that are needed to produce a car—and then applying that concept of "production" to think about the diverse activities that produce "health." The list of activities that contribute to producing health clearly includes healthcare, but it also includes individual decisions to eat healthy foods and exercise regularly; public health measures, such as vaccinations and access to clean drinking water; and regulatory measures, such as highway speed limits. As we learned in Chapter 3, socioeconomic factors also play an important part in determining someone's health status. It has been well established that low socioeconomic status effects individual decisions and behaviors and presents greater challenges in providing appropriately targeted wellness, prevention, and disease management programs (Centers for Disease Control and Prevention, 2013; Woolf et al., 2015). These other "inputs" are important: public health measures account for a large share of the increase in life expectancy that occurred during the twentieth century, and as we saw in Chapter 3, comparison of U.S. and Canadian mortality rates highlights the importance of differential rates of obesity and violence.

While prevention is a critical issue, we must address two challenges to achieve the goal of using prevention effectively:

1. We must identify characteristics of programs that are effective (and also cost-effective).
2. We must develop strategies to induce appropriate patient participation.

Recent headlines articulate the importance of solving the mystery of *how* to design prevention programs that will actually impact behavior:

- "Eating More Fruits, Vegetables Boosts Psychological Well-Being in Just 2 Weeks" (Whiteman, 2017)
- "A Healthy Lifestyle Doesn't Guarantee a Long Life, but It Will Add Life to Your Years" (Dennett, 2017)

Most of us realize that lifestyle choices are important, but this information—alone—does not always spur us to proper action. Alabama strengthened the incentive by implementing a monetary penalty for state employees with "extra pounds" (Fernandez, 2008).

In this chapter, we use the word *prevention* broadly, to encompass a broad range of activities that are designed to prevent adverse outcomes. In addition to activities such as vaccinations that are typically viewed as "prevention programs," we also consider wellness programs, preventive healthcare such as prenatal care, and chronic disease management that is designed to prevent (or postpone) complications associated with chronic disease.

Background: PPACA Focuses Increased Attention on Prevention and Wellness

The Patient Protection and Affordable Care Act (PPACA) has generated a renewed focus on prevention and wellness. This law led to the creation of the National Prevention, Health Promotion and Public Health Council, which is charged with developing strategies to improve the nation's health and coordinate federal prevention, wellness, and public health activities (National Prevention Council, 2011). The council's strategic plan identifies its primary goal: to increase the number of Americans who are healthy at every stage of life. Based on evidence that prevention can reduce healthcare costs and increase productivity, the council identified a four-pronged approach to accomplish this goal:

1. Create, sustain, and recognize health communities
2. Ensure the availability and quality of community preventative services
3. Empower people to make healthy choices
4. Eliminate health disparities

The council established seven evidence-based priorities, to reduce or prevent the leading causes of preventable deaths and major illness:

1. Tobacco-free living
2. Preventing drug and alcohol abuse
3. Healthy eating
4. Active living
5. Injury and violence-free living
6. Reproductive and sexual health
7. Mental and emotional well-being

In addition, the federal Department of Health and Human Services (HHS) provides administrative support for the U.S. Preventive Services Task Force (USPSTF). The USPSTF is an independent body that makes evidence-based recommendations, such as the mammogram screening recommendation discussed in Chapter 3.

Current Issues

To achieve the vision of increased prevention as an essential component of efforts to improve our healthcare system's access, cost, and quality, it will be necessary to address two questions.

First, it is widely recognized that accomplishing these goals will strengthen health. However, it is not clear whether they will reduce cost in the short run (or whether we should view prevention as an "investment" that will produce future health gains).

While many people believe that prevention always "pays," existing evidence does not fully support this view (Russell, 2009; Cohen et al., 2008; Maciosek et al., 2010; RAND Corporation, 2014). This apparent disconnect can be explained by looking at the issue from two perspectives.

1. Prevention clearly pays if we *only* look at individuals who would have developed a disease or condition if they had not participated in prevention. After an individual is diagnosed with cancer, it is easy to conclude that early diagnosis and treatment would have been cheaper and produced a better outcome, compared with the more intensive treatment that may be required after a delayed diagnosis.

2. However, it is generally necessary to provide numerous screening mammograms in order to identify one individual with early-stage treatable cancer (reflect back to our earlier discussion in Chapter 3, where we discussed the cost–benefit analysis of mammography for women between 40 and 49 years of age). Louise Russell summarized the issue succinctly, "Evaluating the claim that prevention reduces medical spending is more complicated than it appears at first glance. Costs that look small when considered per person, or per year, start to mount up. The result is that prevention can cost more than it saves" (Russell, 2009). Instead of simply assuming that all preventive efforts will generate fiscal savings, it may be necessary to target prevention efforts carefully to ensure that prevention dollars are well spent.

Second, some individuals are likely to enjoy substantial benefits from prevention programs, while others may not benefit at all. There is no guarantee that individuals with high potential to benefit will also have a high propensity to participate in the program. It is possible, for example, that a wellness program may seem particularly attractive to people who are already predisposed to be conscientious about engaging in recommended healthy behaviors. The wellness program will not generate a positive net benefit if the couch potatoes (who might have benefited from the wellness program's emphasis on increased exercise) remain comfortably at home, while the people who were already running marathons elect to participate in the program. To be financially viable, programs must be designed to anticipate—and manage—these self-selection issues.

A study of the impact of a subsidized prenatal care program on infant health provides an example of the importance of viewing self-selection as a program management issue. Mukhopadhyay and Wendel (2008) concluded that prenatal care produced statistically significant beneficial impacts on infant health when the mother had specific preexisting diagnoses. Unfortunately—in this sample—these mothers (whose infants are most likely to benefit from prenatal care) did *not* initiate prenatal care early in the pregnancy. This self-selection, which occurs before anyone at the clinic interacts with the pregnant women, impacts the ability of the clinic to produce good outcomes; hence, developing strategies to influence this self-selection process is an important factor that may increase the clinic's overall impact on the patient population.

This problem is not unique to prenatal care. Wendel and Dumitras (2005) reported an analogous misalignment between patients who could potentially benefit from a diabetes disease management program and patients who elected to participate in the program. The program managers envisioned that the program would generate a net financial benefit—because participation would reduce the average number of visits to hospital emergency departments. However, multivariate analysis of the data indicated that patients whose pattern of care focused on physician visits (measured by a relatively high number of physician visits per prescription—and fewer emergency department visits) were more likely to participate in the program, compared with patients with higher numbers of emergency department visits. This mismatch between potential benefit and self-selection patterns reduces the ability of the program to increase population health and demonstrate a positive financial benefit.

The question of *how* to manage self-selection is generating discussion—and the results will clearly impact the design and success of wellness programs. Dee Edington, in the book *Zero Trends* (2009), provides extensive—and very interesting—analyses of the impact of self-selection on the strategic design of employer wellness programs. Dr. Edington concluded that wellness programs should focus primarily on "keeping the healthy people healthy," while others recommend the opposite: that wellness programs should target participation of the less healthy people.

After We Identify Individuals Who Are Most Likely to Benefit from Prevention Programs, Can We Design Programs to Successfully Induce Them to Participate?

The quest to understand people (why they do what they do, and choose what they choose) is pursued by psychologists, sociologists, and anthropologists. One might be surprised to learn that economists also seek to understand decisions and choices. *Behavioral economics* is the study of decision making as it relates to economic issues. (The well-known book and movie *Freakonomics* provided some illustrations of this approach.) Behavioral economists seek to understand factors that influence individual choices, and then use that information to design useful policies and programs.

For example, the British government has a cabinet-level unit, dubbed the "Nudge Unit," that is responsible for using behavioral economics to influence health behaviors, such as obesity and smoking. The unit is nicknamed after the popular book *Nudge*, and it is advised by one of the book's authors (the book's other author heads an analogous unit in the U.S. government). Box 6.1 summarizes three behavioral economics studies.

Behavioral and experimental economics have strong interdisciplinary ties to psychology, as researchers seek to understand individual decision processes. Behavioral economists focus on situations in which individuals systematically make decision errors, in the sense that the decisions are not consistent with the individual's goals. These decision errors are common: retirees wish they had saved more when they were young, smokers intend to quit but do not, and people spend money to join gyms that they do not use. Instead of processing information logically, we anchor on recent information, overemphasize low probabilities, and place undue importance on information that is frequently repeated. Behavioral economists hope to develop sufficient understanding of these decision errors to be able to help individuals make "correct" decisions by structuring incentive systems or decision frameworks.

Behavioral economists examine factors that influence choices, including information, monetary incentives, individual resources, and the decision context. For example, the British Nudge Unit is working to identify specific types, locations, and formats of nutrition labeling that would influence food choices. Will we pay attention—and use the information to increase our production of health—if alcohol content is presented on bar napkins? Or, if yellow tape visually reserves a section of the grocery cart for fresh produce? Research results reported by Elbel et al. (2009) illustrated the intrinsic difficulty of this task. The researchers collected fast-food cash register receipts and survey data in New York City and in nearby Newark, New Jersey, both before and after New York City mandated that restaurants with multiple locations (at least 15) visibly post calorie information for their menu offerings. After analyzing the data in a multivariate difference-in-difference framework, the authors concluded that the law increased the proportion of consumers who saw calorie information, but this information did not influence consumers to reduce the number of calories purchased. Elbel et al. concluded, "In an ideal world, calorie labeling on menus and menu boards would have an immediate and direct impact on everyone's food choices. However, ... greater attention to the root causes of behavior, or multifaceted interventions, or both, will be necessary if obesity is to be greatly reduced in the overall U.S. population" (2009, p. w1117).

BOX 6.1   WHAT IS BEHAVIORAL ECONOMICS? THREE EXAMPLES

Simon: Why Do We Settle for Options That Are Just Good Enough?

The field of behavioral economics is new, but the basic ideas are well established. Herbert Simon, a psychologist, won a Nobel Prize in 1978, for his seminal work on managerial decision making (Simon, 1957). He argued that people balance costs and benefits when they decide how much effort to invest before making a specific decision. Acquiring, organizing, synthesizing, and analyzing information is costly; hence, people frequently use rules of thumb to avoid investing time and effort in a substantive decision process. We park in the same corner of the parking lot every morning, without investing time to search for a better space. Many of us choose a supermarket checkout line after a cursory inspection of the options, without detailed assessment of the amounts and types of goods in each waiting basket, and each checker's speed. Dr. Simon coined the term *satisfice* to encapsulate the idea that we simply choose an option that is "good enough," without investing time and effort to ensure that we select the best option.

Kahneman and Tversky: People Pay More Attention to Losses than to Gains

Daniel Kahneman, another psychologist, won a subsequent Nobel Prize in 2002 for his work with Amos Tversky that demonstrated that individual choices are impacted—in systematic ways—by the decision context. For example, individuals pay more attention to losses than gains; hence, framing a choice as a loss, rather than a gain, will generate a larger response. The www.stickk.com strategy implements this idea—with surprising success (Kahneman, 2011).

Akerlof: Why Do We Procrastinate?

George Akerlof analyzed procrastination (Akerlof, 1991). An embarrassing example of procrastination in his own life motivated him to examine this phenomenon: he promised to mail a box to a colleague, he intended to mail the box every day for a year, his failure to mail the box was embarrassing, and the box was still sitting in his office 1 year later. This forced him to consider the question, why did he make this decision error—repeatedly—for a year? His answer focused on the fact that this type of decision is repeated many times. Each time he considered, "Should I mail the box today?" he weighed the costs and benefits. If he used his time "today" to mail the box (compared with a future day—later in the week), the benefit would be small. His colleague would not really care whether the box arrived a few days later. However, competing time pressures today were clear: if he mailed the box today, he would not complete an immediate task. He concluded that there is a large set of similar decisions, in which individuals make decision errors because they divide time into numerous small segments. The cost of taking the desired action always outweighs the benefit—in any specific segment of time—but the accumulated decisions over a long period of time do not maximize the individual's happiness. In these situations, individuals can benefit from paternalistic schemes designed to prevent procrastination. For example, people hire personal trainers to set rigid times for exercise.

The question of *how* to post nutrition information is clearly important: PPACA mandates that chain restaurants must include nutrition information on their menus. Healthcare adviser E. J. Emanuel (housed in the Office of Management and Budget) is working to figure out optimal strategies for posting that information in a way that will impact decisions: "Where it is likely to impact people, and what's most likely to do it?" (Dorning, 2010). Emanuel conceded that this effort is more typical of Madison Avenue instead of Pennsylvania Avenue, and notes that this is a new role for government.

Another British Nudge Unit project utilizes a website created by two Yale University behavioral economists (Karlan and Ayres, www.stickk.com). This website harnesses evidence that most people pay more attention to losses than to gains. This website allows individuals to create self-financed incentives to quit smoking or lose weight, by depositing money in an account. If the individual succeeds in achieving the goal (the information is self-reported), he or she receives a refund of his or her own money. If he or she fails, then the money will be forfeited. He or she can specify, at the outset, that the forfeited money would be donated to a cause that he or she vehemently dislikes. The researchers report that success rates for www.stickk.com users are higher than success rates in the general population, and they are particularly high for individuals who precommit that forfeited funds will be donated to a cause that the individual dislikes.

While www.stickk.com provides an example of voluntary decision framing at the individual level, behavioral economists typically aim to apply this type of strategy at the system level. The application of behavioral economics to the issue of retirement savings provides a good example. While many people intend to save for retirement, a large proportion of these individuals do not take advantage of the tax advantage offered by employer 401(k) retirement savings plans. After behavioral and experimental economists demonstrated that specifying the "default" option impacts decisions, a large U.S. corporation adopted a new policy for employee retirement savings accounts (Madrian and Shea, 2001). The firm switched from the traditional policy, allowing employees to "opt in" to the decision to open a 401(k) account, to a new system that automatically enrolled new employees in a 401(k) account, but allowed these employees to "opt out." While the decision to open a 401(k) account was optional in both systems, the default option that would occur if the employee took no action switched from not having a 401(k) account to having a 401(k) account. Because inertia appears to exert significant influence on actual behavior, changing the decision framework led to substantial behavior change: 37% of employees opened 401(k) accounts under the opt-in system, while 86% maintained accounts under the opt-out system.

Economists describe this type of manipulation of the decision framework as "beneficent paternalism," to emphasize that it is designed to help individuals achieve goals that they themselves say they want to achieve. This type of policy aims to achieve—on a system level—the types of manipulations that individuals implement when they freeze their credit cards in ice (so the card cannot be used until the ice melts), refuse to keep ice cream or cookies in the house (so these foods will not be conveniently available), or put the alarm clock several feet away from the bed (so they will have to get out of bed to turn the alarm off in the morning). Despite the fine line between helping individuals achieve self-identified goals and incentivizing individuals to achieve goals defined by the employer or health insurance plan, mounting evidence that lifestyle choices exert major impacts on healthcare expenditures (O'Neill and O'Neill, 2008) is generating increasing interest.

If we design wellness and disease management programs without a clear understanding of factors that influence actual decisions, it is unlikely that the programs will be able to help, or induce, individuals to make significant lifestyle changes. In contrast, these programs are likely to be far more successful if the programs and incentives are designed to influence real-world decisions made by real people. Designing such effective programs and incentives, however, requires in-depth understanding of real decision processes—and that conceptual framework is only partially available at this point.

It also raises a more sensitive question: Is this strategy overly manipulative? Advocates of the strategy argue that it is not, because compliance with the policy goal remains voluntary and because (ideally) the strategy is only applied to help individuals make choices that align with those individuals' goals. In the context of retirement savings, the advocates' argument is simply that there has to be a default option (every program must be defined to be either "opt-in" or "opt-out"). Many seniors report—in surveys—that they wish they had saved more when they were younger. We should select the default option that helps people accomplish their goals.

Assuming that the behavioral economics results are useful, how can managed care organizations, disease management, and wellness program managers apply this information? The report of the British Cabinet Office Behavioural Insights Team (2010) provides some interesting examples of applications of these ideas to tackle issues such as smoking cessation, teenage pregnancy, diet and weight management, and diabetes prevention. Some applications are relatively straightforward, such as the development of an opt-out system for authorizing organ donation, to replace the traditional opt-in system. Others are more creative. For example, the report describes a collaboration between Bayer Healthcare and Nintendo DS to develop a device that awards points to diabetic children for consistent blood sugar testing. (The children can use these points on Nintendo games.) The report also describes Volkswagen's hypothesis that fun can be a strong motivator for behavior change:

> The piano stairs was one of the most popular ideas. For one day in a Stockholm metro station, Volkswagen installed motion-sensor piano keys so that musical tunes were played as people climbed the stairs. A before-and-after study showed that 66 per cent more people than normal took the stairs rather than the escalator. (Cabinet Office Behavioural Insights Team, 2010, p. 19)

To have some fun yourself, watch two videos: http://www.thefuntheory.com/ and http://www.youtube.com/watch?v=f-6tNtk_H6s.

Effectiveness of Prevention and Wellness Programs

The passage of the PPACA brought with it greater emphasis and incentives to provide preventative care, wellness, and disease management programs to improve population health, as well as curtailing the escalating cost of health-care. While there continue to be debates surrounding the actual cost savings that preventative and wellness programs generate, there is little argument that they *can* produce high value to society *if* they actually improve lifestyle, reduce the incidence of disability and disease, and slow the progression of some chronic illnesses. Many wellness programs include two compo-nents: lifestyle management and disease management. Lifestyle management includes things like healthy eating, increased activity, and smoking cessa-tion and is focused on disease prevention through risk reduction. Disease management is focused on delaying the progression and complications from the disease and includes programs targeting heart disease, diabetes, and/or pulmonary diseases, such as emphysema and chronic obstructive pulmonary disease (COPD). It makes sense that cost savings could be more immediately noted for disease management programs, as the benefits take effect in the short term, rather than the long-term gains produced by lifestyle changes (RAND Corporation, 2014). A study published in *Health Affairs* (Caloyeras et al., 2014) reported key findings of PepsiCo's Healthy Living Program. The disease management program saved the company $3.78 per dollar invested compared with a savings of just $0.48 from their lifestyle program. The disease management component of their program reduced healthcare costs by $136 per member per month, purportedly driven by a 29% reduction in hospital admissions.

However, a disease management focus doesn't guarantee cost savings. This is exemplified in a Congressional Budget Office report (Nelson, 2012) that looked at Medicare demonstration projects on disease management and care coordination over the previous 10 years. This report looked at 34 programs that provided disease management and care coordination for beneficiaries in the Medicare fee-for-service program and found no effect on hospital readmissions or a reduction in regular Medicare expenditures. One significant finding was that programs with significant direct interaction between primary care providers and patients were more likely to reduce hospital readmissions than programs without this characteristic. This is an important characteristic to note as we gather evidence about what makes a program effective—or not.

More than half of adult Medicaid enrollees have a chronic condition, so finding a mechanism to manage their care that provides both quality and cost-effectiveness has been a priority for the Centers for Medicare and Medicaid Services (CMS). Key findings from a study (Williams, 2004) exam-ining different Medicaid disease management programs over nine states support the need to eliminate the single-disease focus that often exacerbates fragmented care, and to create programs that are patient centered in order to improve disease self-management and positive behavior change.

Earlier in this chapter, we discussed the importance of not only providing effective programs but also identifying ways to target participants that would benefit from these programs. Findings from the CMS disease management study (Williams, 2004) also identify the need for programs to tailor their recruitment and ongoing communications to a population that can be challenging to contact. One of the first steps of program success is actually enrolling participants who may benefit the most from these programs. Another important aspect of effective wellness and prevention programs is identifying barriers to participation. An interesting article in the *Harvard Business Review* (McManamy, 2016) looked at why people do or don't participate in employer-sponsored wellness programs and found that the majority (79%) of those who participated in these programs had positive perceptions of their health, their employer, and their work productivity. Employees that didn't participate in the wellness programs listed lack of information or awareness (this was the primary reason for 69% of nonparticipants), inconvenience and unsupportive company culture, and trust and privacy concerns with their employers as barriers to participation. Both participants and nonparticipants highlighted the need for these programs to be individualized to their needs and to provide support from credible experts who were easy to access and could provide one-on-one support.

Several of these studies lead us to believe that

■ The effectiveness of wellness programs may not be equated to overall healthcare cost savings—other measures may be more meaningful, such as increased worker productivity and sustained healthier behaviors (Mitchell and Bate, 2011).
■ Effective programs need to be individualized, easy to access, and comprehensive (i.e., less one disease specific).
■ Evidence supports a greater role for primary care in prevention and wellness endeavor success.

Conclusions

In this chapter, we examined efficiency strategies aimed at creating and maintaining a healthy populace through the use of wellness, preventative care, and disease management programs. As with other strategies we have explored in earlier chapters of Section II, these strategies offer strong potential to increase efficiency, but they also pose challenges. Effective prevention can reduce long-term healthcare costs and increase productivity of our workforce. However, prevention strategies may not be efficient in all situations and may not actually benefit those who we sought to help. Can we identify characteristics of effective prevention programs? Can we identify those most likely to benefit from these programs, and once we have, how can we ensure that those people will actually participate? What types of incentives can best induce the behaviors we wish to promote? These are questions healthcare providers and policy makers must address in order to obtain the efficiencies these strategies promise. Health professionals (including psychologists, nurses, behavioral counselors, and others who manage programs and interact directly with patients) have much to offer in addressing these challenges.

In the next chapter, we continue to explore strategies to improve healthcare efficiencies, with a look at new provider types and the changing role of patients.

Chapter 7

Regulatory Challenges Posed by New Types of Competition in Healthcare

Introduction

In the influential book *The Innovator's Prescription: A Disruptive Solution for Health Care*, the authors mapped a strategy for reducing the cost of delivering healthcare by dramatically increasing the efficiency of the healthcare industry (Christensen et al., 2008). In recognition of the potential value of vigorous competition in the healthcare industry, the two federal agencies responsible for maintaining competition in the U.S. economy issued a report in 2004 on competition among healthcare providers (Federal Trade Commission and Department of Justice, 2004). This report analyzed the potential benefits of new types of competition emerging in the healthcare industry, regulatory barriers that restrict competition in this industry, and challenges facing regulators. State regulatory policies have evolved since this report was written, yet the issues identified in the report remain salient. Competitive innovation is an essential component of efforts to reduce the cost of delivering healthcare, and regulators face ongoing challenges to develop appropriate consumer protection strategies as the healthcare industry evolves.

In this chapter, we consider the competitive market mechanism that generated significant efficiency gains in other industries, examples of new types of competition emerging in the healthcare industry, and regulatory challenges facing states as the competitive changes unfold.

Background

The starting point for understanding the competitive market process for generating efficiency gains is Joseph Schumpeter's concept of "creative destruction." As this process unfolds, innovators compete with existing organizations, forcing some of them to close (Schumpeter, 1942). The creative destruction process is two-sided, as its name suggests: it delivers innovative efficiency gains (Bureau of Labor Statistics, 2010), but the process also imposes costs on competitors and their communities. We begin by considering two examples outside the healthcare industry, which illustrate issues likely to arise as private-sector innovators work to generate new types of efficiencies in the healthcare industry.

Walmart's impact on the retail industry provides a good example of this dynamic market process that generates both efficiency gains and social controversies. Walmart pursued a low-price and high-volume strategy, while creating new types of efficiencies in its supply chain systems. Walmart's success is documented by a study that concludes that Walmart's low prices generated a statistically significant reduction in the overall rate of U.S. inflation (Business Planning Solutions Global Insight Advisory Services Division, 2005). However, the low prices and the substantial market share raised two types of questions:

1. Do the low prices reflect superior efficiency or unfair tactics?
2. When competitors respond to Walmart's competitive vigor by closing their stores and businesses, how should we weigh the benefits of Walmart's low prices on specific consumer goods against the negative externalities created when businesses close?

The ride-sharing services Uber and Lyft are generating creative destruction in the taxicab market. Uber and Lyft offer lower fares to passengers while challenging the traditional business model of taxicab companies. Notably, taxicab companies in New York City and Chicago responded to the new competition by changing their business practices to increase aspects of service quality valued by passengers (Wallsten, 2015). In many locations, taxicab companies also complained that the ride-sharing companies used unfair competitive practices and the taxicab operators sought to impose regulatory requirements on ride-sharing companies to limit the competitive positions of the new services. In these states, lawmakers and regulators faced two types of issues.

1. Some of the regulatory challenges addressed consumer protection issues, such as the amount of insurance carried by drivers offering ride-sharing services. To address these challenges, regulators must weigh two alternate paradigms for considering the fact that consumers are purchasing rides from new firms that offer lower levels of consumer protection than the established taxicab firms:
   – Consumers understand that riding with Uber and Lyft implies reduced protection from driver insurance policies, but they are willing to accept this reduction in service quality in exchange for low fares.
   – Consumers purchasing the services are not making informed decisions about this trade-off because they do not have sufficient information.
2. Other regulatory initiatives supported by the taxicab companies appear to be straightforward attempts to use regulatory processes to limit competition. For example, the summary of a bill proposed in Nevada (SB485), which was not passed, states,

> Section 2 of this bill requires a passenger using the digital network or software application service of a transportation network company to specify the time at which the passenger wishes to receive transportation services and prohibits a request for transportation services which would commence within 15 minutes after the request is made.

It is not clear that the 15-minute restriction benefits consumers. However, evidence suggests that it could benefit taxi drivers. Wallsten's (2015) analysis indicates that Uber drivers have shorter average response times than taxi drivers (at least in large cities). Prohibiting requests for short response times would limit the potential for Uber drivers to benefit from their ability to offer this type of service quality to consumers.

Current Issues

Traditional healthcare providers serving patients in their local areas face growing competition. We consider two sources of that competition: new types of providers operating in a local area and competition from providers located in larger geographic areas.

1. Retail clinics and single-specialty hospitals (SSHs) offer potential efficiency gains for the healthcare system. These innovators offer services with attractive features—but they generate controversies similar to the issues raised by Walmart and Uber. The success of innovative market newcomers threatens the competitive positions of established entities and generates concerns about the impacts of competitive dynamics on healthcare quality, traditional types of healthcare providers, and communities. While the new types of efficiency create opportunities to address concerns about access and the financial viability of safety net providers, these also generate new types of concerns about consumer protection. We consider the potential benefits offered by retail clinics and specialty hospitals, the implications for general hospitals and primary care physicians (PCPs), and challenges facing policy makers.
2. The emergence of interstate and international competition, including telemedicine providers, presents new types of challenges for local service providers that have traditionally dominated the healthcare industry.

These innovations pose two types of regulatory challenges to states. First, they challenge traditional strategies for defining and ensuring consumer protection. Second, they challenge the traditional system in which healthcare providers are licensed and regulated by states, and healthcare is delivered by physicians located in the same state as the patient.

New Types of Providers: Retail Clinics, SSHs, Telemedicine, and Integrated Care Providers

Retail Clinics

Retail clinics offer a specified set of services at posted prices in a retail setting. The first retail clinics opened at the beginning of the twenty-first century. In 2008, retail clinics were offered in 1000 sites (e.g., Target, Rite Aid, Walmart, and CVS Pharmacy) in 37 states (Laws and Scott, 2008). It is estimated that 2000 clinics were operating in 2016 (Kalorama Information, 2016).

These clinics are staffed by nurse practitioners (NPs) and physician assistants (PAs) who offer a specific list of services, such as school physicals, strep tests, immunizations, blood pressure screenings, and diagnosis and treatment for routine, uncomplicated illnesses. The retail clinic concept focuses on providing cost-effective primary care services for patients, with referrals to higher levels of care as needed. Patients are seen on a drop-in basis, the clinics are typically open the same hours as the retail pharmacy (including evening and weekend hours), prices are posted for specific services, and some clinics offer restaurant-style beepers to permit patients to shop in the store while waiting for care (Rudavsky et al., 2009).

Patient surveys indicate that patients who utilize retail clinics appreciate both the relatively low cost of retail clinic visits and the convenience of drop-in, same-day visits; short wait times; and extended hours. Some physicians have responded to this clear evidence on consumer preferences by offering extended hours and reserving some time slots for drop-in visits (Ahmed and Fincham, 2010).

Retail clinics have sparked legislative opposition in some states. For example, Illinois considered a bill that would have blocked the operation of retail clinics by outlawing the provision of healthcare in a building that also houses the sale of cigarettes. (Proponents of this bill argued that it is not appropriate to create health and destroy health in the same building.) The Federal Trade Commission responded by issuing a letter indicating that this type of regulation would be viewed as anticompetitive, because it would block the process of creative destruction that generates efficiency gains, consumer price reductions, and service quality innovation.

The clinics generated concerns about potential impacts on healthcare quality, physician–patient relationships, and the financial positions of PCPs:

- Substituting care provided by NPs for care provided by physicians could reduce the quality of care provided to patients.
- Each retail clinic visit that substitutes for a PCP visit represents a "missed" opportunity for the PCP to identify chronic conditions and/or coordinate care for those conditions.
- Retail clinic care could disrupt relationships between patients and PCPs.
- Retail clinics could weaken the financial position of PCPs.

Retail clinics have operated long enough to generate useful data for assessing these concerns. Published studies report that the care offered by NPs is comparable to the care offered by physicians for the types of conditions treated at retail clinics (Stanik-Hutt et al., 2013), but at a much lower cost. In addition, Mehrota et al. (2008) analyzed de-identified visit-level data on thousands of retail clinic, PCP, and emergency department visits to assess the validity of these concerns. This data indicates that the quality issues are probably not salient; however, the clinics could pose financial challenges for PCPs.

- These authors report that retail clinics serve a patient population that is not well served by traditional PCP offices. Compared with individuals who visit PCP offices for conditions that can be treated at retail clinics, individuals who utilize retail clinics are more likely to pay out-of-pocket and report that they do not have an established relationship with a PCP.
- Medical records for the patients with retail clinic visits indicate that only 8% of these patients had one or more of the six common chronic conditions (asthma, hypertension, diabetes, chronic obstructive pulmonary disease, congestive heart failure, or depression).
- Most retail clinic visits focus on preventive care, such as immunizations, or acute care for minor ailments. PCP visits that provide this type of care are typically shorter than other PCP visits. Shifting these visits out of PCP offices could reduce scheduling flexibility for PCPs to accommodate patients requiring longer visits. On the other hand, retail clinic visits are less likely to be covered by insurance.

Continued growth of these clinics poses a regulatory challenge for states. The clinics are typically staffed by NPs; hence, clinic operating costs are significantly impacted by state licensure laws that define the scope of practice of NPs and detail the "physician supervision" requirements. These laws permitted NPs to diagnose and treat patients without physician supervision in only one-third of states in 2012, while physician involvement in these processes was required in the remaining two-thirds of states (Bachrach et al., 2015). Clinic growth was most rapid in the "full-practice" states (Kuo et al., 2013), in which

> state practice and licensure law provides for all nurse practitioners to evaluate patients, diagnose, order and interpret diagnostic tests, initiate and manage treatments—including prescribe medications—under the exclusive licensure authority of the state board of nursing. (American Academy of Nurse Practitioners, 2017)

State regulators in other states faced two questions:

1. Do the low-cost and convenience benefits offered by retail clinics outweigh concerns about healthcare quality and coordination?

2. If the clinics generate adverse impacts on the financial position of PCPs, is this issue relevant to the specification of licensure and scope of practice laws?

In response to these issues, some states have expanded the scope of practice defined for NPs: by 2017, half of the states were classified as full-practice states.

Controversies about licensure and scope of practice are not unique to NPs. States also vary with regard to the scope of practice defined for midwives. Some states allow midwives to practice independently, while others require physician supervision of midwives. In addition, Medicaid reimbursement rates for midwives (relative to physicians) vary across states (ACNM Department of Advocacy and Government Affairs Grassroots Advocacy Resources, 2017). Analyses of licensure regulations for an array of occupations indicate that these regulations stem from a mix of efforts to promote consumer protection and efforts to protect the competitive position of individuals who already work in the regulated occupation. If these policies are designed to ensure patient safety, the rationale for variation across states is not clear. However, Adams et al. (2003) report that strict regulation does reduce the proportion of births that are attended by certified nurse midwives (CNMs).

States face similar trade-offs as they consider licensure and scope of practice for dental professionals. Vermont, Maine, and Minnesota permit dentists to hire "dental therapists" to deliver preventive and routine restorative care (Koppelman, 2016). These midlevel providers can fill cavities, place temporary crowns, and extract diseased or loose teeth. At least 10 additional states are exploring this option. Wind and Marier (2014) report that regulations restricting the activities of midlevel providers lead to significantly higher prices (by 10%–12%). In addition, allowing insurers to directly reimburse hygienists leads to higher utilization of their services (by 3–4 percentage points).

Three factors create pressure to consider increased utilization of advanced practice nurses (NPs, CNMs, certified registered nurse anesthetist [CRNAs], and clinical nurse specialists [CNSs]) and other types of medical professionals:

■ Current and projected PCP shortages, particularly in poor and rural areas.
■ Patient Protection and Affordable Care Act (PPACA) provisions that expand healthcare coverage and increase the number of people who may seek care.
■ Rising costs for healthcare.

Medicare reimbursement rates for PAs, NPs, and CNSs are set at 85% of the physician fee schedule, while rates for CNMs are set at 65% of the physician fee schedule. The differential between the payment rates for physicians and other medical professionals creates incentives for organizations with capitated payments to utilize nonphysician professionals. Competitive pressure from retail clinics creates additional incentive for PCP practices to develop strategies for increasing utilization of PAs and NPs in traditional primary care settings. In these settings, NPs can provide protocol-driven care to patients with less complex conditions, while physicians can focus on patients with more complex conditions.

State regulatory policies regarding licensure and scope of practice, along with state consumer protection strategies, are becoming increasingly important as increasing proportions of consumers have high-deductible health insurance plans coupled with health savings accounts (HSAs). Individuals with this type of health insurance have strong incentives to "shop" for healthcare, and to make careful trade-offs between prices offered by competing healthcare providers and the nonprice characteristics of the services offered by those providers. Similarly, the majority of individual private-sector insurance plans purchased through the health insurance exchanges are silver or bronze plans (which typically pay 60%–70% of healthcare expenses, while gold and platinum plans cover 80%–90%). Individuals purchasing these plans face substantial deductibles and copayments when they use healthcare services, which creates strong financial incentives to shop for low-price providers. (Individuals with income between 100% and 250% of the FPL may receive federal cost sharing reduction subsidies, to help cover these costs.) In addition, New Hampshire implemented a "right-to-shop" program, and Maine is considering a right-to-shop bill that would require insurers to:

■ Notify consumers of their right to shop.
■ Provide accurate information on the cost of services offered by local providers.
■ Share savings generated by consumer efforts to find and utilize lower-cost providers.

If additional states (or insurers) adopt right-to-shop strategies, consumer shopping could generate significant incentives for physician practices to increase utilization of midlevel providers, and it could create pressure for state regulators and lawmakers to broaden the scope of practice regulations for midlevel providers.

Single-Specialty Hospitals

The competitive challenge posed by SSHs raises additional questions. As their name implies, SSHs focus on one specific type of treatment or procedure. In 2003, a report by the U.S. General Accounting Office (2003) noted that 100 SSHs were in operation, with an additional 26 under development. Most of these hospitals were clustered in seven states, with 26% of the U.S. population: Arizona, California, Texas, Oklahoma, South Dakota, Louisiana, and Kansas. The authors of *The Innovator's Prescription* highlighted specialty hospitals as a competitive innovation with strong potential to help make our healthcare system more efficient (Christensen et al., 2008). Their logic focused on process efficiency. Whereas a general hospital organizes flexible work processes to provide customized treatment for any type of patient who might arrive at the hospital, a specialty hospital organizes a small number of streamlined work processes to treat specific types of cases. This permits specialty hospitals to be more efficient in treating those specific types of cases than equally well-managed general hospitals.

Despite this potential efficiency advantage offered by specialty hospitals, CMS imposed an 18-month moratorium on billing by new specialty hospitals in 2003–2004. This moratorium reflected concern about two issues:

1. SSHs are typically owned and operated by the physicians who diagnose patient conditions and refer patients to their own hospitals for treatment. This type of self-referral generates the same types of concerns as those generated when an auto mechanic provides diagnosis and repair as a bundled service.

2. Policy makers have expressed concern about the impact of specialty hospitals on the financial viability of general hospitals (Federal Trade Commission, 2004, p. 17). Our current system expects for-profit and nonprofit general acute care hospitals to provide uncompensated care to uninsured and underinsured patients and to generate the revenue needed to support this activity by earning profit (or positive net revenue) on other types of care. SSHs exert competitive pressure on general hospitals—because they compete for *insured* patients who require specific types of care (primarily orthopedic or oncology care).

Analysts also debate whether SSHs actually reduce cost versus select healthy patients. Barro et al. (2006) examined Medicare claims for cardiac patients in 1993, 1996, and 1999 and conclude,

> We find support for both sides of this debate. Markets experiencing entry by a cardiac specialty hospital have lower spending for cardiac care without significantly worse clinical outcomes. In markets with a specialty hospital, however, specialty hospitals tend to attract healthier patients and provide higher levels of intensive procedures than general hospitals.

The policy question is whether we should respond to this dilemma by

■ Limiting the expansion of the specialty hospital industry (to protect the *"net revenue over cost"* of general hospitals, so they can continue to offer uncompensated care)
■ Developing a more transparent system for funding uncompensated care, so that general hospitals can compete on a more level playing field
■ Revising Medicare payment rates for cardiac surgery to more accurately reflect patient complexity

Our current system for financing care for uninsured patients requires insured patients to pay high enough rates to generate sufficient revenue to cover the cost of providing care to uninsured patients. This cross-subsidy mechanism for financing uncompensated care is attractive to politicians because it is not transparent. It does not require a visible tax increase to finance the care for uninsured patients—but it imposes a hidden tax on insured patients whose rates must be sufficient to cover these hospital expenditures. Economists refer to the cross-subsidy mechanism of financing social programs as "taxation by regulation" because the uncompensated care regulations impose a "tax" on insured patients—in the form of higher premiums (Posner, 1971).

If the authors of *The Innovator's Prescription* are correct in predicting that specialty hospitals will produce specific types of care more efficiently (and effectively) than general hospitals, then blocking this new type of competition will increase *total* healthcare expenditures—because it will prevent the substitution of a lower-cost option for a higher-cost option. Allowing this new type of innovation will require, however, transitioning from the cross-subsidy strategy for financing uncompensated care, and care for individuals enrolled in Medicaid programs, to a more transparent strategy based on tax revenue. While no one likes to think about raising taxes, economic logic suggests that the tax strategy may reduce our total expenditure for healthcare. A transparent tax-based approach is also likely to permit the development of a more fair distribution of the burden of financing care for the uninsured. (Opponents of SSHs argue that blocking SSHs reduces the *average cost* of patients treated in general hospitals—because low-risk patients are not permitted to elect treatment at the SSH. However, forcing the low-risk patients to obtain treatment in a relatively high-cost facility is not a cost-effective strategy. Instead, this strategy increases *total cost*—which is a much more relevant variable.)

In recognition of the cost implications of protecting cross-subsidy arrangements, the federal agencies responsible for antitrust enforcement recommend that states consider replacing the cross-subsidy system for financing uncompensated care with a transparent financing mechanism.

> Governments should reexamine the role of subsidies in health care markets in light of their inefficiencies and potential to distort competition. Health care markets have numerous cross-subsidies and indirect subsidies. Competitive markets compete away the higher prices and supra-competitive profits necessary to sustain such subsidies. Such competition holds both the promise of consumer benefits and the threat of undermining an implicit policy of subsidizing certain consumers and types of care. Competition cannot provide resources to those who lack them; it does not work well when certain facilities are expected to use higher profits in certain areas to cross-subsidize uncompensated care. In general, it is more efficient to provide subsidies directly to those who should receive them, rather than to obscure cross subsidies and indirect subsidies in transactions that are not transparent. Governments should consider whether current subsidies best serve their citizens' health care needs. (U.S. Department of Justice and Federal Trade Commission, 2004, p. 23)

The use of cross-subsidy financing to pay for socially beneficial goods and services is not unique to healthcare. Landline telephone service provides a good example. Universal access to telephone service is a long-held social goal. It was widely recognized, decades ago, that some households could not afford to pay monthly payments that would cover the cost of providing monthly service. Landline telephone service was provided by regulated monopolies, and the regulators set monthly rates that asked some customers to pay higher rates, to generate subsidies for other customers. The resulting rate represented a complex set of cross-subsidies: urban customers subsidized the expenditures required to extend lines to rural customers, and business customers subsidized residential customers. This system worked smoothly until new technology offered a cost-saving strategy for transmitting telephone calls. When MCI applied for permission to use microwave transmission technology to transmit business customer telephone calls between St. Louis and Chicago, it was clear that the new technology would compete for the profitable segment of telephone business—and this would undercut the financial viability of the cross-subsidy system. Regulators faced a choice: the new technology would reduce overall costs, but it would also make it impossible to maintain the cross-subsidy system for financing the social goal of universal access to telephone service.

Similar cross-subsidy rate systems were built into regulated transportation and electricity rates, and similar dilemmas occurred when new technology and new types of competitors attempted to enter those industries. In each case, the new competitors aimed to compete for the profitable business, without contributing to the cross-subsidy—which is known as "skimming the cream" (in the sense that the new entrant hopes to enjoy the best part of the business without helping to finance the cross-subsidy). Efforts to protect the cross-subsidy financing system focused on blocking the entry of new competitors. However, in each case, the cross-subsidy system was eventually dismantled.

U.S. health policy makers face similar limitations in their ability to protect cross-subsidy systems. Policy makers can block development of new specialty hospitals, but they cannot block the development of an international industry providing similar services. For example, a 2009 article in the *Wall Street Journal* described large cardiac and eye specialty hospitals in India that provide care at prices significantly lower than the typical U.S. hospital prices. This article reports that the average price charged for coronary artery bypass graft surgery was $20,000–$42,000 for Medicare patients treated in U.S. hospitals, and $2000 for patients treated at the Narayana Hrudayalaya Hospital in India. Some of the cost savings achieved by this hospital reflect volume: two large hospitals in the United States (Cleveland Clinic and Massachusetts General Hospital) performed 1367 and 536 of these procedures, respectively, while the number performed at the Narayan Hrudayalaya Hospital in the same year (2008) was 3174 (Anand, 2009).

The hospital in India is one example of a growing market for "medical tourism." The idea of traveling to a foreign country for medical care (including surgery) raises a series of questions:

■ Will the hospital be accredited? And if not, does this actually indicate that there are quality or safety problems?
■ How will the patient travel home after the surgery?
■ How will the patient pay for the surgery in the foreign country—and follow-up care in the United States?
■ If adverse outcomes occur, will the patient be able to sue for malpractice?

However, these issues are being addressed:

■ Joint Commission International (JCI), the organization that accredits hospitals in the United States, also accredits hospitals in more 80 countries (http://www.jointcommissioninternational.org/about-jci/jci-accredited-organizations/).
■ Medical tourism facilitators can earn certification through the Medical Tourism Association.
■ BlueCross and BlueShield of South Carolina announced in 2008 plans to organize an infrastructure to support travel by its members to obtain healthcare in foreign countries (Einhorn, 2008).
■ Employers can purchase insurance to cover possible liability resulting from the implementation of an overseas medical care benefit option from Compass Benefits Group, medical tourism facilitators can purchase facilitator liability insurance, and patients can purchase patient medical malpractice insurance from AOS Assurance Company Limited.

Telemedicine

Advancements in technology supporting telemedicine raise salient questions about the appropriate geographic scope of healthcare competition for state policy makers. Telemedicine can potentially offer healthcare services to patients living in underserved areas. Telemedicine can also potentially create new types of competition from healthcare providers located in distant states. Telemedicine also challenges the traditional model for physician licensure that occurs at the state level. Currently, physicians are licensed to practice in a specific state. An individual physician can be licensed to practice in multiple states; however, this would require paying licensure fees in each of those states.

This model restricts telemedicine across state lines because the location of a medical service is typically defined to be the location of the patient. Thus, a physician located in Arizona must be licensed to practice in Nevada before he or she can provide care via telemedicine to a patient located in Nevada. Two initiatives have been launched to address this issue.

1. A federal bill has been proposed to enable physicians licensed in one state to provide telemedicine care to patients in other states without obtaining medical licensure in those other states. The American Medical Association (AMA) and Federation of State Medical Boards (FSMB) oppose the bill. These organizations argue that the bill would erode the current level of consumer protection. For example, consumers would have fewer options for addressing problems that arise due to the telemedicine visits. Others argue that the opposition voiced by the AMA and the FSMB reflects concerns about the potential for interstate care to generate new types of competition for physician services (Terry, 2015).

2. AMA supports, instead, the nascent interstate licensure compact. States joining this compact agree that a physician licensed in one state will be able to become licensed in other compact states through a streamlined procedure. However, these physicians will be required to pay the licensure fee in each state that grants them a license. Telemedicine advocates view this as a significant obstacle to increased use of this technology to provide care across state lines.

Network Economies

Some analysts suggest that increased interstate competition, increased use of telemedicine and health information technology, and increased reliance on analysis of "big data" to manage healthcare systems will generate *network economies*. The Microsoft antitrust case provided a clear illustration of the benefits and challenges of network economies. As Microsoft solidified a dominant market position for the Windows operating systems, Microsoft's success generated controversy about the question of whether this success reflected consumer preference for a superior product or unfair market tactics against competitors. Microsoft Windows standardized a previously fragmented market and made it easy for coworkers and friends to share word processing and spreadsheet files. This convenience generated network economies in the sense that the value enjoyed by one individual using

Microsoft products, such as Word, is an increasing function of the number of coworkers and friends who also use this software. The coworkers who will potentially share these Word files form a "network," and the value gained by each member of the network increases as the size of the network grows. This phenomenon, that larger networks produce value *because* they are large, is known as network economies. This generates a competitive advantage for the firm with the largest market share—because it is difficult for small firms to compete with the firm that sells the large-network product.

The PPACA encourages just such network economies. As healthcare systems integrate primary, secondary, and tertiary care through new delivery systems and models (like accountable care organization [ACOs]) and acquire robust health information technology, they will generate the ability to create network economies. While this may lead to better care coordination, it raises concerns similar to those identified with Microsoft.

Integrated Care Providers

Healthcare providers are responding to the increased use of quality-based payment incentives and capitated payment systems by developing new models for healthcare delivery. These provider organizations compete to sign contracts with insurance companies, to function as "preferred providers" within insurance plans. This competition creates incentives for provider organizations to develop new care delivery strategies to reduce per capita costs while strengthening health outcomes. Some organizations are attempting to accomplish these goals through integrated care. For organizations that provide care to individuals covered under publicly funded programs (chiefly Medicare or Medicaid), this private-sector innovation is developing within the context of government-defined quality-based payment incentives and government-defined capitated payment designs. In this case, it is payment system issues (rather than regulatory issues) that play a significant role in shaping a private-sector innovation.

Integration of care can have a variety of different meanings. *Integrated care* does *not* mean that each individual healthcare practitioner interacts with patients in a silo, without a system for coordinating care. Integrated care can mean simply an addition of a case manager to examine the care that the patient is receiving and to attempt to coordinate it in some way, for example, to ensure that there is no duplicate testing or to check for medications that may interact to produce harmful effects. These efforts obviously can also reduce costs.

More generally, *integrated care* refers to team-based care in a primary care clinic, where the PCP works with a colocated behavioral health professional, such as a social worker or a clinical psychologist. This strategy can produce more efficient care for several reasons:

■ The fractionated delivery design in which physical and mental healthcare are delivered through separate care delivery systems (which are also often uncoordinated) does not offer any clear benefits.

■ Many patients presenting in primary care also have behavioral problems, such as depression and anxiety, or a lifestyle problem, such as smoking and obesity.

■ Many of these diagnoses were missed in the average, often very short (e.g., 15 minutes), traditional primary care visit.

■ Even when these diagnoses were made or suspected, the PCP making an external referral to a mental health professional usually did not work—research indicated that usually about 80% of patients failed to show up to this referral.

■ The PCPs often had an orientation to treat acute problems like strep or lacerations but did not have the time to deal with chronic disease problems like diabetes, and having a behavioral health provider on a primary care team helped the patient deal with all the psychological and behavioral complexities of managing his or her chronic disease.

■ There is some evidence that patients liked this "one-stop shopping," where both behavioral and mental health could be received under one roof.

■ There is some evidence that this integrated arrangement produced what is called "medical cost offset"—a reduction in overall healthcare costs (see O'Donohue and Maragakis, 2015).

It is also important to note that integrated care is not simply colocating traditional mental health services inside a medical setting. In an integrated care setting, the behavioral health specialists adapt to and adopt the ecology of the primary care medical practice. The behavioral health provider quickly screens and assesses, just like the PCP. If the behavioral health provider sees that the problem is complex or will require lengthy treatment, he or she refers the patient to an external mental health specialist—just as the PCP would if the cardiac problem were complex and required the specialized treatment that only a cardiologist could provide. In integrated care settings, treatment is also often brief and intermittent—three to five half-hour sessions are typical. Like primary care medicine, primary care behavioral health is touching a large number of individuals, but briefly, whereas specialty care is often touching a lower number of individuals for longer time periods.

However, there have been significant challenges to successfully designing and implementing effective integrated care practices. First, there are a set of operational questions that needed to be answered:

■ What is the proper ratio of full-time PCPs to full-time behavioral health providers? (Roughly, the answer seems to be for every three to five PCPs, there should be one behavioral care physician.)

■ What, if any, behavioral health screens should be used to identify possible behavioral health problems? (Many integrated care settings seem to be overly fixed on depression and screen for this, but then do not screen for myriad other behavioral health problems, such as anxiety, substance abuse, and personality disorders.)

■ Are there really any evidence-based protocols for the brief three to five half-hour sessions that behavioral health providers utilize?

■ Are there proper referrals for external specialty mental healthcare—and does this "case finding" make this service delivery more expensive?

■ What is the proper mix of patients the behavioral provider should be seeing—mental health problems, such as depression, versus medical problems, such as chronic disease management, versus wellness and prevention interventions?

In addition, integrated care seems to be developing the same problems that have plagued mental health practice for decades:

■ Mental health practitioners delivering interventions that are not evidence based but rather are delivered because the practitioner has become enamored with particular interventions for some reason

■ Deep debates about when psychotropic medications should be used versus when psychotherapy should be prescribed

■ Controversies concerning what type of mental health professional ought to be placed in an integrated care setting—a social worker, a master's-level psychologist, or a doctoral-level psychologist?

Thus, in integrated care a specialty-trained behavioral health provider joins the primary care medical team to help the team identify, treat, or refer behavioral health problems that are seen in the primary care delivery system. It is an important innovation and may represent savings as a patient is more accurately and more comprehensively diagnosed (e.g., medical tests are not done to search for the physical cause of fatigue when depression is diagnosed, and the fatigued is now found to be a part of the depression symptom complex), when lower-cost behavioral health services are substituted for higher-cost medical diagnostics and treatment, and when the "low-hanging fruit" of lifestyle problems, such as smoking, diet, and exercise, are targeted for intervention to produce more wellness and less sickness. However, more outcomes research is needed, and these delivery systems need to be implemented in the context of quality improvement systems to measure the degree to which they are actually both faithful to the integrated care model and producing appropriate outcomes (O'Donohue and Maragakis, 2016).

Conclusion

As we conclude this discussion of new types of providers and new roles for patients, it is important to note that these types of innovations can potentially lead to radical changes in the healthcare system.

Markets for healthcare services have traditionally been confined to local areas—partly due to preferred provider lists and state-level regulation of insurance—but these innovations may change this. HSAs may create more price-conscious patients who are willing to invest time to locate and utilize high-quality and cost-effective providers. For nonemergency care, some of these patients will be increasingly willing to travel outside their local areas to obtain care.

The wide availability of medical information on the Internet and public reporting of quality measures has the potential to produce consumer behavior changes. The role of patients in demanding particular diagnostics, medications, and/or treatments raises some of the same issues we explored when examining the managed care backlash. However, the most serious concerns may focus on the potential—and yet unknown—impact these innovations may have on individuals with low health literacy, low income, or high-cost health conditions.

In summary, the strategy of harnessing competitive market forces offers strong upside potential, but it also raises concerns about the impacts on individuals with low health literacy, low income, or high-cost health conditions. The strident political debate about health reform reflects, in part, differing assessments of the relative strengths of the positive and negative impacts of this strategy. Increased competitive vigor will highlight the importance of consumer behavior, provider quality data, licensure issues, coordination of care across multiple providers, and competition from out-of-area providers.

Chapter 8

HIT = EMR + HIE

Introduction

Building a strong health information technology (HIT) infrastructure has been a major component of the current federal strategy for increasing quality and reducing cost. Before the passage of the Affordable Care Act, the federal government provided hundreds of millions of dollars to healthcare organizations so that they could convert from paper records to electronic health records. HIT includes two components:

- electronic medical record (EMR) systems used by providers, to replace the current paper record systems, and
- health information exchange (HIE) that permits providers to exchange electronic information, even if it is generated by different proprietary EMR systems. (Systems that can exchange information through the HIE are said to be "interoperable." The telephone system provides a good analogy. We purchase—and use—cell phones that rely on a variety of operating systems. These phones are produced by several manufacturers. However, a telephone exchange permits us to call each other, regardless of the type of phone we are using). The Veterans Affairs (VA) healthcare system has some of the longest experience with EMRs that are shared among all VA providers. Empirical evidence indicates that this system has effectively generated efficiencies (Yaisawarnga and Burgess, 2006). Evidence indicating that HMOs successfully reduced the rate of preventable hospital admissions (Zhan et al., 2004) suggests that integrated care management can successfully utilize HIT to strengthen

healthcare quality and reduce expenditures. It is widely assumed that a strong infrastructure for exchanging electronic health information among independent provider organizations can support broader application of these strategies.

Congress passed the Health Information Technology for Economic and Clinical Health (HITECH) Act in 2009, to incentivize and facilitate widespread adoption of EMRs and HIE. The effort is overseen by a federal agency, the Office of the National Coordinator (ONC), within the federal Department of Health and Human Services. Most of the funds were allocated to provide subsidies to induce physicians and hospitals to purchase and implement EMR software, and to induce states to develop HIE infrastructure to facilitate exchange of electronic information across providers. To qualify for the subsidies, physicians and hospitals were required to purchase and implement EMR systems, treat a sufficient proportion of Medicaid or Medicare patients, and demonstrate Meaningful Use (MU) of these systems. To demonstrate MU, physicians must exchange electronic health information with other entities, and report data on a substantial number of new quality measures.

The idea that widespread adoption of interoperable electronic health records could boost the efficiency of the U.S. healthcare system was not new in 2009. President Bush advocated widespread adoption of interoperable electronic health records in 2004. At that time, healthcare providers were already using information technology to organize, coordinate, and streamline care. Most claims for payment were submitted in an electronic format, diagnostic test results were frequently transmitted to providers electronically, and some prescription information was sent electronically. Providers were using standard systems for coding hospital admissions (Diagnostic Related Group [DRG] codes), diagnoses (International Classification of Diseases [ICD] codes), and procedures (clinical procedural terminology [CPT] codes). Electronic claims processing systems generated large databases that were supporting substantial analyses of patterns of care and the efficacy of an array of healthcare interventions (e.g., prevention, disease management, wellness, and prenatal care programs).

Research conducted by the RAND Corporation on the potential benefits of widespread utilization of EMRs and HIE was widely discussed prior to passage of the HITECH Act in 2009 (Girosi et al., 2005; Hillestad et al., 2005). Advocates of federal subsidies and incentives for increased adoption and utilization of HIT cited the RAND predictions that expanded use of HIT could potentially generate several types of improvements:

- Coordination across multiple providers
- Reduction of duplicate tests
- Convenient clinician access to relevant patient-specific guideline information
- Efficient systems to monitor and report proportions of physician decisions that are consistent with guideline recommendations
- New types of quality reporting
- Research on process effectiveness

These studies concluded that effective use of HIT could *potentially* generate significant improvements in healthcare quality and sufficient cost savings, even after accounting for the cost to purchase, implement, and maintain the EMR and HIE systems. Similarly, Buntin and Cutler (2009) cited published estimates of the magnitude of inefficient expenditures in the U.S. healthcare system, and argued that increased utilization of HIT is an essential component of a comprehensive strategy to reduce cost and strengthen healthcare quality.

A 2008 Congressional Budget Office (CBO) report reviewed the evidence on costs and benefits of HIT, including the RAND research. This report cautioned that the RAND report provided estimates of potential cost savings, but it did not provide estimates of likely cost savings. Further, the CBO concluded that likely cost savings were substantially smaller than the potential savings noted in the RAND research. The CBO report also noted that surveys indicated that only one-fourth of physicians were using EMR systems at that time, and the adoption rate differed significantly by practice size. The adoption rate was significantly lower among small practices than large practices. In addition, area-wide HIE systems were not widely available.

Background

In this section, we consider four types of background information: alternate explanations for the low adoption rates, the logic for federal investment in the HITECH subsidies, adoption rates prior to 2009, and barriers to widespread use of HIT identified by the CBO in 2008.

If HIT Can Generate Net Benefits, Why Are Federal Subsidies Needed to Boost Adoption?

Economists suggest two broad possibilities:

1. The expected benefits of these systems might not be sufficient to justify the cost of purchasing and implementing these.
2. Market failures could exist that might block implementation of these systems.

Understanding the reasons underlying slow diffusion of HIT is important for structuring health policy. Federal intervention could be useful if the fundamental problem stems from market failures. However, federal subsidies might be unwise—or ineffective—if the fundamental problem lies in the relationship between costs and benefits.

Expected Benefits versus Costs

Some evidence suggests that the fundamental reason for the slow adoption rate was straightforward: providers may not have been convinced that the likely benefits outweigh the substantial investment of time and money required to implement HIT systems and adjust workflows sufficiently to gain benefits from the systems. Mazanec (2016) summarizes evidence indicating that EMR costs exceeded benefits gained in the first few years, for many hospitals and physicians (although the MU payments provided by the HITECH Act filled this gap for many of these organizations). Difficulties faced by organizations considering EMR adoption included

- The systems were expensive and the benefits were uncertain.
- The systems were not viewed as user-friendly.
- Implementing the new systems required significant training time and significant changes in hospital and physician work processes.

Potential Market Failures

On the other hand, three types of market failure could potentially explain the slow adoption of HIT prior to the HITECH Act:

1. Patients and healthcare payers may have low willingness to pay for improvements in healthcare quality, due to inability to accurately assess the quality of care provided by specific providers.

2. Organizations that invest in HIT may not be the beneficiaries of monetary benefits generated by those investments. For example, primary care physicians might utilize EMR-generated information to enhance the quality of care in ways that reduce inappropriate emergency department visits. Healthcare payers benefit if the affected patients are insured, and hospitals benefit if the relevant patients are uninsured. However, the current reimbursement system does not generate any benefits for the primary care physicians who made the initial investments.

3. Interdependence among disparate organizations could block adoption, if the ability to exchange information is essential to organizations that implement EMR systems. In this situation, providers would not purchase EMR systems if there were no mechanism to exchange electronic health information with other providers, and investors would not develop HIE capability because providers do not have any electronic information to exchange. This problem is not unique to the healthcare industry. Advocates of universal access to telephones in the 1970s argued that the value of any individual telephone depends on the number of other people with telephones who are potentially available for phone conversations. Economists use the term *network externalities* to describe the idea that your decision to purchase a telephone enhances the value of the phones owned by your friends.

EMRs and HIE exhibit some characteristics of *public goods*. Economists use the term *public good* to characterize a good that has two characteristics:

1. All members of a community benefit from public goods, whether they pay for the good or not. Economists use the term *nonexcludable* to describe this idea. National defense is a classic example of a public good. If the country has sufficient national defense to prevent an attack, everyone in the country benefits. It is not possible for one individual or group within a country to ensure that it is defended from attack by a foreign country, without also ensuring that all residents in the country are equally defended. In contrast, emergency medical care does not meet this criterion for categorization as a public good, as defined by economists. It may not be desirable, but it would be conceptually possible for a group to organize a system that would provide emergency care for members of the group, while refusing to provide this service to nonmembers.

2. When one individual enjoys the benefit of a public good, it does not reduce the ability of others to enjoy the good simultaneously. Economists use the term *nonrivalrous* to describe this idea. National Public Radio (NPR) is another classic example of a public good. When NPR broadcasts its 5:00 p.m. news show, any number of individuals can listen to the show on car radios, without impairing the ability of other drivers to listen at the same time. Note that ice cream cones do not exhibit this characteristic. When one individual is savoring an ice cream cone, a second individual cannot simultaneously savor the same cone—at least without affecting the first person's consumption experience.

If HIT successfully boosts healthcare quality while reducing cost, HIT would exhibit these two characteristics. First, healthcare cost reductions would be passed on to individuals in the form of lower health insurance premiums. Even if one individual refused to allow his personal health information to be exchanged via HIE, he would benefit from the reduced health insurance premium. Second, the systematic provision of high-quality care would benefit all individuals simultaneously. Once a healthcare provider begins using electronic information systems to support delivery of high-quality care, all patients could benefit.

The CBO (2008) report discussed these market failure issues, and concluded that market failures could justify federal action to subsidize and incentivize adoption of EMRs and HIE.

Rationale for Investing Taxpayer Dollars in HITECH Subsidies

Nonetheless, committing significant funds to subsidize EMR adoption and statewide HIE under the HITECH Act was a risky federal gamble. It was not clear, at that time, whether physicians would respond to the incentives to adopt EMR systems, and it was not clear whether state HIE strategies would be financially viable once the subsidies were terminated (the failure rate of early area-wide HIEs was disappointing). We might wonder, why did Congress take this risk, instead of waiting for these technologies to diffuse through the healthcare industry via market forces? The natural diffusion process would have been substantially slower, but less visible—and therefore less risky. To understand the strategic vision embedded in the HITECH Act of 2009, it is useful to examine the impacts of major technology innovations on other industries.

In the first half of the 1800s, transportation of raw materials and finished goods was slow and uncertain (Chandler, 1977). Therefore, most businesses focused on purchasing inputs and selling outputs in their immediate geographic neighborhoods. In the middle of that century, rapid railroad construction knit together diverse regions of the country, and drastically altered the economic landscape. As it connected markets in new ways, the railroad infrastructure generated a new type of vigorous competition that transformed American industry. Friedman (1999) tells a similar story in *The Lexus and the Olive Tree* about the role of Internet connections in generating new types of global commerce. Both of these innovations generated lower prices for consumers, along with vigorous competition among new types of businesses. These innovations also generated controversy, as many existing businesses found that they could not compete against the new firms that offered lower prices (perhaps because the innovators incurred lower costs because they did not build brick-and-mortar stores) and new types of goods and services.

Analysts looking at the efficiency impacts of new technology in other industries predicted or hoped that the new HIT "information highway" could potentially generate an analogous explosion of innovation and efficiency improvements in healthcare. However, the 2008 CBO report that surveyed evidence on the likely impacts of a federal HIT initiative concluded that there were no credible estimates of the overall impact of an HIT initiative.

This lack of evidence of the potential value of new HIT reflected the fact that HIT is expected to produce two types of impacts:

1. Some benefits, such as eliminating the medical transcription process (because providers presumably will enter information directly into the EMR system—although this is not universally true in actual practice), are relatively straightforward. Cost savings generated by these impacts can be estimated with reasonable confidence. However, this type of efficiency was not expected to generate sufficient cost savings to justify the expense of adopting HIT.
2. The impacts that were expected to generate more substantial benefits are far more difficult to predict. If the new HIT information highway facilitates development of new strategies for delivering and coordinating care, the benefits could be significant. However, it is difficult to estimate the value of potential innovations that do not currently exist.

The fact that proponents of the HITECH subsidies envision this technology supporting transformative change makes it difficult to conclude—even now—whether the decision to invest in the HITECH subsidies was visionary or ill-advised.

HIT Adoption Rates Prior to the HITECH Act

Estimates of the proportions of providers utilizing EMRs or HIE must be interpreted with caution, because these systems are complex and multifaceted. Some providers may use only the basic components of an EMR system, while other providers may use advanced features. Similarly, some providers may exchange only basic types of information with other providers, while others utilize HIE more intensively. Nonetheless, analysts concur that the diffusion of EMR and HIE systems among hospitals and physicians was occurring prior to the 2009 HITECH Act. While large hospitals and large physician practices were more likely to implement EMR systems than smaller organizations, the numbers of organizations utilizing EMR systems had been increasing gradually. However, substantial numbers of healthcare providers were still relying on paper medical records: 60% of hospitals owned by hospital systems were using two key features of EMR technology—physician documentation and computerized practitioner order entry (CPOE)—while 48% of the smaller independent hospitals were using these features of EMR systems (Dranove et al., 2015).

Challenges

The 2008 CBO also identified challenges hindering widespread adoption of EMRs and HIE, which continue to raise issues today:

■ Exchanging health information across provider organizations requires matching information about individual patients to ensure that the test result for the patient named "John Smith" is assigned to the health information record for the correct individual with that name. Individual provider organizations have systems for assigning medical record numbers to records for individual patients within each organization, but the United States does not have a system of unique patient identifiers that are common across organizations. In the past, Medicare utilized Social

Security numbers for this purpose. However, the 2015 Medicare Access and CHIP Reauthorization Act mandates that the Centers for Medicare and Medicaid Services (CMS) stop using Social Security numbers for this purpose by 2019.

- On a wider scale, there is a continuing lack of clearly specified technical standards for information exchange. This leads to increased costs for information exchange across vendor platforms, and for connecting EMR systems to HIE platforms.

- Patient privacy and confidentiality issues are ongoing. Some states permit patients to opt out of HIE systems, while other states require HIE to manage systems to allow patients to opt in to these systems. Some patient advocates argue that patients should be permitted to designate the precise set of information that may be exchanged, and the precise set of approved recipients for each type of information. Interstate HIE will have to address interstate variations in requirements.

- The outlook for the long-term financial sustainability of the statewide HIE incentivized under the HITECH Act is unclear.

- Information in an individual patient's record includes data entered by an array of providers, diagnostic labs, and pharmacies. To ensure data integrity, HIE organizations must implement processes to identify and correct data errors. The specification of appropriate opportunities for patients to request changes or corrections is not clear.

- The software varied in quality on important dimensions such as ease of use, reliability, and options, and some of the electronic health record (EHR) programs were difficult to use and not reliable.

Impact of the HITECH Act

In this section, we consider the impact of the HITECH Act on HIT adoption, the impacts of HIT on outcomes, and the evolution of enterprise HIE operating alongside the statewide HIE organizations that were subsidized under the HITECH Act.

Impact on HIT Adoption

Swain et al. (2015) reported a substantial increase in hospital engagement in HIE following implementation of the HITECH subsidies and incentives.

In 2015, 75% of hospitals exchanged information with hospitals outside their hospital systems, compared with only 15% engaged in this activity in 2008.

Dranove et al. (2015) provide detailed analysis of hospital EMR adoption, which is a precursor to HIE. This analysis supports two conclusions:

1. Some hospitals did respond to the HITECH subsidies by implementing new EMR systems; however, the increase in adoption was small.

    In 2011, 76% of hospitals were using the physician documentation and CPOE features of EMR systems. The model developed by Dranove et al. (2015) predicts that 66% of hospitals would have been using these EMR features in 2011 if the pre-HITECH trends had continued without introduction of the HITECH subsidies and MU incentives. Without the HITECH subsidies, 76% of hospitals would have been using these features two years later, in 2013.

2. The HITECH program was also costly.

    The average federal subsidy expenditure per additional hospital EMR implementation was $47 million. Individual hospitals did not receive payments of this magnitude. However, hospitals that demonstrated MU of HIT were potentially eligible for HITECH subsidy payments (if they also met the additional criteria), whether they implemented EMR systems prior to 2009 or after 2009. Thus, a substantial portion of the subsidy payments went to hospitals that were already implementing EMR systems prior to passage of the HITECH Act. Supporters of the HITECH strategy argue that the subsidy payments to pre-2009 adopters were useful because the subsidies incentivized these hospitals to use more advanced features of their EMR systems in order to meet the MU requirements.

Impact on Outcomes

Evidence that increased utilization of HIT strengthened healthcare cost and quality outcomes is mixed and inconclusive. Rahurkar et al. (2015) report the results of a meta-analysis that examined 27 studies of the impact of HIE on cost, utilization, and quality of care. These authors conclude,

> Overall, 57% of published analyses reported some benefit from HIE. However, articles employing study designs with strong internal validity, such as randomized controlled trials or

quasi-experiments, were significantly less likely than others to associate HIE with benefits. Among six articles with strong internal validity, one study reported paradoxical negative effects, three studies found no effect, and two studies reported that HIE led to benefits.... Overall, little generalizable evidence currently exists regarding benefits attributable to HIE.

Two studies estimate impacts of hospital IT on efficiency and patient mortality using a different strategy (Lee et al., 2012; McCullough et al., 2013). Using detailed analysis of large data sets, these authors reach two conclusions:

1. A hospital EMR generates statistically significant positive impacts on efficiency, but the effects are small.
2. While hospital IT does not impact mortality for all patients, it does generate statistically significant mortality reductions for complex patients.

These HIT impacts are valuable, but they do not appear to affect healthcare cost and quality on the scale envisioned by analysts who predicted that HIT infrastructure could support transformational change in the healthcare industry. However, it is important to note the dates on these studies. Some analysts expect the impacts to grow over time, as hospitals gain experience utilizing the information provided by HIT and as the HIT systems mature.

Statewide versus Private-Sector HIE

Progress toward building HIT infrastructure is occurring in two separate, but overlapping, realms. Private healthcare providers, particularly large hospitals, large physician groups, and integrated provider organizations, have been implementing EMR systems and exploring strategies for using the new information as a tool to strengthen patient care and generate efficiencies for many years. Some of these organizations are building systems to exchange information among providers that are part of the provider group. For example, a hospital might purchase EMR software and offer software licenses, data warehousing, and IT support to physicians who admit patients to that hospital. Alternately, providers participating in an accountable care organization (ACO) have an incentive to develop an efficient system for exchanging information among participants in that ACO. These private-sector HIE initiatives are known as "enterprise HIE."

Investing in enterprise HIE may yield two benefits for the hospitals organizing these efforts, compared with the strategy of relying on a statewide HIE. First, a hospital-supported HIE is specifically designed to accomplish tasks that are strategically important for that organization. Hospitals indicate that they value the ability to tailor the system to meet strategic priorities, and they value the ability to act in a timely manner, without working through the slower decision process that is likely to occur in a multistakeholder statewide HIE organization (Vest and Kash, 2016). Second, obtaining value from the HIT infrastructure may require substantial organizational effort to standardize and coordinate information entry and analysis processes. It may be easier to structure these processes within a small group of providers, compared with the task of achieving efficiencies among a larger and more diverse group.

Advocates of statewide HIE express concern that these organizations may be creating "neighborhood" HIE rather than statewide HIE. Interviews of HIE organization leaders suggest that individual hospital creation of enterprise HIE weakens the business case for those hospitals to support statewide HIE organizations (Vest and Kash, 2016). This issue is important because the long-term financial viability of statewide HIE organizations, that were subsidized under the HITECH Act, is not clear. In a separate national survey conducted in 2014, Adler-Milstein et al. (2016) found that half of the surveyed statewide HIE organizations reported that they were not generating sufficient revenue to cover operating costs. Further, they found fewer statewide HIEs operating in 2014 ($n = 106$) than the number found during a similar survey in 2012 ($n = 119$).

Conclusions

Christenson et al. (2009) described the ongoing process of substantive innovation and industry restructuring that is occurring in the healthcare industry. HIT could provide essential infrastructure to support this innovation process. For example, private-sector initiatives, such as the High Value Healthcare Collaborative (HVHC), are developing methodologies for using shared EMR data to support analytics. The HVHC described its goal as follows:

> The HVHC is a provider learning network committed to improving health care value through data and collaboration. Members of this organization contribute data that is merged with Medicare claims

data, to support analysis of strategies for improving healthcare efficiency and quality.

Founding members of this organization include the high-profile healthcare innovators Intermountain Healthcare, the Mayo Clinic, and The Dartmouth Institute. HVHC is partially funded by a 3-year Center for Medicare and Medicaid Innovation (CMMI) grant. Under this grant, the HVHC will use data analytics to generate savings by improving quality of care for patients with specific clinical conditions, such as congestive heart failure or diabetes. Millenson (2006) summarized the competitive challenge embraced by organizations such as HVHC: "Our ultimate challenge is [to figure out] how to use IT as an enabling tool to supplement the art of medicine."

Cutler (2010) analyzed factors that impede innovation in the healthcare industry and concluded that two features of our current system create significant inertia:

1. Medicare and Medicaid payment systems tend to focus on the volume of care inputs, rather than the value of treatment outputs.
2. It is difficult to modify these payment systems because we do not have sufficient information about the quality of care.

Efforts are underway to address both of these issues. CMS is working to move toward value-based payment systems, and payers are working to use the new information generated by EMRs and HIE to create meaningful measures of care quality.

The new HIT is also welcomed by advocates of strategies to support individual decisions, as they select providers and insurers that deliver high-quality and cost-effective care. To date, consumers have not had sufficient information to compare prices and quality metrics across healthcare treatment options. New HIT data could potentially support user-friendly systems to help individuals engage in meaningful comparisons of quality and price across providers.

Conclusion to Section II

In this section, we examined several efficiency strategies and explored the promises and challenges related to these innovations. In Chapter 4, we explored strategies to align incentives through payment system redesign. We conclude that current Medicare rate structures create inefficient silos, that some proposed cost-cutting efforts may create unintended consequences related to provider competition, and that any strategies to address the rate-setting issues must include a quality component. In Chapter 5, we looked at lessons learned from the era of managed care in hopes of anticipating and possibly avoiding similar issues with the expansion of accountable care organizations (ACOs) and medical homes. Consumer protection is a complex issue, definitions of *quality* will need to be redesigned, and market power, solvency issues, adverse selection, and public reporting of provider quality measures must be addressed. Chapter 6 revealed that wellness programs, preventive care, and disease management will only achieve their promised results if we can identify cost-effective programs and find ways to incentivize participation by the individuals who could most benefit from them. Chapter 7 explored new types of providers emerging in the healthcare industry (e.g., retail clinics and specialty hospitals), and the new role of the consumer in this "disruptive innovation" environment. We noted that these innovations present opportunities to gain new types of efficiencies, and they also present issues related to competition, access, and the financial viability of safety net providers. Finally, in Chapter 8, we discussed the potential for health information technology (HIT) to organize, coordinate, and streamline care. However issues related to federal funding to incentivize HIT adoption, barriers related to inadequate infrastructure, and patient privacy challenges need to be addressed in order to fully realize the positive impact of this strategy.

After Section I demonstrated that we must increase efficiency within the healthcare system, Section II provided an overview of a diverse array of public-sector and private-sector strategies designed to achieve this goal. Change is occurring; we should expect

■ More competition
■ More consumer financial responsibility
■ More efforts to design incentive structures to spark and support innovation

Identified issues that must be addressed to fully actualize these efficiencies include

■ Competition is not compatible with cross-subsidy systems (a direct general tax subsidy is needed).
■ More consumer "direction" may imply more inequality, particularly for those individuals with low health literacy.
■ The Centers for Medicare and Medicaid Services (CMS) incentive structure issue is complex because it is difficult for government to play this role—because of the strong role of private-sector innovation.
■ Government regulation will have to change—to allow the innovations that could deliver on the promises for a better healthcare system (e.g., the Stark law and legal liability constraints).

Conclusion

As we experience substantial changes in the way we access and finance healthcare in the coming years, your familiarity with economic issues and trends will help you navigate these changes in ways that best serve you and your patients. Armed with this perspective, you will be able to assess practice opportunities and threats, identify viable strategies for adapting to the changes, participate in policy debates, and identify sound policy options. Over the course of this book, we identified pressures for change within our healthcare system, efficiency strategies, "lessons learned" from earlier attempts, and new pressures generated by these new initiatives.

In Section I, we identified issues surrounding access, cost, and quality, and in Section II, we explored potential options for addressing these issues within an economic framework. Specifically:

- In Chapter 1, our focus was on issues of the uninsured, who they were, and why those with access to insurance don't always take up the insurance offer. We then went on to explore solution options such as employer mandates, expanded public programs, and offering tax credits to purchase health insurance.
- In Chapter 2, we looked at issues related to cost of healthcare and concluded that the main driver of escalating healthcare costs is technology. Three possible solutions to check the increasing cost for healthcare include reducing research and development, accepting reduced consumption of goods that are not healthcare related, or entertaining some rationing scheme.
- We concluded Section I with a discussion on issues related to quality in Chapter 3. We explored data that suggest that other countries achieve better health outcomes for less money, looked at the impact medical

errors have on quality of care, and discovered regional variations in quality and utilization. We then reviewed current solutions to the quality issues, which included Total Quality Management (TQM), clinical pathways, and clinical guidelines.

In Section I, we concluded that that these three issues can only be resolved by increasing the efficiencies within our healthcare system.

In Section II, we focused our discussion on strategies for increasing efficiency, and the potential benefits and challenges of each. We based this exploration on current proposals as well as previous attempts to innovate our healthcare system from a "lessons learned" perspective:

- The problems within our healthcare system are long-standing and complex.
- All healthcare providers must understand the issues and be actively engaged in finding and implementing the solutions.
- "Lessons learned" from other industries and past efforts to fix our healthcare system must be applied to new innovations and policy proposals in order to achieve the benefits we seek.

As you face the challenges that lie ahead, you can rely on what you have learned from the content of this book to assist you in evaluating and negotiating the ever-changing healthcare landscape. The changes will not be smooth; they will generate controversy. As new controversies arise, evidence-based assessments of the debates and policy proposals will help you positively and proactively navigate these changes.

We close with three illustrations of the insights into policy controversies that can be gained by applying the ideas discussed in this book.

1. In 2017, the Republican proposal for replacing the PPACA included a provision to permit health insurers to increase the differential between premiums for policies purchased by young adults and premiums for policies purchased by older (non elderly) adults. What forces underlie such a proposal? As we noted in Chapter 1, average healthcare expenditures for older (non elderly) adults are five times greater than average healthcare expenditures for younger adults. Under the PPACA, the older-adult premiums could not be more than three times the premiums for policies offered to younger-adults.

The economics lens for comparing the two policy options is straightforward:

■ The PPACA strategy implies that younger adults will subsidize health-care expenditures for older adults and the proposed change would allow health insurers to eliminate this subsidy by setting premiums to cover expected expenditures in each age category.

■ Economic analysis could add more detail about the dollar amounts of the subsidy, the impact of the PPACA-mandated subsidy on premiums for policies offered to young adults (young-adult premiums will be higher under the PPACA strategy than under the proposed change), and the impact of the higher young-adult premiums on the willingness of those young adults to purchase insurance.

■ Economic analysis could also estimate the impacts of the PPACA-mandated subsidy and the proposed change on premiums offered to older (non elderly) adults (the older-adult premiums will be lower under the PPACA strategy), and the impact of the lower older-adult premiums on the willingness of those individuals to purchase insurance.

■ Finally, economic data provides summary statistics on the relative incomes of individuals in the two age groups.

The information provided by economic theory and evidence can inform this policy debate but it cannot settle the issue. Others will view the issue through other lenses, that focus on social cohesion or the health benefits offered by healthcare delivered to individuals across the age spectrum. The value of such social goals is properly debated in the political arena, while the economics information provides a framework for assessing the costs of pursuing such social goals. Economic analysis can clarify the trade-offs among those goals.

2. The PPACA expanded the role of Health Savings Accounts (HSAs) in the U.S. health insurance system, and the 2017 Republican proposal for replacing the PPACA placed even greater emphasis HSAs. Suppose, for example, an employer is willing to allocate $6000 annually, per employee, to cover the employee's healthcare expenditures. That employer could either use the $6000 to purchase a traditional insurance policy or the employer could use some of that $6000 to purchase a high-deductible catastrophic health insurance policy and deposit the rest of the money in an HSA that would be owned by that employee. Most employees would not spend enough money on healthcare, in most years, to meet their deductibles. In this situation, the employees

would use the funds deposited in the HSA account to pay directly for each healthcare episode. Under either insurance strategy, most of that employee's healthcare expenditures would be covered by the employer's $6000. Funds remaining in the HSA at the end of the year would remain in the account for future years.

Proponents of high-deductible catastrophic health insurance with HSAs hope to encourage consumers to "price-compare" before accessing healthcare services, thus incentivizing healthcare providers to offer lower, competitive prices. Economists provide information about the impacts of the two incentive structures on healthcare utilization patterns: When individuals switch from traditional insurance to an HSA-plus-catastrophic insurance policy, healthcare expenditures decrease on average. Economists and business strategy experts also provide evidence from dramatic efficiency gains achieved in non healthcare industries. This evidence suggests that consumer shopping for low prices is an important driver of innovations that generate efficiency gains.

Economists may also provide analyses of:

- The difficulty of "shopping" for goods such as healthcare for which quality characteristics are difficult to observe, and implications of this shopping on product and service quality, and
- The level of healthcare literacy required for this type of shopping, consumer habits related to searching for relevant information, and the ability of technology applications to facilitate the process of acquiring relevant information.

These pieces of economic analysis can inform the debate. However, it will not be realistic to expect precise estimates of the potential long-term benefits of increased consumer awareness of healthcare costs. Proponents predict that increased consumer "shopping" will facilitate and fuel an efficiency revolution in the healthcare industry, but the magnitude, timing, and "shape" of such a revolution cannot be predicted with accuracy. In the face of this uncertainty, individuals viewing the issue through other lenses may place higher priority on non-efficiency goals, such as ensuring consumer protection for vulnerable groups.

3. The PPACA sought to increase the quality of healthcare through a greater emphasis on incentives and penalties for both individual providers and healthcare organizations. High-quality performers will have opportunities to receive greater reimbursement through Medicare and Medicaid, while low performers will face lower reimbursements and

possible penalties. While few disagree that improving quality is a good thing, many question the potential for improving quality through the specific strategies outlined in the PPACA.

Examining the potential impact of this policy on hospitals through an economic lens can help inform policymakers about questions raised by this strategy:

- Do we have a set of robust quality measures that support meaningful analysis of healthcare quality? There has been vigorous debate on the specific measures that will be used and the confounding factors that complicate this analysis.
- Are hospitals that admit and treat relatively complex patients unfairly penalized under current policy? Hospitals located in more urban areas and teaching hospitals may be particularly vulnerable.
- Do the reporting system requirements to collect, monitor, and report these quality measures place greater financial pressure on hospitals that are already financially constrained?
- If low performing hospitals face reduced reimbursement, will they be able to invest in better processes, technology, and employees that can ultimately generate better outcomes?

All health policies have the potential for unintended consequences. Examining the potential economic impact of these policies prior to enacting them can help inform the debates, expose potential "trade-offs," and ultimately lead to more effective policies.

References

Abraham, J. M., and Feldman, R. 2010. What will happen if employers drop health insurance? A simulation of employees' willingness to purchase insurance in the individual market. *National Tax Journal* 63(2): 191–213.

ACNM Department of Advocacy and Government Affairs Grassroots Advocacy Resources. State fact sheet: Alabama American College of Nurse-Midwives. Silver Spring, MD: American College of Nurse-Midwives. Retrieved from http://www.midwife.org/acnm/files/ccLibraryFiles/Filename/000000005600/ACNMStateFactSheets8-21-15.pdf.

Adams, A., Ekelund, R., and Jackson, J. 2003. Occupational licensing of a credence good: The regulation of midwifery. *Southern Economic Journal* 69(3): 659–675. doi: 10.2307/1061700.

Adler, N. E., Boyce, T., Chesney, M. A., Cohen, S., Folkman S., Kahn R. L., and Syme S. L. 1994. Socioeconomic status and health. *The Challenge of the gradient. American Psychologist* 49: 15–24.

Adler, N. E., and Coriell, M. 1997. Socioeconomic status and women's health. In Health care for women: Psychological, social, and behavioral influences, ed. S. J. Gallant, G. P. Keita, and R. Royak-Schaler, Washington, DC: American Psychological Association, p 11–23.

Adler-Milstein, J., Lin S. C., and Jha, A. K. 2016. The number of health information exchange efforts is declining, leaving the viability of broad clinical data exchange uncertain. *Health Affairs* 35(7): 1278–1285.

Ahmed, A., and Fincham, J. E. 2010. Physician office vs retail clinic: Patient preferences in care seeking for minor illnesses. *Annals of Family Medicine* 8(2): 117–123.

Aizer, A. 2007. Public health insurance, program take-up, and child health. *Review of Economics and Statistics* 89: 400–415.

Aizer, A., and Grogger, J. 2003. Parental Medicaid expansions and health insurance coverage. National Bureau of Economic Research Working Paper 9907. Cambridge, MA: National Bureau of Economic Research.

Akerlof, G. A. 1970. The market for "lemons": Quality uncertainty and the market mechanism. *Quarterly Journal of Economics* 84(3): 488–500.

Akerlof, G. A. 1991. Procrastination and obedience. *American Economic Review* 81(2): 1–19.

American Academy of Nurse Practitioners. 2017. State practice environment. Austin, TX: American Academy of Nurse Practitioners. Retrieved from https://www.aanp.org/legislation-regulation/state-legislation/ state-practice-environment.

American College of Physicians. 2012. What is the patient-centered medical home? Washington, DC: American College of Physicians. Retrieved from http://www. acponline.org/running_practice/pcmh/understanding/what.htm.

American Diabetes Association. 2012. Economic Costs of Diabetes in the U.S. in 2012.. *Diabetes Care 2013 Apr.* 33(4): 1033–1046. Retrieved from https://doi. org/10.2337/dc12-2625.

American Diabetes Association. 2008b. Standards of medical care in diabetes—2008. *Diabetes Care* 31(Suppl. 1): S12–S54. Retrieved from https:// doi.org/10.2337/dc08-S012.

Anand, G. 2009. The Henry Ford of heart surgery: In India, a factory model for hospitals is cutting costs and yielding profits. *Wall Street Journal*, November 25. Retrieved from http://online.wsj.com/article/SB125875892887958111.html.

Anderson, A. 2017. Sears's bankruptcy and auto repair AG settlements. Retrieved from http://www.law.columbia.edu/center_program/ag?exclusive=filemgr. download&file_id=92512&crtcontentdisposition.

Anderson, G. 2004. *Chronic Conditions: Making the Case for Ongoing Care.* Baltimore, MD: Johns Hopkins University.

Bachrach, D., Frohlich, J., Garcimonde, A., and Nevitt, K. 2015. *Building a Culture of Health: The Value Proposition of Retail Clinics.* Princeton, NJ: Robert Wood Johnson Foundation.

Baicker, K., Cutler, D., and Song, Z. 2010. Workplace wellness programs can generate savings. *Health Affairs* 29(2): 304–311.

Bansak, C., and Raphael, S. 2006. The effects of state policy design features on take-up and crowd-out rates for the State Children's Health Insurance Program. *Journal of Policy Analysis and Management* 26: 149–175.

Barro, J. R., Huckman, R. S., and Kessler, D. P. 2006. The effects of cardiac specialty hospitals on the cost and quality of medical care. *Journal of Health Economics* 25: 702.

Berg, W. 2010. Benefits of screening mammography. *Journal of the American Medical Association* 303(2): 168–169.

Bipartisan Policy Center and Center for the Study of the American Electorate. (2012). Report on the turnout and registration in the American election, 2012. Washington, DC, Bipartisan Policy Center.

Blumberg, L. J., Buettgens, M., Feder, J., and Holahan, J. 2011. Why employers will continue to provide health insurance: The impact of the Affordable Care Act. Washington, DC: Urban Institute, February 1.

Blumenthal, D., Abrams, M., and Nuzum, R. 2015. The Affordable Care Act at 5 years. *New England Journal of Medicine* 372: 2451–2458.

Bono, E. 1985. *Six Thinking Hats.* New York: Little Brown and Company.

Bourdon, K. H., Rae, D. S., Narrow, W. E., Manderschild, R. W., and Regier, D. A. 1994. National prevalence and treatment of mental and addictive disorders. In *Mental Health: United States*, ed. R. W. Mandershild, and A. Sonnenschein. Washington, DC: Center for Mental Health Services.

Brown, J. G. 1995. Memorandum from the Department of Health and Human Services, Inspector General.

Buchmueller, T., Cooper, P., Simon, K., and Vistnes, J. 2005. The effect of SCHIP expansions on health insurance decisions by employers. *Inquiry* 42(3): 218–231. Retrieved from http://www.jstor.org/stable/29773202.

Bundorf, M. K., Levin, J. D., and Mahoney, N. 2008. Pricing and welfare in health plan choice. National Bureau of Economic Research Working Paper 14153. Cambridge, MA: National Bureau of Economic Research.

Buntin, M. B., and Cutler, D. 2009. The two trillion dollar solution saving money by modernizing the health care system. Washington, DC: Center for American Progress. Retrieved from https://www.americanprogress.org/issues/healthcare/reports/2009/06/24/6168/the-two-trillion-dollar-solution/.

Bureau of Labor Statistics. 2010. Preliminary multifactor productivity trends. Washington, DC: Bureau of Labor Statistics. Retrieved from http://www.bls.gov/news.release/pdf/prod3.pdf.

Business. 1999. MCI WorldCom Inc.: Company profile, information, business description, history, background information on MCI WorldCom, Inc. Retrieved from http://www.referenceforbusiness.com/history2/10/MCI-WorldCom-Inc.html.

Business Planning Solutions Global Insight Advisory Services Division. 2005. The economic impact of Wal-Mart. Washington, DC: Government Printing Office, November. Retrieved from http://www.ihsglobalinsight.com/publicDownload/genericContent/11-03-05_walmart.pdf.

Cabinet Office Behavioural Insights Team. 2010. Applying behavioural insight to health. London: Cabinet Office Behavioural Insights Team. Retrieved from http://www.cabinetoffice.gov.uk/sites/default/files/resources/403936_BehaviouralInsight_acc.pdf.

Calabresi, G., and Bobbitt, P. 1978. Tragic Choices. New York: W.W. Norton & Company.

Caloyeras, J. P., Lui, H., Exum, E., Broderick, M., and Mattke, S. 2014. Managing manifest diseases, but not health risks, saved PepsiCo money over seven years. *Health Affairs* 33(1): 124–131. doi: 10.1377/hlthaff.2013.0625.

Canadian Institute for Health Information. 2017. National health expenditures: How much does Canada spend on health care? Ottawa: Canadian Institute for Health Information, February. Retrieved from https://www.cihi.ca/en/nhex2016-topic4.

Carroll, A. 2012. JAMA forum: the iron triangle of healthcare: access, cost, and quality. *The JAMA Forum*, October 3. Retrieved from http://newsatjama.jama.com/category/the-jama-forum.

Cartwright-Smith, L., and Rosenbaum, S. J. 2009. Fair process in physician performance rating systems: Overview and analysis of Colorado's physician designation disclosure act. BNA's Health Care Policy Report. Arlington, VA: BNA.

Cavanaugh, S. 2014. ACOs moving ahead. The CMS Blog, December 22. Retrieved from http://aspenhealthcareconsulting.com/content/acos-moving-ahead.

Centers for Disease Control and Prevention. 2013. Morbidity and Mortality Weekly report: CDC health disparities and inequities report. Vol. 62, no. 3. Atlanta: Centers for Disease Control and Prevention, 1–189.

Centers for Medicare and Medicaid Services. 2015. National Health Expenditures 2015 Highlights. Retrieved from https://www.cms.gov/Research-Statistics-Data-and-Systems/Statistics-Trends-and-Reports/NationalHealthExpendData/Downloads/highlights.pdf.

Centers for Medicare and Medicaid Services 2016a. The Boards of Trustees Federal Hospital Insurance and Federal Supplementary Medical Insurance Trust Funds. The 2016 annual report of the boards of trustees of the federal hospital insurance and federal supplementary medical insurance trust funds. Retrieved from http://www.cms.gov/Research-Statistics Data-and-Systems/Statistics-Trends-and-Reports/ReportsTrustFunds/downloads/tr2010.pdf.

Centers for Medicare and Medicaid Services. 2016b. Medicare Trustees Report Shows Continued Slow Cost Growth, June 22. Retrieved from https://www.cms.gov/Newsroom/MediaReleaseDatabase/Press-releases/2016-Press-releases-items/2016-06-22.html.

Chandler, A. D. 1977. *The Visible Hand: The Managerial Revolution in American Business*. 4th ed. Cambridge, MA: Harvard University Press.

Chandra, A., and Skinner, J. 2011. Technology growth and expenditure growth in health care. National Bureau of Economic Research Working Paper 16953. Cambridge, MA: National Bureau of Economic Research. Retrieved from http://www.nber.org/papers/w16953.

Chen, K. 2002. Railroad to settle EEOC litigation over genetic test. *Wall Street Journal*, May 9.

Christensen, C. M., Grossman, J. H., and Hwang, J. 2008. *The Innovator's Prescription: A Disruptive Solution for Health Care*. 1st ed. New York: McGraw-Hill.

Christenson, J., Andrusiek, D., Everson-Stewart, S., Kudenchuk, P., Hostler, D., Powell, J., Callaway, C. W., et al. 2009. Chest compression fraction determines survival in patients with out-of-hospital ventricular fibrillation. *Circulation* 120(13): 1241–1247.

Claxton, G., and Damico, A. 2011. Snapshots: Employer health insurance costs and worker compensation. Menlo Park, CA: Henry J. Kaiser Family Foundation, February 27.

Clemens J., and Gottlieb, J. D. 2014. Do physicians' financial incentives affect medical treatment and patient health? *American Economic Review*, 104(4): 1320–1349.

Cohen, J. T., Neumann, P. J., and Weinstein, M. C. 2008. Does preventive care save money? Health economics and the presidential candidates. *New England Journal of Medicine* 358: 661–663.

Cohen, R.A. 2017. Long-term trends in health insurance: Estimates from the National Health Interview Survey, United States, 1968–2015. National Center for

Health Statistics. February. Retrieved from https://www.cdc.gov/nchs/health_policy/coverage_and_access.htm.

Collins, S. R., Gunja, M., Doty, M. M., and Beutel, S. 2015. How high is Americas health care cost burden? New York: Commonwealth Fund, November 20.

Committee on Quality of Health Care in America, Institute of Medicine. 2001. *Crossing the Quality Chasm: A New Health System for the 21st Century.* Washington, DC: National Academy Press.

Commonwealth Fund. 2012. *Commission on a High Performance Healthcare System. Rising to the Challenge: Results from a Scorecard on Local Health System Performance.* New York: Commonwealth Fund.

Congressional Budget Office. 2008. Key issues in analyzing major health insurance proposals. Washington, DC: Congressional Budget Office, December. Retrieved from http://www.cbo.gov/sites/default/files/cbofiles/ftpdocs/99xx/doc9924/12-18-keyissues.pdf.

Congressional Budget Office. 2016. Key issues in analyzing major health insurance proposals. Washington, DC: Congressional Budget Office, November 4.

Congressional Budget Office. 2017. The 2017 Long-Term Budget Outlook, March. Retrieved from https://www.cbo.gov/system/files/115th-congress-2017-2018/reports/52480-ltbo.pdf.

Conklin, A., Morris, Z. S., and Nolte, E. 2010. *Involving the Public in Healthcare Policy: An Update of the Research Evidence and Proposed Evaluation Framework.* Cambridge: RAND Europe.

Conover, C. J., and Sloan, F. A. 1998. Does removing certificate-of-need regulations lead to a surge in health care spending? *Journal of Health Politics, Policy and Law* 23(3): 455–481. doi: 10.1215/03616878-23-3-455.

Consumer Purchase Disclosure Project. 2008. Patient chart for physician performance measurement, reporting and tearing programs. San Francisco.

Coriell, M., and Adler, N. E. 1996. Socioeconomic status and women's health: How do we measure SES among women? *Women's Health* 2(3): 141–156.

Cox, C., Levitt, L., and Claxton, G. 2017. Insurer financial performance in the early years of the Affordable Care Act. April 24. Menlo Park, CA: Henry J. Kaiser Family Foundation.

Cox, C., Semanskee, A., Claxton, G., and Levitt, L. 2016. Explaining health care reform: Risk adjustment, reinsurance, and risk corridors. October 5. Menlo Park, CA: Henry J. Kaiser Family Foundation. Retrieved from http://kff.org/health-reform/issue-brief/explaining-health-care-reform-risk-adjustment-reinsurance-and-risk-corridors/.

Cubanski, J., and Schauffler, H. 2002. Mandated health insurance benefits: Tradeoffs among benefits, coverage, and costs? U.S. California Health Policy.

Cunningham, P., Rudowitz, R., Young, K., Garfield, R., and Foutz, J. 2016. Understanding Medicaid hospital payments and the impact of recent policy changes. June 9. Menlo Park, CA: Henry J. Kaiser Family Foundation.

Cutler, M. D., and McClellan, M. 2001. Is technological change in medicine worth it? When costs and benefits are weighed together, technological advances have proved to be worth far more than their costs. *Health Affairs* 20: 11–29.

Cutler, D. M, McClellan, M., and Newhouse, J. P. 1998. What has increased medical-care spending bought?. *American Economic Review* 82(2): 132–136.

Cutler, D. M., McClellan, M., and Newhouse, J. P. 2000. How does managed care do it? *RAND Journal of Economics* 31(3): 526–548.

Cutler, D. 2010. Where are the health care entrepreneurs? The failure of organizational innovation in health care. National Bureau of Economic Research Working Paper 16030. Cambridge, MA: National Bureau of Economic Research.

Dafny, L., Duggan, M., and Ramanarayanan, S. 2009. Paying a premium on your premium? Consolidation in the U.S. health insurance industry. *American Economic Review* 102(2): 1161–1185.

Darby, M., and Karni, E. 1973. Free competition and the optimal amount of fraud. *Journal of Law and Economics* 16(1): 67–88.

DeAngelis, C. D., and Fontanarosa, P. B. 2010. US Preventive Services Task Force and breast cancer screening. *Journal of the American Medical Association* 303(2): 172–173.

Deming, W. E. 1993. *The New Economics for Industry, Government & Education.* Cambridge, MA: Massachusetts Institute of Technology Center for Advanced Engineering Study.

Dennett, C. 2017. A healthy lifestyle doesn't guarantee a long life, but it will add life to your years. *Washington Post*, April 18.

Dorning, M. 2010. Obama adopts behavioral economics. *Blumberg Businessweek*, June 24. Retrieved from https://www.bloomberg.com/news/articles/2010-06-24/obama-adopts-behavioral-economics.

Doyle, J. J., Jr., Ewer, S. M., and Wagner, T. H. 2008. Returns to physician human capital: Analyzing patients randomized to physician teams. National Bureau of Economic Research Working Paper 14174. Cambridge, MA: National Bureau of Economic Research.

Dranove, D., Garthwaite, C., Bingyang L., and Ody, C. 2015. Investment subsidies and the adoption of electronic medical records. *Journal of Health Economics* 44: 309–319.

Eddy, D. M., Hasselblad, V., McGivney, W., and Hendee, W. 1988. The value of mammography screening in women under age 50 years. *Journal of the American Medical Association* 259: 1512–1519.

Edington, D. 2009. *Zero Trends: Health as a Serious Economic Strategy.* Ann Arbor, MI: Health Management Research Center.

Editors. 2009. Auto workers: Rescue them or not? *New York Times*, March 9.

Einhorn, B. 2008. Medical travel is going to be part of the solution. *Bloomberg Business Week*, March 17.

Elbel, B., Kersh, R., Brescoll, V. L., and Dixon, L. B. 2009. Calorie labeling and food choices: A first look at the effects on low-income people in New York City. *Health Affairs* 28(6): w1110–w1112. Retrieved from https://www.ncbi.nlm.nih.gov/pubmed/19808705.

Emanuel, E. J., and Fuchs, V. R. 2009. Who really pays for health care? The myth of shared responsibility. *Journal of the American Medical Association* 299(9): 1057.

Enthoven, A. C., and Singer, S. J. 1998. The managed care backlash and the task force in California. *Health Affairs* 17(4): 95–110.

Every, N. R., Hochman, J., Becker, R., Kopecky, S., and Cannon, C. P. 2000. Archived: Breast cancer: Screening. Final update summary: Breast cancer: Screening—US Preventive Services Task Force. Washington, DC: U.S. Department of Health and Human Services, U.S. Preventive Services Task Force.

Federal Reserve Bank of San Francisco. 2003. Federal Reserve Bank San Francisco economic letter: The fiscal problem of the 21st century. Federal Reserve Bank of San Francisco, September 13.

Federal Trade Commission and Department of Justice. 2004. *Improving Health Care: A Dose of Competition.* Washington, DC: Federal Trade Commission and Department of Justice.

Feeg, V. D. 1996. The bittersweet maternal health policy victory. *Pediatric Nursing* 22(5): 366–445.

Feinstein, C. D. 1990. Deciding whether to test student athletes for drug use. *Interfaces* 20(3): 80–87.

Fernandez, D. 2008. Alabama "obesity penalty" stirs debate. CBS News, August 25. Retrieved from http://www.cbsnews.com/news/alabama-obesity-penalty-stirs-debate.

Fisher, E. S., and Bell, J. E. 2010. Dartmouth Atlas project finds substantial variation in joint replacement surgery. States News Service. Dartmouth Institute for Health Policy and Clinical Practice.

Fisher, E. S., Bynum, J. P., and Skinner, J. S. 2009. Slowing the growth of health care costs: Lessons from regional variation. *New England Journal of Medicine* 360: 849–852.

Fisher, E. S., and O'Donohue, W. 2006. *Practitioner's Guide to Evidence-Based Psychotherapy.* New York: Springer.

Fisher, E. S., Wennberg, D. E., Stukel, T. A., Gottlieb, D. J., and Lucas, F. L. 2003. The implications of regional variations in Medicare spending. Part 1: The content, quality, and accessibility of care. *Annals of Internal Medicine* 138: 273–287.

Frank, R. G., Glazer, J., and McGuire, T. G. 1998. Measuring adverse selection in managed health care. National Bureau of Economic Research Working Paper 6825. Cambridge, MA: National Bureau of Economic Research.

Frean, M., Gruber, J., and Sommers, B. D. 2016. Disentangling the ACA's coverage effects: Lessons for policymakers. *New England Journal of Medicine* 375(17): 1605–1608.

Friedman, M. 2001. How to cure health care. *Public Interest* 142(3): 2001–2030.

Friedman, T. L. 1999. *The Lexus and the Olive Tree.* Garden City, NY: Anchor Books.

Fuchs, V. R. 2013. The gross domestic product and health care spending. *New England Journal of Medicine* 369: 107–109.

Garber, A., and Skinner, J. 2008. Is American health care uniquely inefficient? National Bureau of Economic Research Working Paper 14257. Cambridge, MA: National Bureau of Economic Research.

Gazmararian, J. A., Koplan, J. P., Cogswell, M. E., Bailey, C. M., Davis, N. A., and Cutler, C.M. 1997. Maternity experiences in a managed care organization. *Health Affairs* 16(3):198–208. doi:10.1377/hlthaff.16.3.198.

Gechert, S. 2010. Supplementary private health insurance in selected countries: Lessons for EU governments? *CESIFO Economic Studies* 56(3): 444–464.

George, M. G., Tong, X., Sonnenfeld, N., and Hong, Y. 2012. Recommended use of aspirin and other antiplatelet medications among adults: National Ambulatory Medical Care Survey and National Hospital Ambulatory Medical Care Survey, United States, 2005–2008. *Morbidity and Mortality Weekly Report (MMWR)*. 2012;61(suppl):11–18.

Gerteis, J., Izrael, D., Deitz, D., LeRoy, L., Ricciardi, R., Miller, T., and Basu, J. 2014. *Multiple Chronic Conditions Chartbook*. AHRQ Publication Q14-0038. Rockville, MD: Agency for Healthcare Research and Quality.

Girosi, F., Robin, M., and Scoville, R. 2005. *Extrapolating Evidence of Health Information Technology Savings and Costs*. Santa Monica, CA: RAND Corporation.

Glans, M., 2017. Research & commentary: Direct primary care can help New Jersey's primary care shortage. Heartland Institute Research and Commentary. Arlington Heights, IL: Heartland Institute, May. Retrieved from https://www. heartland.org/about-us/who-we-are/matthew-glans.

Glazer, A., and Rothenberg, L. S. 2005. *Why Government Succeeds and Why it Fails*. Cambridge, MA: Harvard University Press.

Gold, J. 2013. 9 pioneer ACOs jump ship after first year. Kaiser Health News, July 16. Retrieved from http://khn.org/news/9-pioneer-acos-jump-ship-after-first-year/.

Goldsmith, J., and Kaufman, N. 2015. Pioneer ACOs: Anatomy of a "victory." Health Affairs Blog, June 18. Retrieved from http://healthaffairs.org/blog/2015/06/18/ pioneer-acos-anatomy-of-a-victory/.

Grady, D. 2009. Premature births are fueling higher rates of infant mortality in U.S., report says. *New York Times*, November 3. Retrieved from http://www.nytimes. com/2009/11/04/health/04infant.html.

Gravalle, H., and Siciliani, L. 2009. Third degree waiting time discrimination: Optimal allocation of a public sector healthcare treatment under rationing by waiting. *Health Economics* 18: 977–986.

Grove, A. 2005. Efficiency in the health care industries. *Journal of the American Medical Association* 294(4): 490–492.

Gruber, J. 1994. The incidence of mandated maternity benefits. *American Economic Review*, 84(3): 622–641. Retrieved from http://www.jstor.org/stable/2118071.

Hall, R. E., and Jones, C. I. 2007. The value of life and the rise in health spending. *Quarterly Journal of Economics* 122: 39–72.

Hastie, T., Tibshirani, R., and Friedman, J. 2009. *The Elements of Statistical Learning: Data Mining, Inference, and Prediction*. 2nd edn. New York: Springer.

Heckman, J. J. 2012. The Developmental Origins of Health. *Health Econ* 21(1): 24–29.

Herring, B. 2005. The effect of the availability of charity care to the uninsured on the demand for private health insurance. *Journal of Health Economics* 24(2): 225–252.

Herszenhorn, D. M. 2009. Senate blocks use of new mammogram guidelines. *New York Times*, December 3.

Hillestad, R., Bigelow J., Bower, A., Gurosi, F., Meili, R., Scoville, R., and Taylor, R. 2005. Can electronic medical record systems transform health care? Potential health benefits, savings, and costs. *Health Affairs* 24(5): 1103–1117.

Honig, M., and Dushi, I. 2005. Offers or take-up: Explaining minorities' lower health insurance coverage. Economic Research Initiative on the Uninsured Working Paper 40. Ann Arbor, MI: University of Michigan, August. Retrieved from https://ssrn.com/abstract=803006.

Horn, S., and Backofen, J. 1987. Ethical issues in the use of a prospective payment system: The issue of a severity of illness adjustment. *Journal of Medicine and Philosophy* 12(2): 145–153.

Institute for Healthcare Improvement. 2017. IHI Triple Aim Initiative. Cambridge, MA: IHI. Retrieved from http://www.ihi.org/Engage/Initiatives/TripleAim/Pages/default.aspx.

Institute of Medicine. 1994. America's Health in Transition: Protecting and Improving Quality. Washington, DC: The National Academies Press. Retrieved from https://doi.org/10.17226/9147.

Insel, T. R. 2008. Assessing the economic costs of serious mental illness. *American Journal of Psychiatry* 165(6): 663–665.

James, J. T. 2013. A new, evidence-based estimate of patient harms associated with hospital care. *Journal of Patient Safety* 9(3): 122–128.

Jensen, G. A., and Morrisey, M. A. 1999. Employer-sponsored health insurance and mandated benefit laws. *Milbank Quarterly* 77(4): 425–59.

Jewell, K., and McGiffert, L. 2009. *To Err Is Human—To Delay Is Deadly*. Austin, TX: Consumers Union.

Johnson, R. C. 2011. Health dynamics and the evolution of health inequality over the life course: The importance of neighborhood and family background. *B.E. Journal of Economic Analysis and Policy* 11(3).

Joint Commission on Accreditation of Healthcare Organizations. 2017. Sentinel event policy and procedures. Oakbrook Terrace, IL: Joint Commission on Accreditation of Healthcare Organizations, February 17.

Jones, L. C. 2005. More life versus more goods, explaining rising health expenditures. Federal Reserve Bank San Francisco Economic letter. Federal Reserve Bank San Francisco, May 27.

Kahneman, D. 2011. *Thinking Fast and Slow*. New York: Farrar, Straus and Giroux, p. 499.

Kaiser Family Foundation. 2004. Uninsured workers in America. Menlo Park, CA: Kaiser Family Foundation.

Kaiser Family Foundation. 2006. Trends in health insurance enrollment. Section 2, chapter 5, p. 147. March 15. Menlo Park, CA: Kaiser Family

Foundation. Retrieved from http://www.kff.org/insurance/7031/ti2004-list. cfm?RenderForPrint=1=44470.

Kaiser Family Foundation. 2007. State health facts. Menlo Park, CA: Kaiser Family Foundation.

Kaiser Family Foundation. 2011. Individual market guaranteed issue (not applicable to HIPAA eligible individuals). Menlo Park, CA: Kaiser Family Foundation. Retrieved from http://www.kff.org/other/state-indicator/individual-market-guaranteed-issue-not-applicable-to-hipaa-eligible-individuals/?currentTimeframe=0&sortModel=%7B%22colId%22:%22Location%22,%22sort%22:%22asc%22%7D

Kaiser Family Foundation. 2012. Health research and educational trust. Employer health benefits: 2012 annual survey. September. Menlo Park, CA: Kaiser Family Foundation.

Kaiser Family Foundation. 2013. Health research and educational trust. Employer health benefits: 2013 annual survey. September. Menlo Park, CA: Kaiser Family Foundation.

Kaiser Family Foundation. 2016. Key facts about the uninsured population. September 29. Retrieved from http://www.kff.org/uninsured/fact-sheet/key-facts-about-the-uninsured-population.

Kaiser Family Foundation. 2017. Polling data note: Beyond the ACA, the affordability of insurance has been deteriorating since 2015. Menlo Park, CA: Kaiser Family Foundation.

Kaiser Permanente Division of Research. 2009. Press Release: Low blood sugar events increase dementia risk in elderly patients with type 2 diabetes, Kaiser Permanents study finds. Northern California, April 9. Retrieved from https://divisionofresearch.kaiserpermanente.org/pressrelease?Id=3401.

Kalorama Information. 2016. Retail clinics 2016: Growth of clinics, revenue forecasts, sales of IVD products of clinics, customer satisfaction & other trends. Rockville, MD: Kalorama Information.

Khrushchev, N. 2011. Great-Quotes.com. Retrieved from http://www.great-quotes.com/quote/215785.

Kohn, L. T., Corrigan, J. M., and Donaldson, M. S. 2000. *To Err Is Human: Building a Safer Health System.* Washington, DC: Committee on Quality of Health Care in America, Institute of Medicine.

Koppelman, J. 2016. States expand the use of dental therapy: Access to care increases when dentists are authorized to hire midlevel providers. Washington, DC: Pew Charitable Trusts Research and Analysis. Retrieved from http://www.pewtrusts.org/en/research-and-analysis/analysis/2016/09/28/states-expand-the-use-of-dental-therapy.

Kramer, M. S., Barros, F. C., Demissie, K., Liu, S., Keily, J., and Joseph, K. S. 2005. Does reducing infant mortality depend on preventing low birth weight? An analysis of temporal trends in the Americas. *Paediatric and Perinatal Epidemiology* 19: 447–448.

Kuo, Y.-F., Loresto, F. L., Jr., Rounds, L. R., and Goodwin, J. S. 2013. States with the least restrictive regulations experienced the largest increase in patients seen by nurse practitioners. *Health Affairs* 32(7): 1236–1243.

Lamb, G. C., Smith, M. A., Weeks, W. B., and Queram, C. 2013. Publicly reported quality-of-care measures influenced Wisconsin physician groups to improve performance. *Health Affairs* 321(3): 536–543.

Landau, E. 2010. "Landmark" cancer vaccine gets FDA approval. CNN Health, April 29. Retrieved from http://www.cnn.com/2010/HEALTH/04/27/provenge.prostate.cancer.fda/index.html.

Laws, M., and Scott, M. K. 2008. The emergence of retail-based clinics in the United States: Early observations. *Health Affairs* 27(5): 1293–1298.

Lee, J., McCullough, J. S., and Town, R. J. 2012. The impact of health information technology on hospital productivity. National Bureau of Economic Research Working Paper 18025. Cambridge, MA: National Bureau of Economic Research.

Lemaire, J. 2005. The cost of firearm deaths in the United States: Reduced life expectancies and increased insurance costs. *Journal of Risk and Insurance* 72: 359–374.

Lichtenberg, F. 2003. The benefits to society of new drugs: A survey of the econometric evidence. In *Science & Cents: Exploring the Economics of Biotechnology,* edited by, John Duca and Mine Yucel. Dallas, TX: Federal Reserve Bank of Dallas, September, pp. 43–59.

Lichtenberg, F. R. 2009. The quality of medical care, behavioral risk factors, and longevity growth. National Bureau of Economic Research Working Paper 15068. Cambridge, MA: National Bureau of Economic Research.

Lichtenberg, F. R. 2010. Has medical innovation reduced cancer mortality? National Bureau of Economic Research Working Paper 15880. Cambridge, MA: National Bureau of Economic Research.

Maciosek, M. V., Coffield, A. B., Flottemesch, T. J., Edwards, N. M., and Solberg, L. I. 2010. Greater use of preventive services in U.S. health care could save lives at little or no cost. *Health Affairs* 29(9): 1656–1660.

Madrian, B. C., and Shea, D. F. 2001. The power of suggestion: Inertia in 401(k) participation and savings behavior. *Quarterly Journal of Economics* 116(4): 1149–1187.

Mandelblatt, J. S., Stout, N. K., Schechter, C. B., van den Broek, J. J., Miglioretti, D. L., Krapcho, M., Trentham-Dietz, A. et al., 2016. Collaborative modeling of the benefits and harms associated with different U.S. breast cancer screening strategies. *.Annals of Internal Medicine* 164(4):215–225.

Mathews, A. W. 2013. To save, workers take on health-cost risk. *Wall Street Journal,* March 17.

Mazanec, D. 2016. EMR ROI—Prognosis for doctors and hospitals: guarded. Dorsata. Medicare Improvements for Patients and Providers Act 154. 2008.

McCaul, K. D., Branstetter, A. D., Schroeder, D. M., and Glasgow, R. E. 1996. What is the relationship between breast cancer risk and mammography screening? A meta-analytic review. *Health Psychology* 15(6): 423–429.

McClellan, M., McKethan, A. N., Lewis, J. L., Roski, J., and Fisher, E. S. 2010. A national strategy to put accountable care into practice. *Health Affairs* 29(5): 982–990.

McCullough, J. S., Parente, S., and Town, R. 2013. Health information technology and patient outcomes: The role of organizational and informational complementarities. National Bureau of Economic Research Working Paper 18684. Cambridge, MA: National Bureau of Economic Research.

McGlynn, E. A., Asch, S. M., Adams, J., Keesey, J., Hicks, J., DeCristofaro, A., and Kerr, A. 2003. The quality of health care delivered to adults in the United States. *New England Journal of Medicine* 348(26): 2635–2645.

McManamy, S. 2016. Why people do—and don't—participate in wellness programs. *Harvard Business Review.* Retrieved from https://hbr.org/2016/10/why-people-do-and-dont-participate-in-wellness-programs.

McWilliams, J. M., Landon, B. E., Chernew, M. E., and Zaslavsky, A. M. 2014. Changes in patients' experiences in Medicare accountable care organizations. *New England Journal of Medicine* 371: 1715–1724.

Meara, E., Rosenthal, M. B., Sinaiko, A. D., and Baicker, K. 2007. State and federal approaches to health reform: What works for the working poor? *Frontiers in Health Policy Research* 10: Article 5.

Mehrota, A., Wang, M. C., Lave, J. R., Adams, J. L., and McGlynn, E. A. 2008. A comparison of patient visits to retail clinics, primary care physicians, and emergency departments. *Health Affairs* 27(5): 1272–1282.

Millenson, M. L. 2006. The promise of personalized medicine: A conversation with Michael Svinte. *Health Affairs* 25(2): w54–w60.

Miller, D., Gust, C., Dimick, J., Birkmeyer, N., Skinner, J., and Birkmeyer, J. 2011. Large variations in Medicare payments for surgery highlight savings potential from bundled payment programs. *Health Affairs* 30(11): 2107–2115. doi: 10.1377/hlthaff.2011.0783.

Miller, R. H., and Luft, H. S. 1997. Does managed care lead to better or worse quality of care? *Health Affairs* 16(5): 7–25.

Miller, R. H., and Luft, H. S. 2002. HMO plan performance update: An analysis of the literature, 1997–2001. *Health Affairs* 21(4): 63–86.

Mitchell, R. J., and Bate, P. 2011. Measuring health-related productivity loss. *Population Health Management* 14(2): 93–98.

Mukhopadhyay, S., and Wendel, J. 2008. Are prenatal care resources distributed efficiently across high-risk and low-risk mothers? *International Journal of Health Care Finance and Economics* 8(3): 163–179.

Mullin, R. 2014. Tufts study finds big rise in cost of drug development. *Chemical and Engineering News*, November 20. Retrieved from http://cen.acs.org/articles/92/web/2014/11/Tufts-Study-Finds-Big-Rise.html.

Murphy, A. 2010. Mammography screening for breast cancer: A view from 2 worlds. *Journal of the American Medical Association* 303(2): 166–167.

Nardin, R., Himmelstein, D., and Woolhandler, S. 2009. Massachusetts' plan: A failed model for health care reform. Chicago: Physicians for a National Health Program. Retrieved from http://www.pnhp.org/mass_report/mass_report_Final.pdf.

Narins, C. R., Dozier, M., Ling, F. S., and Zareba, W. 2005. The influence of public reporting of outcome data on medical decision making by physicians. *Archives of Internal Medicine* 165: 83–87.

National Association of State Budget Officers. 2016. State expenditure report. Washington, DC: National Association of State Budget Officers, November 17. Retrieved from http://www.nasbo.org/mainsite/reports-data/state-expenditure-report.

National Committee for Quality Assurance. 2011. HEDIS & performance measurement. Washington, DC: National Committee for Quality Assurance. Retrieved from http://www.ncqa.org/hedis-quality-measurement.

National Conference of State Legislatures. 2017. Affordable Care Act Medicaid expansion. Washington, DC: National of State Legislatures, May 1. Retrieved from http://www.ncsl.org/research/health/affordable-care-act-expansion.aspx.

National Prevention Council. 2011. National Prevention Strategy. Washington, DC: U.S. Department of Health and Human Services, Office of the Surgeon General, June. Retrieved from https://www.surgeongeneral.gov/priorities/prevention/strategy/.

Nelson, L. 2012. Lessons from Medicare's demonstration projects on disease management, care coordination and value-based payment. Congressional Budget Office Working Paper 2012-01. Washington, DC: Congressional Budget Office, January. Retrieved from https://www.cbo.gov/sites/default/files/112th-congress-2011-2012/workingpaper/WP2012-01_Nelson_Medicare_DMCC_Demonstrations_1.pdf.

Newman, T. B., Johnston, B. D., and Grossman, D. C. 2003. Effects and costs of requiring child-restraint systems for young children traveling on commercial airplanes. *Archives of Pediatrics & Adolescent Medicine* 157(10): 969.

Nordhaus, W. D. 2003. The health of nations: The contribution of improved health to living standards. In *Measuring the Gains from Medical Research: An Economic Approach*, edited by K. Murphy and R. Topel. Chicago, IL: Chicago University Press.

Nyweide, D. J., Lee, W., Cuerdon, T. T., Pham, H. H., Cox, M., Rajkumar, R., and Conway, P. H. 2015. Association of pioneer accountable care organizations versus traditional Medicare fee for service with spending, utilization, and patient experience. *Journal of the American Medical Association* 313(21): 2152–2161.

O'Donohue, W., and Cucciare, M. 2005. The role of psychological factors in medical presentations. *Journal of Clinical Psychology in Medical Settings* 12(1): 13–24.

O'Donohue, W., and Maragakis, A. 2015. *Integrated Primary and Behavioral Care: Role in Medical Homes and Disease Management*. New York: Springer.

O'Donohue, W., and Maragakis, A. 2016. *Quality Improvement in Mental Health*. New York: Springer.

Okeke, E. N., Hirth, R. A., and Grazier, K. 2010. Workers on the margin: Who drops health coverage when prices rise? *Inquiry: A Journal of Medical Care Organization, Provision and Financing* 47(1): 33–47.

Okunade, A. A., and Murthy, V. N. 2002. Technology as a "major driver" of health care costs: A cointegration analysis of the Newhouse conjecture. *Journal of Health Economics* 21(1): 147–159.

O'Neill, J. E., and O'Neill, D. M. 2008. Health status, health care and inequality: Canada vs. the U.S. *Forum for Health Economics & Policy* 10(1): article 3.

Organization for Economic Cooperation and Development. 2015. Organization for Economic Cooperation and Development health data. Paris: Organization for Economic Cooperation and Development, June.

Orzag, P. 2007. The long-term outlook for health care spending: Sources of growth in projected federal spending on Medicare and Medicaid. Washington, DC: Congressional Budget Office, November.

Pauly, M. V. 2001. Making sense of a complex system: Empirical studies of employment-based health insurance. *International Journal of Health Care Finance and Economics* 1(3/4): 333–339. Retrieved from http://www.jstor.org/stable/3528911.

Pear, R. 2005. Medicare officials insisting on wider choices in drug benefits. *New York Times*, June 15. Retrieved from http://www.nytimes.com/2005/06/15/health/15drug.html?_r=1&pagewanted=print.

Polsky, D., Stein, R., Nicholson, S., and Bundorf, M. K. 2005. Employer health insurance offerings and employee enrollment decisions. *Health Services Research* 40: 1259–1278.

Posner, R. A. 1971. Taxation by regulation. *Bell Journal of Economics and Management Science* 2(1): 22–50. Retrieved from http://www.jstor.org/stable/3003161.

Rahurkar, S., Vest, J. R., Menachemi, N. 2015. Despite the spread of health information exchange, there is little evidence of its impact on cost, use and quality of care. *Health Affairs* 34(3): 477–483.

RAND Corporation. 2014. Do workplace wellness programs save employers money? Research Brief 9744. Santa Monica, CA: RAND Corporation. Retrieved from http://www.rand.org/content/dam/rand/pubs/research_briefs/RB9700/RB9744/RAND_RB9744.pdf.

Regier, D. A., Narrow, W. E., Rae, D. S., Manderscheid, R. W., Locke, B. Z., and Goodwin, F. K. 1993. The de facto US mental and addictive disorders service system. *Archives of General Psychiatry* 50(2): 85.

Robinson, P. 2009. Medical analysis by milton friedman. *Forbes*, June 19. Retreived from https://www.forbes.com/2009/06/18/milton-friedman-medical-insurance-opinions-columnists-health-care.html

Rock, R. C. 1985. Assuring quality of care under drug-based prospective payment. *Medical Decision Making* 5(1): 531–534.

Rosoff, J. A. 2001. Evidence-based medicine and the law: The courts confront clinical practice guidelines. *Journal of Health Politics, Policy and Law* 26(2): 327–368.

Rotter, T., Kinsman, L., James, E., Machotta, A. Gothe, H., Willis, J., Snow, P., and Kugler, J. 2010. Clinical pathways: Effects on professional practice, patient outcomes, length of stay and hospital costs. Cochrane Database of Systematic Review, 3(3): CD006632. doi:10.1002/14651858.CD006632.pub2.

Rudavsky, R., Pollack, C. E., and Mehrotra, A. 2009. The geographic distribution, ownership, prices, and scope of practice at retail clinics. *Annals of Internal Medicine* 151(5): 315–320.

Rudowitz, R., Artiga, S., Damico, A., and Garfield. R. 2016. A closer look at the remaining uninsured population eligible for Medicaid and CHIP. Menlo Park, CA: Henry J. Kaiser Family Foundation, June 9.

Russell, L. B. 1994. *Educated Guesses: Making Policy about Medical Screening Tests.* Berkeley, CA: University of California Press.

Russell, L. B. 2009. Perspective preventing chronic disease: An important investment, but don't count on cost savings: An overwhelming percentage of preventive interventions add more to medical costs than they save. *Health Affairs* 28(1): 42–45.

Savings, H., and Goodman, J. 2013. Why do some states spend more on health care? Health Affairs Blog, March 25. Retrieved from http://healthaffairs.org/blog/2013/03/25/why-do-some-states-spend-more-on-health-care/.

Scanlon, W. 1998. Health Insurance Standards: New Federal Creates Challenges for Consumers, Insurers, Regulators. 1998 US General Accounting Office. GAO/HEHS-98-67, p. 30.

Schumpeter, J. A. 1942. *Capitalism, Socialism, and Democracy.* 3rd ed. New York: Harper Perennial.

Sen, A. (2002). Why health equity? *Health Economics.* 11:659–666.

Simon, H. A. 1957. *Models of Man: Social and Rational; Mathematical Essays on Rational Human Behavior in Society Setting.* New York: John Wiley & Sons.

Singh, G. K., and Siahpush, M. 2006. Widening socioeconomic inequalities in U.S. life expectancy, 1980–2000. *International Journal of Epidemiology* 35: 969–979.

Smith, J. 2007. Diabetes and the rise of the SES health gradient. National Bureau of Economic Research Working Paper 12905. Cambridge, MA: National Bureau of Economic Research.

Smith, M. A., Wright, A., Queram, C., and Lamb, G. C. 2012. Public reporting helped drive quality improvement in outpatient diabetes care among Wisconsin physician groups. *Health Affairs* 31(3): 570–577.

Sloan, F. A., and Conover, C. J. 1998. Effects of state reforms on health insurance coverage of adults. *Inquiry: A Journal of Medical Care Organization, Provision and Financing* 35(3): 280–293.

Sommers, B. D. 2006. Insuring children or insuring families: Do parental and sibling coverage lead to improved retention of children in Medicaid and CHIP? *Journal of Health Economics* 25(6): 1154–1169.

Song, Y., Skinner, J., Fisher, E., Wennberg, J., Bynum, J., and Sutherland, J. 2010. Considering moving? Where you go determines whether you will be told you're sick. Dartmouth Institute for Health Policy and Clinical Practice.

Sowell, T. 1993. *Is Reality Optional? And Other Essays.* Stanford, CA: Hoover Institution Press, p. 83.

Sowell, T. 1995. *The Vision of the Anointed.* New York: Basic Books, p. 113.

Stanik-Hutt, J., Newhouse, R. P., White, K. M., Johantgen, M., Bass, E. B., Zangaro, G., Wilson, R., Fountain, L., Steinwachs, D. M., Heindel, L., and Weiner, J. P. 2013. The quality and effectiveness of care provided by nurse practitioners. *Journal for Nurse Practitioners* 9(8): 492–500.

Sturm, R., and Pacula, R. 1999. State mental health parity laws: Cause or consequence of differences in use? *Health Affairs* 18(5): 182–192.

Sun, E. C., Jena, A. B., Lakdawalla, D. N., Reyes, C. M., Philipson, T. J., and Goldman, D. P. 2009. an economic evaluation of the war on cancer. National Bureau of Economic Research Working Paper 15574. Cambridge, MA: National Bureau of Economic Research.

Swain, M., Charles, D., Patel V., and Searcy, T. 2015. Health information exchange among U.S. non-federal acute care hospitals: 2008–2014. ONC Data Brief 24. Washington, DC: Office of the National Coordinator for Health Information Technology, April 19. Retrieved from http://www.healthit.gov/sites/default/files/data-brief/ONC_DataBrief24_HIE_Final.pdf.

Temkin, E. 1999. Driving through: Postpartum care during World War II. *American Journal of Public Health* 89(4): 587–595.

Tengs, T. 1996. An evaluation of Oregon's Medicaid rationing algorithms. *Health Economics* 5(3): 171–181.

Terry, K. 2015. Interstate licensing bill for telemedicine gathers support. *Medscape Medical News*, August 18.

Thorpe, K. E., Florence, C. S., and Joski, P. 2004. Which medical conditions account for the rise in health care spending? *Health Affairs* 437–445.

Thurm, S. 2013. Will companies stop offering health insurance because of the affordable care act? *Wall Street Journal*, June 16.

Timmins, N. 2010. Letter from Britain: Across the pond, giant new waves of health reform. *Health Affairs* 29(12): 2138–2141.

Town, R., and Vistnes, G. 2001. Hospital competition in HMO networks. *Journal of Health Economics* 20(5): 733–753.

Tsugawa, Y., and Jena, B. A. 2017. Research: Higher U.S. physician spending doesn't lead to better patient outcomes. *Harvard Business Review*, March 13. Retrieved from https://hbr.org/2017/03/research-higher-u-s-physician-spending-doesnt-lead-to-better-patient-outcomes.

Tuerck, D. G., Bachman, P., and Head, M. 2011. The high price of Massachusetts health care reform. Boston: Beacon Hill Institute. Retrieved from http://www.beaconhill.org/BHIStudies/HCR-2011/BHIMassHealthCareReform2011-0627.pdf.

U.S. Census Bureau, American Community Survey. 2015. Table S2701. Selected characteristics of health insurance coverage in the United States. 2015 American Community Survey 1-Year Estimates. Retrieved from https://factfinder.census.gov/faces/tableservices/jsf/pages/productview.xhtml?pid=ACS_15_1YR_S2701&prodType=table.

U.S. Department of Health and Human Services, National Center for Chronic Disease Prevention and Health Promotion. 2003. *The Power of Prevention: Reducing the Health and Economic Burden of Chronic Disease.* Retrieved from http://www.ibhworklife.com/Documents/Wellness/power_of_prevention.pdf.

U.S. Department of Health and Human Services, National Center for Health Statistics, Centers for Disease Control and Prevention. 2016. Health, United States, 2015. With special feature on racial and ethnic health disparities (June

22, 2017). Washington, DC: U.S. Department of Health and Human Services. Retrieved from https://www.cdc.gov/nchs/data/hus/hus15.pdf.

U.S. Department of Health and Human Services, National Institute of Mental Health. Any mental illness (AMI) among adults. Washington, DC: U.S. Department of Health and Human Services. Retrieved from http://www. nimh.nih.gov/health/statistics/prevalence/any-mental-illness-ami-among-adults. shtml.

U.S. Department of Justice and Federal Trade Commission. 2014. Improving health care: A dose of competition. Washington, DC: U.S. Department of Justice, July.

U.S. General Accounting Office. 2003. Specialty hospitals: Geographic locations, services provided and financial performance. GAO-04-167. Washington, DC: U.S. General Accounting Office.

U.S. Preventive Services Task Force. 2009a. Screening for Breast Cancer (December). Retrieved from http://www.uspreventiveservicestaskforce.org/usp-stf/uspsbrca.htm.

U.S. Preventive Services Task Force. 2009b. Screening for Breast Cancer: U.S. Preventive Services Task Force Recommendation Statement. Annals of Internal Medicine (November 17). Vol. 151, no. 10.

U.S. Preventive Services Task Force. 2016. Breast Cancer: Screening (January). Retrieved from https://www.uspreventiveservicestaskforce.org/Page/Document/UpdateSummaryFinal/breast-cancer-screening1.

Van Den Bos, J., Rustagi, K., Gray, T., Halford, M., Ziemkiewicz, E., and Shreve, J. 2011. The 17.1 billion problem: The annual cost of measurable medical errors. *Health Affairs* 30(4): 596–603.

Vest, J. R., and Kash, B. A. 2016. Differing strategies to meet information-sharing needs: Publicly supported community health information exchanges versus health systems' enterprise health information exchanges. *Milbank Quarterly* 94(1): 77–108.

Vistnes, J., and Monheit, A. C. 2011. The health insurance status of low-wage workers: The role of workplace composition and marital status. *Medical Care Research and Review* 68(5): 607–623.

Vita, M. G. 2001. Regulatory restrictions on selective contracting: An empirical analysis of any-willing-provider regulations. *Journal of Health Economics* 20(6): 955–966.

Wachenheim, L., and Leida, H. 2012. The impact of guaranteed issue and community rating reforms on states' individual insurance markets. Washington, DC: America's Health Insurance Plans. Retrieved from http://www.ahipcoverage. com/wp-content/uploads/2012/03/Updated-Milliman-Report.pdf.

Waidmann, T., Garrett, B., and Hadley, J. 2004. Explaining differences in employer sponsored insurance coverage by race, ethnicity and immigrant status. Economic Research Initiative on the Uninsured Working Paper 42. Ann Arbor, MI: University of Michigan.

Walker, D. M. 2007. Long-term budget outlook: Saving our future requires tough choices today. Patient Protection and Affordable Care Act. Washington,

DC: U.S. Department of Labor, Employee Benefits Security Administration. Retrieved from http://www.dol.gov/ebsa/healthreform/.

Wallsten, S. 2015. The competitive effects of the sharing economy: How is Uber changing taxis? Arlington Heights, IL: Heartland Institute Freedom Rising. Retrieved from https://www.heartland.org/publications-resources/publications/the-competitive-effects-of-the-sharing-economy-how-is-uber-changing-taxis.

Wanamaker, B., and Bean, D. 2013. Seize the ACA: The innovator's guide to the Affordable Care Act. September. Lexington, MA: Clayton Christenson Institute for Disruptive Innovation. Retrieved from https://www.christenseninstitute.org/wp-content/uploads/2013/09/Seize_the_ACA_midres.pdf.

Wendel, J., and Dumitras, D. 2005. Treatment effects model for assessing disease management: Measuring outcomes and strengthening program management. *Disease Management* 8(3): 155–168.

Wendel, J., and Paterson, M. 1996. Managing risk in a changing health care system. *Journal of Health Care Finance* 22(3): 15–22.

Werner, R. M., Kolstad, J. T., Stuart, E. A., and Polsky, D. 2011. The effect of pay-for-performance in hospitals: Lessons for quality improvement. *Health Affairs* 30(4): 690–698.

Whalen, J. 2005. Britain stirs outcry by weighing benefits of drugs versus price. *Wall Street Journal*, November 22, A1.

Whiteman, H. 2017. Eating more fruits, vegetables boosts psychological well-being in just 2 weeks. *Medical News Today*, February 10.

Williams, C. 2004. Medicaid disease management: Issues and promises. Menlo Park, CA: Henry J. Kaiser Family Foundation, September 1.

Wind, C., and Marier, A. 2014. Effects of occupational regulations on the cost of dental services: Evidence from dental insurance claims. *Journal of Health Economics* 34: 131–143.

Wisconsin Policy Research Institute. 2006. The history of health care costs and health insurance. Wisconsin Policy Research Institute Report, vol. 10, no. 10. Thiensville, WI: Wisconsin Policy Research Institute.

Woloshin, S., and Schwartz, L. M. 2010. The benefits and harms of mammography screening: Understanding the trade-offs. *Journal of the American Medical Association* 303: 164–165.

Woolf, S. 2010. The 2009 breast cancer screening recommendations of the U.S. Preventive Services Task Force. *Journal of the American Medical Association* 303(2): 162–163.

Woolf, S. H., Aron, L., Dubay, L., Simon, S. M., Zimmerman, E., and Luk, K. X. 2015. How are income and wealth linked to health and longevity? Washington, DC: Urban Institute, Center on Society and Health. Retrieved from http://www.urban.org/sites/default/files/publication/49116/2000178-How-are-Income-and-Wealth-Linked-to-Health-and-Longevity.pdf.

Yaisawarnga, S., and Burgess, J. E., Jr. 2006. Performance-based budgeting in the public sector: An illustration from the VA health care system. *Health Economics* 15: 295–310.

Zhan, C., Miller, R. M., Wong, H., and Meyer, S. G. 2004. The effects of HMO penetration on preventable hospitalizations. *Health Services Research* 39(2): 345–361.

Zutshi, A., Peikes, D., Smith, K., Azur, M., Genevro, J., Parchman, M., and Meyers, D. 2013. The medical home: What do we know, what do we need to know? A review of the earliest evidence on the effectiveness of the patient-centered medical home model. AHRQ—PCMH Resource Center. Rockville, MD: Agency for Healthcare Research and Quality. Retrieved from https://pcmh.ahrq.gov/sites/default/files/attachments/the-medical-home-what-do-we-know.pdf.

Index

1942 Stabilization Act, 46
1973 Health Maintenance Organization Act, 140
1996 Health Insurance Portability and
    Accountability Act (HIPAA), xxii, 43
  prohibited restrictive practices, 47–49
  state reforms, 49–50
1996 Mental Health Parity Act, 144
1996 Newborns' and Mothers' Health
    Protection Act, 144
2003 Medicare Modernization Act, xxii
2009 American Recovery and Reinvestment
    Act, xxxv
2009 Health Information Technology for
    Economic and Clinical Health
    (HITECH) Act, xxi, xxxv, 132,
    198, 200, 206
  HIT adoption rates prior to, 204
  impact of, 205
  investing taxpayer dollars in, 202–204
2015 Medicare Access and CHIP
    Reauthorization Act (MACRA), xxii,
    xxxiv, xxxvii, 132–133, 205

A

ACA, *see* Affordable Care Act (ACA)
Accountable care organizations (ACOs), 128,
    139, 148–149, 159–160, 207
Administrative expenditures, 63
Affordable Care Act (ACA), 7, 197
Affordable expenditures, concept of, 6
Agency for Healthcare Research and Quality
    (AHRQ), 101

Akerlof, George, 169
Alternative Payment Model
    (APM), 133
AMA, *see* American Medical
    Association (AMA)
American Association of Health Plans, 101
American College of Physicians, 139
American Medical Association
    (AMA), 101, 190
"America's Health in Transition: Protecting
    and Improving" report, 92
Annals of Internal Medicine, 103
Aon Hewitt, 38–39
AOS Assurance Company Limited, 189
APM, *see* Alternative Payment
    Model (APM)
Arrow, Kenneth, 117
AT&T, 20

B

Bayer Healthcare, 172
Behavioral and experimental
    economics, 167–172
Behavioral health services, 193–194
Beneficent paternalism, 171
Berwick, Donald, 96, 97
BlueCross and BlueShield, 46, 189
Bono, Edward, xxvii
British Cabinet Office Behavioural Insights
    Team, 172
Bundled payment, 122–123, 128–129
Bush, George W., 198

C

CAFE, *see* Corporate Average Fuel
        Economy (CAFE)
Cancer-related mortality, 88–89
CBO, *see* Congressional Budget
        Office (CBO)
Center for Medicare and Medicaid
        Innovation (CMMI), 209
Centers for Disease Control and
        Prevention, 89
Centers for Medicare and Medicaid Services
        (CMS), xxxiv, 60, 84, 97, 124–125,
        132, 173, 185, 205, 209
Certificate of need (CON) programs, 123
Certified nurse midwives (CNMs), 183, 184
Clayton Christensen Institute, 115
Clinical guidelines, 101–109
    benefits and harms of screening
        program, 109
    costs and benefits, 103–104
    quality of evidence, 102–103
    statistical and math modeling, 104–109
Clinical pathways, 100–101
CMMI, *see* Center for Medicare and
        Medicaid Innovation (CMMI)
CMS, *see* Centers for Medicare and Medicaid
        Services (CMS)
CNMs, *see* Certified nurse
        midwives (CNMs)
Coding systems, xxiii
Commercial Insurance, 135–137
Compass Benefits Group, 189
CON, *see* Certificate of need
        (CON) programs
Congressional Budget Office (CBO), 23, 66,
        119, 173, 199, 202, 203, 204
Consumer Price Index, 81
Consumer protection, 144–148
Continuous quality improvement (CQI), 98
Corporate Average Fuel Economy
        (CAFE), 119
Cost, 61–62; *see also* Healthcare costs
        and benefits
Cost containment, 69
Cost Sharing Reduction (CSR), 54, 184
Countervailing market power, 151

CQI, *see* Continuous quality
        improvement (CQI)
Creative destruction process, 178
Critical pathways, *see* Clinical pathways
*Crossing the Quality Chasm: A New Health
        System for the 21st Century,* 92
Cross-subsidy pricing system, 20,
        137, 186–188
CSR, *see* Cost Sharing Reduction (CSR)

D

Damaged Care, As Good as It Gets, 142
Darden Restaurants, Inc., 38
Dartmouth Atlas, 94
Decision Sciences, 105
Deming, Edwards, 97
Department of Health and Human Services
        (HHS), 110, 160, 165, 198
Department of Justice (DoJ), 151
Dern, Laura, 142
Diabetes disease management program, 167
Diagnostic Related Group (DRG), 122,
        125–127, 129, 130, 135, 144
Direct primary care (DPC), 128
Disease management, 163, 171–174
Disruptive Innovation, 115
DME, *see* Durable medical
        equipment (DME)
Doctor Ranking Model Code, 157
DoJ, *see* Department of Justice (DoJ)
DPC, *see* Direct primary care (DPC)
DRG, *see* Diagnostic Related Group (DRG)
Durable medical equipment (DME), 129

E

Eddy, David, 104, 108
Edington, Dee, 167
Educated Guesses, 107
Electronic medical record (EMR), xxxv, 197,
        198, 201, 204–206
Emanuel, E. J., 170
Employee Benefit Research Institute, 35
Employer mandate, 50
Employer-sponsored health
        insurance, 22–39

shifting cost onto workers, 24–39
   actual and equilibrium wage, 26
   affecting equilibrium wage, 29–31
   bargaining power, 31–34
   coverage for low-income
      workers, 37–39
   equilibrium wage concept, 27–29
   not accepting wage cuts, 34–36
   quantity supplied and quantity
      demanded, 25–26
   supply and demand, 24–25
   wage–health insurance tradeoff, 36–37
   workers pay for, 23–24
Employer-sponsored insurance (ESI), 8, 39
EMR, *see* Electronic medical record (EMR)
Enterprise HIE, 207
Environmental Protection Agency (EPA), 76
EPCs, *see* Evidence-based Practice
      Centers (EPCs)
ESI, *see* Employer-sponsored insurance (ESI)
Evidence-based Practice Centers (EPCs), 101
Expected value, 21

F

FDA, *see* Food and Drug
      Administration (FDA)
Federal Aviation Administration, 75
Federal expenditures, 63
Federal Reserve Bank, of San Francisco, 66
Federal Trade Commission (FTC), 151, 181
Federation of State Medical Boards
      (FSMB), 190
Fee-for-service (FFS) payments, 117,
      122, 123–124, 140
Food and Drug Administration (FDA), 81
Freakonomics (book), 167
Freakonomics (movie), 167
Friedman, Milton, 16
FSMB, *see* Federation of State Medical
      Boards (FSMB)
FTC, *see* Federal Trade Commission (FTC)

G

GDP, *see* Gross domestic product (GDP)
Grisham, John, 142

Gross domestic product (GDP),
      59–60, 66, 132
Grove, Andy, 100
Guaranteed issue regulations, 49, 50
Guns and butter decision, 108

H

Harvard Business Review, 174
Health Affairs, 173
Healthcare
   markets, 116–117
      addressing failures, 118–119
      principal–agent relationship, 117–118
      reducing patient incentives, 118
   regulatory challenges and competition
      emerging in, 177–195
      concept of "creative
         destruction," 178–179
      integrated care providers, 191–194
      issues, 179–180
      overview, 177
      retail clinics, 180–184
      single-specialty hospitals, 185–189
      telemedicine, 189–191
   spending of physicians, 95
Healthcare, access to, 5–58
   accepting/rejecting sponsor
      insurance, 39–42
   demographic characteristics and
      uninsurance, 8–12
   employer-sponsored insurance, 22–39
      shifting cost onto workers, 24–39
      workers pay for, 23–24
   insurance sources and trends, 6–8
   overview, 5–6
   PPACA, 51–56
      impacts, 55–56
      strategy for increasing health
         insurance, 52–55
   private insurance markets, 12–22
      premiums, 19, 20–22
      principles and managing risk, 13–16
      principles application for health
         insurance, 16–19
   restrictive insurance company
      practices, 42–47

lemons problem, 43–47
    reasons, 43
  solution strategies, 47–51
    pre-PPACA estimates, 50–51
    pre-PPACA legislation, 47–50
  uninsured people, 12
Healthcare costs and benefits, 69–70,
    71, 77–83
  implementing policies to constrain
    Medicare expenditures, 82–83
  price and profit regulations, 80–82
  reducing technological innovation
    rate, 80
  restraining quantities of healthcare
    services, 78–80
    ration by price, 78–79
    ration by setting priorities, 79–80
    ration by wait time, 79
  spending on healthcare, 77–78
Healthcare expenditures, 16, 36, 59, 61–62
  sources of funding for, 63–77
    impact of technology, 70–72
    increasing life expectancy, 72–74
    public expenditures
      sustainability, 65–70
    strategies for analyzing healthcare
      issues, 74–77
    value *vs.* treatment costs, 72
  by type, 62–63
Health information exchange (HIE), xxxv,
    197, 198, 201, 204–205, 207–208
Health information technology (HIT),
    96, 197, 203
  adoption rates prior to HITECH Act, 204
  impact on adoption, 205–206
  impact on outcomes, 206–207
  overview, 197–199
  structuring health policy and federal
    subsidies, 200–202
    expected benefits *vs.* costs, 200
    potential market failures, 200–202
Health insurance exchanges (HIXs), 5, 6, 52
Health insurance markets
  lemons problem in, 44–45
Health maintenance organizations (HMOs),
    140, 142, 148–149, 151
Health Savings Accounts (HSAs), 215–216

Heckman, James, 114
HHS, *see* Department of Health and Human
    Services (HHS)
HIE, *see* Health information exchange (HIE)
High Value Healthcare Collaborative
    (HVHC), 208–209
HIPAA, *see* 1996 Health Insurance
    Portability and Accountability
    Act (HIPAA)
Hispanic workers and insurance, 41, 42
HIT, *see* Health information
    technology (HIT)
HITECH, *see* 2009 Health Information
    Technology for Economic and
    Clinical Health (HITECH) Act
HIXs, *see* Health insurance
    exchanges (HIXs)
HMOs, *see* Health maintenance
    organizations (HMOs)
Homicide and suicide rates, 89
HSAs, *see* Health Savings Accounts (HSAs)
HVHC, *see* High Value Healthcare
    Collaborative (HVHC)

I

Incentives
  for hospitals, 122–125, 129–130, 132–133
  impact of, 152–153
  for organizations, 184
  quality-based payment, 191
Independent Payment Advisory Board
    (IPAB), 82–83
Infant mortality, 89–90
Inflation, 23
*The Innovator's Prescription: A Disruptive
    Solution for Health Care,*
    177, 185, 186
Institute of Medicine (IOM), 85, 91–92
Insurance sources, and trends, 6–8
Integrated care pathways/care maps, *see*
    Clinical pathways
Integrated Care Providers, 191–194
Investment activities, 63
IOM, *see* Institute of Medicine (IOM)
IPAB, *see* Independent Payment Advisory
    Board (IPAB)

J

JAMA, *see Journal of the American Medical Association* (JAMA)
James, Brent, 96, 97
JCAHO, *see* Joint Commission on Accreditation of Healthcare Organizations (JCAHO)
JCI, *see* Joint Commission International (JCI)
John Q, 142
Joint Commission International (JCI), 189
Joint Commission on Accreditation of Healthcare Organizations (JCAHO), 92–93, 98
Journal of the American Medical Association (JAMA), 102

K

Kahneman, Daniel, 169
Kaiser Permanente, 99
Kelley Blue Book, 44
Khrushchev, Nikita, 84

L

Lean Six Sigma, 92
Lemons problem, 43–47
    employer-sponsored health insurance mitigates, 45–47
    in health insurance markets, 44–45
The Lexus and the Olive Tree, 203
Life expectancy, 72–74
Live birth, 90
Lyft, 178–179

M

MACRA, *see* 2015 Medicare Access and CHIP Reauthorization Act (MACRA)
Mammogram screenings, 102–103, 107–108
Managed care backlash, 141, 142–144, 149
Managed care organizations
    backlash, 142–144
    definition of quality, 148–149
    historical trends, 141–142
    market power issues, 149–152

provider laws and countervailing market power, 151–152
    reduced provider reimbursement rates, 150–151
    mental health parity, 154–157
    overview, 140–141
    physician rating systems, 157–159
    physician risk taking and solvency regulation, 152–154
Managed care plans, 140
Market power issues, 149–152
    provider laws and countervailing market power, 151–152
    reduced provider reimbursement rates, 150–151
McDonald, 19
Meaningful Use (MU), 132, 133, 198
Medicaid, 8, 40, 51, 54–56, 66–67, 135–137, 173
Medical arms race, 124
Medical care expenditures and expenses, 16; *see also* Healthcare expenditures
Medical cost offset, 192
Medical errors, 85–86, 91–93
Medical Expenditure Panel Survey (MEPS), 42
Medical Tourism Association, 189
Medicare, xxiii, 8, 65, 135–137, 173
    expenditures growth, 82–83
    payments, 124–125
    transfer patient, 129
    trust fund report, 65–66
Medicare Shared Savings Program (MSSP), 159
Mental health practice, 193
MEPS, *see* Medical Expenditure Panel Survey (MEPS)
Merit-based Incentive Payment System (MIPS), 133
Microsoft Windows, 190–191
MIPS, *see* Merit-based Incentive Payment System (MIPS)
MSSP, *see* Medicare Shared Savings Program (MSSP)
MU, *see* Meaningful Use (MU)
Multivariate statistical analysis, 94

N

Narayana Hrudayalaya Hospital, 188
National Committee on Quality Assurance (NCQA), 158
National Guideline Clearinghouse, 101
National Health Accounts, 62
National Health Expenditures, 62
National Institute for Health and Care Excellence (NICE), 104
National Patient Safety Goals, 93
National Public Radio (NPR), 202
NCQA, *see* National Committee on Quality Assurance (NCQA)
Net revenue over cost, 135–136
Network Economies, 190–191
New York Times, 148
NICE, *see* National Institute for Health and Care Excellence (NICE)
Nicholson, Jack, 142
Nintendo DS, 172
NPR, *see* National Public Radio (NPR)
NPs, *see* Nurse practitioners (NPs)
Nudge Unit, 168, 170
Nurse practitioners (NPs), 182, 184

O

Occupational Safety and Health Administration (OSHA), 109
Office of the National Coordinator (ONC), 198
OSHA, *see* Occupational Safety and Health Administration (OSHA)
Out-of-pocket expenditures, 63, 64

P

P4P, *see* Pay-for-performance (P4P) programs
PAs, *see* Physician assistants (PAs)
Patent system, 81
Patient-centered medical homes (PCMHs), 139, 159–160
Patient-Centered Primary Care Collaborative, 160

Patient Charter for Physician Performance Measurement, Reporting and Tiering Programs, 158
Patient Protection and Affordable Care Act (PPACA), xxi–xxii, xxxiii–xxxiv, 6, 19, 34, 40, 42, 43, 82, 113, 155, 214–215
  assessment of, xxxvi
  debates about, xxxvii–xxxviii
  focuses on prevention and wellness, 164–167
  impacts, 55–56
  issues addressed by, xxxiv–xxxvi
  strategy for increasing health insurance, 52–55
    exemption from mandate, 52
    expanding Medicaid eligibility for adults, 54–55
    state-level health insurance exchanges, 52–54
Pay-for-performance (P4P) programs, 130–131
Payment system design, 121
  bundled payment, 128–129
  capitated payment for physicians, 128
  DRG payment for hospital services, 125–127
  FFS payments for hospital services, 123–124
  overview, 121
  pay-for-performance (P4P) programs, 130–131
  public and private payment systems, 134–138
  rate redesign, 124–125
  RBRVS and MACRA, 132–133
  selective contracting, 129–130
  types of payment structure, 121–123
  value-based purchasing (VBP) for hospitals, 132
PCMHs, *see* Patient-centered medical homes (PCMHs)
PCPs, *see* Primary care physicians (PCPs)
PepsiCo's Healthy Living Program, 173
Personal healthcare, 62–63
PHO, *see* Physician hospital organization (PHO)

Physician assistants (PAs), 184
Physician hospital organization (PHO), 151
Physician Quality Reporting System
 (PQRS), 132, 133
Physician rating systems, 157–159
Physician risk taking, 152–154
PPACA, *see* Patient Protection and
 Affordable Care Act (PPACA)
PPOs, *see* Preferred provider
 organizations (PPOs)
PPS, *see* Prospective payment system (PPS)
PQRS, *see* Physician Quality Reporting
 System (PQRS)
Pre-1983 FFS system, 125, 126
Preferred provider organizations (PPOs), 140
Premier Inc., 131
Premiums, insurance, 19, 20–22
Pre-PPACA
 estimates, 50–51
 employer mandate, 50
 Medicaid coverage, 51
 tax credit, 51
 legislation, 47–50
 prohibited restrictive practices, 47–49
 state reforms, 49–50
Prevention and wellness programs, 164–167
 designing policies, 167–172
 effectiveness of, 172–174
 PPACA focuses on, 164–167
Price, 61–62
 elasticity, 40–41
 rationing, 78–79
 regulation, 80–82
Primary care physicians (PCPs), 181–182
Priority setting and rationing, 79–80
Private insurance markets, 12–16
 application for health insurance, 16–19
 insuring risk *vs.* subsidizing
  expenditure, 17–19, 20
 preexisting conditions, 17
 principles and managing risk, 13–16
 premium for specific type of
  insurance, 13–14
 purchasing insurance, 14–16
Private insurance payments, 63–64
Profit regulations, 80–82
Prospective payment system (PPS), 125

Public health activities, 63
Public health insurance, 64

Q

Quality-adjusted life-years (QALYs), 104
Quality care, 85–111
 diagnosing problem, 91–96
 preventable medical errors, 91–93
 variations in regional treatment
  patterns, 94–96
 overview, 85–87
 strategies for strengthening, 109–111
 systematic healthcare system, 96–109
 clinical pathways and
  guidelines, 100–109
 total quality management
  principals, 96–100
 types of evidence, 87–91
 healthcare system, 90–91
 international comparisons, 87–90
Quality improvement, *see* Continuous
 quality improvement (CQI)

R

RA, *see* Risk adjustment (RA) systems
Rainmaker, 142
RAND, 94, 198
Randomized controlled trial (RCT), 102
Rate redesign, 124–125
Rate-setting regulations, 49, 50
RBRVS, *see* Resource-Based Relative Value
 Scale (RBRVS)
RCT, *see* Randomized controlled trial (RCT)
Regence BlueShield, 157
Research expenditures, 63
Resource-Based Relative Value Scale
 (RBRVS), 132–133
Retail clinics, 180–184
Revealed preference information, 75
"Right-to-shop" program, 184
Risk adjustment (RA) systems, 155
Risk pooling concept, 154
Risk sharing, 152
Risk *vs.* subsidy, 17–19, 20
Russell, Louise, 107, 166

S

Satisfice, 169
SCHIP, *see* State Children's Health Insurance
    Program (SCHIP)
Schumpeter, Joseph, 178
Sears Holdings Corp., 38
Selective contracting, 129–130
SES, *see* Socioeconomic status (SES),
    and health
SGR, *see* Sustainable Growth Rate (SGR)
SID, *see* Supply-induced demand (SID)
Simon, Herbert, 169
Single-payer system, 84
Single-Specialty Hospitals (SSHs), 185–189
Six Sigma, *see* Lean Six Sigma
"Skimming the cream," 188
Smith, Mary, 123, 126
Socioeconomic status (SES), and health, 56
Solvency regulation, 152–154
Solvency requirements, 153–154
Sowell, Thomas, xxxiii
SSHs, *see* Single-Specialty Hospitals (SSHs)
State Children's Health Insurance Program
    (SCHIP), 8, 40
Statewide *vs.* private-sector HIE, 207–208
Statistical life-year, 76
Statistics Canada, 88
Stimulus bill, *see* American Recovery and
    Reinvestment Act (2009)
Subsidy, risk *vs.*, 17–19, 20
Supply-induced demand (SID), 117
Sustainable Growth Rate (SGR), 132–133

T

"Taxation by regulation," 186
Tax credit, 51, 53–54
Telemedicine, 189–191
*To Err Is Human: Building a Safer Health
    System,* 85, 92

*To Err Is Human—To Delay Is
    Deadly,* 85
Total Quality Management (TQM), 96–100
Triple Aim, 52, xxxvi
Tversky, Amos, 169

U

Uber, 178–179
Uninsured people, 12
United States, employer-sponsored
    insurance in, 46
Urban Institute, 52
U.S. General Accounting Office, 185
U.S. Government Printing Office, 51
U.S. National Center for Health
    Statistics, 88
U.S. Preventive Services Task Force
    (USPSTF), 101, 103, 107, 108, 165

V

VA, *see* Veterans Affairs (VA)
Value-based purchasing (VBP), 132
Veterans Affairs (VA), 197
Volkswagen's hypothesis, 172

W

Wait time rationing, 79
Walker, David, 67
Wall Street Journal, 19, 40, 109, 188
Walmart, 178
Washington, Denzel, 142
Washington State Medical Association, 157
Wellness program, 166, 173
World Health Organization, 90

Z

Zero Trends, 167